"What a rich and wonderful resource! Busy preachers and pastors will find the beautifully written and easy-to-navigate *Easter Fire* invaluable as they preach the weekday liturgies of Easter. I am struck, not only by the depth of the exegesis, illustrations, and liturgical/historical notes, but also by their breadth and expression. Bishop Sklba and Rev. Juknialis draw upon their own insights and experiences as well as those of a variety of theologians, poets, artists, psychologists, historians, and lay faithful. The result is a practical and hope-filled resource—a deep well that preachers can draw from on a daily basis throughout the Easter Season for both homiletic and personal inspiration."

—Susan McGurgan, DMin
Director, Lay Pastoral Ministry Program
Assistant Professor of Pastoral Theology
The Athenaeum of Ohio/Mount St. Mary's Seminary

EASTER FIRE

Fire Starters for the Easter Weekday Homily

Richard J. Sklba and Joseph J. Juknialis

LITURGICAL PRESS
Collegeville, Minnesota

www.litpress.org

1   2   3   4   5   6   7   8   9

Library of Congress Cataloging-in-Publication Data

Names: Sklba, Richard J.
Title: Easter Fire : fire starters for the Easter weekday homily / Richard J. Sklba and Joseph J. Juknialis.
Description: Collegeville, Minnesota : Liturgical Press, 2016.
Identifiers: LCCN 2015033960 | ISBN 9780814648667 | ISBN 9780814648919 (ebook)
Subjects: LCSH: Eastertide—Sermons. | Bible. Acts—Sermons. | Catholic Church—Sermons.
Classification: LCC BV4259 .S54 2016 | DDC 252/.63—dc23
LC record available at http://lccn.loc.gov/2015033960

O God, who through your Son
bestowed upon the faithful the fire of your glory,
sanctify this new fire, we pray,
and grant that,
by these paschal celebrations,
we may be so inflamed with heavenly desires,
that with minds made pure
we may attain festivities of unending splendor.
Through Christ our Lord. Amen.

May the light of Christ rising in glory
dispel the darkness of our hearts and minds.

—The Blessing of the Easter Fire, *The Roman Missal*

Contents

Introduction

Easter begins with the first flickering light of the Easter fire against the darkness of Holy Saturday night. Blessed, and carried reverently, that light is accompanied by the congregation's triple praise for "Christ the Light of the World." One by one the holy flame is shared among those gathered in the assembly of believers, ever vigilant for the first signs of new life. Still surrounded by the darkness of a sinful world, the solemn announcement of the Lord's history-changing resurrection is sung as the jubilant message of the *Exultet* illumines the church together with the wider world. The Lord has been raised. Death has been conquered. The Word made flesh has been set free. All of creation is made new by his eternal light and life-giving presence.

Ever since that history-changing resurrection, the Good News has been proclaimed from the housetops, announced in the gathered assemblies of his disciples, and whispered to the hearts of those who seek him. Indeed, "how can they call on him in whom they have not believed? And how can they believe in him of whom they have not heard? And how can they hear without someone to preach?" (Rom 10:14). Yet what is it that one does when he or she preaches? Over the course of two thousand years of Christian preaching the answer to that question has taken on many different forms. In one way or another it has usually echoed St. Paul's wisdom in his Second Letter to Timothy that "all scripture is inspired by God and is useful for teaching, for refutation, for correction, and for training in righteousness" (3:16).

Apologetics and the refutation of error found predominance during the time of the early church fathers and again during the Reformation. Doctrinal preaching in the form of catechetics and a focus upon correct and right moral living became the norms following Trent and into the first two-thirds of the twentieth century. More recently, liturgical preaching has taken on the nature of the homily that seeks to proclaim the works of God in our lives, pointing to the ways that God is present in the context of our relationships—i.e., in righteousness and spirituality.

That more recent shift in liturgical preaching came as a result of the Second Vatican Council's document on the reform and renewal of the liturgy, *Sacrosanctum Concilium*. "The sermon, moreover, should draw its content mainly from scriptural and liturgical sources, for it is the proclamation of God's wonderful works in the history of salvation, which is the mystery of Christ ever made present and active within us" (35).

That understanding was further developed in this country by the foundational document on preaching published by the United States Bishops' Committee on Priestly Life and Ministry, *Fulfilled in Your Hearing* (1982), which noted that the "the purpose (of the homily) is not conversion from radical unbelief to belief. A homily presupposes faith. Nor does the homily concern itself with a systematic theological understanding of the faith. The liturgical gathering is not primarily an educational assembly." Moreover, the same document also states that "the response that is most general and appropriate 'at all times and in every place' is the response of praise and thanksgiving (Eucharist)."

In 2012 the United States Conference of Catholic Bishops' Committee on Clergy, Consecrated Life, and Vocations published the document *Preaching the Mystery of Faith: The Sunday*

Homily. It once more emphasized that, "Every homily . . . must therefore be about the dying and rising of Jesus Christ and his sacrificial passage through suffering to new and eternal life for us. By means of that pattern, the People of God can understand their own lives properly and be able to see their own experience in the light of the Death and Resurrection of Jesus . . . reflecting on our personal and collective experience in the light of the Paschal Mystery."

The same focus for contemporary liturgical preaching has been highlighted by Pope Francis in *Evangelii Gaudium* (The Joy of the Gospel, 2014) in which he points out that "in the homily, truth goes hand in hand with beauty and goodness. Far from dealing with abstract truths or cold syllogisms, it communicates the beauty of the images used by the Lord to encourage the practice of good. The memory of the faithful, like that of Mary, should overflow with the wondrous things done by God. Their hearts, growing in hope from the joyful and practical exercise of the love which they have received, will sense that each word of Scripture is a gift before it is a demand" (142).

Finally and most recently, the decree of the Congregation for Divine Worship and the Discipline of the Sacraments has published *Homiletic Directory* (June 29, 2014). It succinctly articulates the homiletic wisdom that has unfolded since the Second Vatican Council.

All of these sources have brought us to understand that effective liturgical preaching proclaims the *kerygma*—that is, it names where and how the passion, death, and resurrection of the Lord Jesus continues to take place today among believers, in the church, and in society. In other words, the task of liturgical preaching is to name the actions of God, to point to what God is doing today, "to show how and where the mystery of our faith, focused upon that day's Scripture readings, is occurring in our lives" (FIYH).

How to Use *Easter Fire*

The preacher will find offered here both biblical background and homiletic suggestions for the weekday's scriptures of the seven weeks of the Easter season. The material for each day begins with "God's Story Proclaimed," offering exegetical material for the first reading of the day (from Luke's Acts of the Apostles), the psalm and gospel acclamation, and the gospel reading for that day.

There are also on occasion literary and historical notes that provide further background and context for the texts chosen by the Lectionary for a particular day.

Interspersed among the biblical background are paragraphs indicated by an icon as Homiletic Spark. The sentence highlighted in bold denotes the core focus of a possible homiletic message, always noting what it is that God is continuing to do in our lives. Generally these paragraphs offer only generic examples, with the expectation that the homilist can uncover specific examples common to those in the gathered assembly.

Among the Homiletic Sparks here are paragraphs highlighted in gray with the heading "God's Story Made Present." These point to an activity of God in our lives as a focus for a possible homily. However, they also offer a specific, concrete instance of how and where it is that God continues to enflesh his Word in the lives of believers today. These examples may come from the media, literature, society, or simply daily human living.

None of the Homiletic Sparks offered in this volume are offered as homilies in themselves, but rather with the hope that they might spark in the preacher a recognition of where similar occurrences are taking place in his or her world and community and the personal lives of those gathered.

Throughout this work the Homiletic Sparks that are offered are of two kinds. They may be metaphors of illustration or metaphors of participation. For example, in a homily a preacher may suggest that just as waves wash over the shoreline, smoothing rocks, cliffs, and crevices, so God washes over our lives eroding our sin and bringing us to the image of Jesus. That image is a *metaphor of illustration*, an image to compare how God may work in our lives. On the other hand, the preacher may point out how God actually does work in our lives to make us holy through spouses who challenge one another, through parents who raise children into goodness, or through the forces of society that insist upon cooperation and goodness. Such moments are the very activity of God eroding our sinfulness and smoothing our rough images. Such an image is a *metaphor of participation*. Metaphors of illustration are activities that parallel or imitate the activity of God, but they are not direct actions of God upon our lives. Metaphors of participation, on the other hand, are actual examples of God's moving activity in our lives. Throughout this book you will find both types of metaphors. The latter is usually more forceful than the former simply because it is more concrete, although both can be effective.

Finally, as part of the process of preparation the preacher may consider asking some of the following questions as a means of naming concrete examples of God's movement in human life.

- How is God's Story my story? Our story?
- What is the good news found in this text? What is the challenge?
- Where have I seen this Good News enfleshed in the lives of parishioners?
- What new vision does this Scripture offer?
- What darkness does it dispel?
- Where does this text suggest healing might be taking place?
- What promise of God does it make known?
- What might it offer to those who live in fear?
- What specific difficulties or conflicts might this text help negotiate?
- How does it tell the story of the community?
- In what ways does this Scripture passage offer hope to individuals living faith? To your community? To those who feel lost?

Our hope is that these pages and the thoughts they offer may become sparks to the weekday homilies of busy pastors and preachers during the glorious fifty days of each year's Easter season. May the paschal mystery we celebrate continue to illumine our journey into the new life we now share because of the baptism we have received.

—Joseph J. Juknialis
—Richard J. Sklba

The Octave
of Easter

Monday of the Octave of Easter

God's Story Proclaimed

Acts of the Apostles

This is the second volume of Luke's gospel. Initially written for an affluent and educated segment of first-century society, Jesus is presented as a prophetic figure like Elijah, a new yet ancient voice reforming society and summoning care for the poor. This "Part Two" brings that same message to the wider world of nations and describes the way in which the God of Pentecost used the apostle Peter and the newly converted Saul (Paul) to bring the Good News of Jesus to the larger world. The Gospel is proclaimed first to Jews and then to Gentiles, culminating in Paul's preaching in Rome, the first-century center of imperial power. Words of faith first spoken two thousand years ago have again become the treasure of contemporary Christianity, annually renewing people of every age in faith and charity. This global gospel may be seen as part of the New Evangelization to which we are called anew. The entire church is its messenger.

ACTS 2:14, 22-33
God raised this Jesus; of this we are all witnesses.

Raised Up by God

The primary proclamation of Easter is the triple announcement that Jesus has been (1) raised by God (vv. 24, 32) and personally released from the "throes of death" (v. 24), (2) exalted to the "right hand of God," and (3) made the occasion for the final pouring out of the Holy Spirit upon the entire cosmos (v. 33). This is the fundamental good news of the Gospel of Jesus the Christ. This is the essence of Christianity, the truly astonishing *kerygma* ("announcement") around which we shape our lives, our celebrations, and our world. This is also our faith: received, welcomed, and embraced. Acts was written by Luke to document the spread of that faith throughout the known Western world of the first century AD. Today's first weekday Eastertide reading places the entire contemporary church once again among the curious crowd gathered to hear Peter's words amid the initial confusion of Pentecost. People felt somehow compelled to stop and see what was happening. Easter and Pentecost are thus liturgically telescoped into a unity more characteristic of John's gospel (cf. John 20:1-23). During this first week of Easter the entire church hears again the initial proclamation of the Gospel from the lips of Peter immediately after the history-shaking event of that first Pentecost.

Believers hear a different song sung. Being a believer can at times feel like being sidelined, as if one is out of step with the rest of what is going on around us. Slowly, however, if one is faithful, one begins to hear a different tune being sung and a different rhythm at the heart of life. It is the Spirit of the risen Christ that has found a home in us, then, a voice to which we have stopped to listen, a new person who has taken over our lives. It is God's Spirit that propels us to stop and care about someone's distress even when time is of the essence. It brings us to soup kitchens and bedsides, and it enables us to love even those who seem unlovable.

In "An Old Cracked Tune" poet Stanley Kunitz reflected upon the difficulties of his own life, something that led him to a different place. "I dance, for the joy of surviving, / on the edge of the road," is how he wrote it. He explained that for him life was a matter of "dancing on the edge of the road, not in the middle where the heavy traffic flows. Maybe one of the secrets of survival is to learn *where* to dance."[1] Surely persons of faith have learned *where* it is that they choose to dance, at times becoming a place that differs from many others.

3

Wondrously Mining the Psalms

In this speech, Luke describes Peter quoting Psalm 16, the song of David about a mysterious figure whom God would not abandon to the abode of the dead nor allow to experience corruption (v. 10). Repeatedly Acts describes the early apostolic speeches as rooted in the Scriptures of Israel, and it interprets the life, death, and resurrection of Jesus in their light. In Psalm 16, the Hebrew word for the "nether world," namely, *Sheol* (v. 27), is made in the Hebrew text a parallel to *shahath* ("pit"), which the Greek text, however, has curiously chosen to translate as a place of decay and corruption. A comparison between the English translation of the psalm response (v. 10 in the Hebrew Psalter) and the reading from Acts (v. 27) illustrates the development. Thus we can see how the Greek translation of the Psalms was used at times by the early apostolic preachers to clarify their understanding of the destiny of Jesus and to describe his mission of salvation. For a Greek-speaking world, they used the Greek Scriptures.

Catechetical note: Just as the Scriptures deepened their understanding from earlier to later books, we continue that process when we understand our own lives better as a result of those inspired writings and the insights of our Christian faith. This is especially helpful when more difficult things come along in life or when we can view them in retrospect. We Christians have received the benefit of these deepened insights. When any psalm is applied to Jesus, it also offers an interpretation of our own lives as baptized followers of the risen Lord.

God's promise is life. Rivers and lakes are renewed. Cities gentrify. The earth reboots in springtime. Bodies mend. Relationships heal and are rebuilt. Hope is discovered anew. There is something at the heart of all that is that will not lie still in death. The believer recognizes it as the action of a life-giving God.

We Are All Witnesses

Earlier the text of Acts described the process by which Matthias had been chosen by lot to take the place of the ill-fated Judas and restore the apostolic "college" to the symbolic number of twelve (1:15-26). By definition they had been chosen as apostles because they each had witnessed the primary events of salvation. Peter proudly accepted the title of *martus* ("witness") to the fact that God had raised Jesus from death (v. 32). All subsequent generations of Christians are likewise expected to be witnesses (*marturēs*), that is, to give ample demonstration of the effects of the Lord's resurrection in their own lives as a result of the grace of their baptism. The Greek word for witness, "martyr," quickly came to describe someone who gave witness by a faith-filled death. This also reflected and shared the Lord's entrance into the paschal mystery.

Note to the Preacher

By ordination and the canonical faculty to preach, even contemporary twenty-first-century preachers can be said to be the church's officially designated witnesses to the Lord's resurrection! Moreover, if we claim membership in a church that is truly apostolic, even as it is "one and catholic," all who preach the Gospel are also expected to offer their own apostolic witness to the risen Lord at work in our world.

God's Story Made Present

God stirs us to give witness. Each of us in the circumstances of our own lives finds ourselves attesting to the faith in which we stand.

Fr. Lawrence Jenko was the Catholic priest held hostage in Beirut along with journalist Terry Anderson and multiple other Americans in 1985. Sometime later, well after his return to this country, he told the story of coming to his mother's bedside just before she died. When he walked into the hospital room around noontime, her first weak words to him—and her last as it turned out—were "Did you have lunch yet?" Shortly thereafter she died. Later on, Fr. Jenko reflected upon that moment with a bit of wistfulness, wishing that his mother's final words might have been more reflective or faith-filled or in some way more memorable. "Did you have lunch yet?" seemed much too unimpressive for the banner one carries in the procession through death's archway. Yet the more he thought about it, the more appropriate those words seemed for that had been the way his mother had lived—always attentive to someone else's needs. It had always been the lens through which she looked upon life, the Spirit of Jesus that gave life to her days.

ANTIPHON—PSALM 16:1

Keep me safe, O God; you are my hope. (or: Alleluia)

Psalm 16:1-2a, 5, 7-8, 9-10, 11

Commentators vary in their suggestions regarding the original purpose of this psalm. Some see its expression of trust as a fitting prayer uttered by the people of Judah upon return from exile in Babylon in the sixth century BC to face the daunting task of rebuilding the walls of Jerusalem. Others prefer a time four hundred years later when God's faithful people courageously practiced their faith amid the threat of harsh Hellenistic punishments, even death. Taken as a whole, the psalm has also been viewed at times as a prayer of conversion that rejects false gods and reaffirms devotion to YHWH alone. The psalm's three themes of enduring trust (v. 1), return home (v. 6), and restoration to life (v. 10) also made the psalm a suitable prayer for the lips of the risen Jesus, Jewish to the core. In today's Eucharist the risen Jesus again expresses total permanent trust in his heavenly Father. Jesus returns home to his Father's home forever.

The Refrain

As noted above, the liturgy uses the first verse of the psalm as a prayer placed on the lips of Jesus. Here in the Easter liturgy as a communal response, the same verse becomes the prayer for all the baptized who have been granted a share in Christ's redemptive forgiveness and in the promise of eternal life in Christ. Preservation from full and final corruption (v. 10) becomes the hope of the entire assembly as a result of our baptism. Christ's prayer is now our prayer when faced by trial or hardship because of the Easter mysteries in which we have shared. Our hardships, large and small, are sacramentally linked to the Lord's paschal mystery.

GOSPEL ACCLAMATION—PSALM 118:24

Throughout this entire first week of Eastertide, the same alleluia verse from Psalm 118 is offered as an alternative to the solemn sung alleluia. It is as if the "day" of Easter (v. 24) is prolonged in time and extended for an initial octave of utter jubilation. It may also be helpful to note that the same Hebrew verb, *'asah*, like its Latin equivalent *facere*, can mean both to "make" and to "act" or "do." Although God may have "made" or "created" the day of Easter, it seems much more faithful to the Easter event to acclaim this day as the one in which God has definitively intervened by means of the resurrection of Jesus! Indeed, "this is the day in which the Lord has acted decisively!"

At an even more profound level, it may be helpful to recall that the sacred name of YHWH is a verb, usually translated simply as LORD. Conjectural though its original form and meaning may be (because at the time of Jesus it was never spoken except by the high priest once a year), the word could probably be translated as "He who will be what he will be" or "He who will make happen what will happen" (Exod 3:13-15). Thus the very name of God signals the

One who freely and diversely intervenes for the world's salvation.

Lectionary note: Curiously, the gospel for Easter Sunday (John 20:1-10) does not include any account of meeting the risen Lord Himself. Each day during this first week of Easter, however, the Lectionary chooses a different gospel reading from the various scriptural accounts of the early church's experience of Jesus newly risen. In that way, the modern assembly at prayer is exposed again each year to all the various reports of the church's first experiences of the risen Lord. Thereafter during the remaining fifty days of Easter, the Lectionary continues its presentation of passages from Acts as a first reading but then concentrates almost exclusively on John for the day's gospel text.

The Gospel of Matthew. This gospel is patterned after the Pentateuch with five discourses of Jesus interspersed by five accounts of the messianic healing actions by Jesus for the poor and ailing. It addresses a community comprised of early Torah-observant Jewish converts as well as Gentiles, concluding with the command of Jesus to bring the Gospel to all nations (28:18) and to baptize them into the very life of the Trinity! Jews and Gentiles are bound together by God's will forever.

Matthew 28:8-15

Go tell my brothers to go to Galilee, and there they will see me.

Lectionary note: This gospel's final chapter is divided into three parts. The first begins with an initial description of a terrifying meeting of the two women with an angel at the open empty tomb (vv. 1-6) and his command that they should convey to the apostles the risen Lord's invitation to meet in Galilee (v. 7). In Matthew's gospel today's passage (vv. 8-15) is then immediately followed by the final meeting of the Eleven with Jesus in Galilee and his great farewell commission of instruc-

tion and baptism for the whole world (vv. 16-20). This solemn conclusion reinforces Matthew's concern for the eventual definitive cooperation and united witness of Jews and Gentiles in God's kingdom.

True and False Witnesses

Historians tell us that it was an early Jewish custom to visit a tomb for three days, perhaps to make sure that the speedy burial required in pre-embalmment ages did not accidentally inter someone still living. The theme of personal witness is clearly a primary concern for this first day's liturgy after the feast of Easter. The church's Lectionary first presents two Marys, the Magdalene and another Mary (the same individuals who had stood beneath the cross, cf. 27:56), who joyfully encounter the risen Lord (v. 9) and are deputed "apostles to the apostles" with his promise that the Eleven would also meet the risen Jesus, but in Galilee. His first words to the women were "Do not be afraid" (v. 10), repeating the very same admonition as had been given earlier by the angel at the tomb (v. 5). This expression echoes the angel's announcement to Mary (Luke 1:30), as well as the constant encouragement given to all the early faith-filled witnesses, especially those who faced opposition and skepticism. In the next portion of the chapter (vv. 16-28), the apostles will be gathered in Galilee and introduced to their eventual mission—namely, that of sharing the good news with the larger world. The practice of Israel was to require two men as a joint credible witness team to support each other's truthfulness. From the beginning the gospels, however, also include women among potential witnesses to the resurrection. Their witness included the experience of the empty tomb as well as the report of their meeting with the risen Jesus. From the earliest days our Christian faith has highlighted the unique way in which God constantly uses fearless women as heralds of hope for God's new world, even in our own time. Who are the fearless women of today that speak to your own faith?

By way of contrast, subtly emphasizing the women's positive witness, Matthew's gospel deftly reverts to the tale of the guards of the tomb (v. 11) who were bribed to claim the theft of the body of Jesus during the night. To make such an assertion as having happened while they were asleep, however, and therefore unable to witness anything, renders their testimony ludicrously empty and incredulous. They were protected by temple authorities (v. 12) even though they had shirked their responsibilities. They offered false witness to nonevents. They received money for lying (v. 15). The contrasting scenes are stark and striking. By ignorance, indifference, or downright sinfulness we also can give false nonwitness about the work of God in our world today.

God's Story Made Present

Faith gives new eyes for seeing. Each of us discerns that call to faith, or we do not. It is much like the contrast between the two Marys, on the one hand, and the guards, on the other.

> **Monday of the Octave of Easter**

If God is not always so obvious, then how does one know if one's experience is of God or not? The psychologist William James suggests four marks: (1) the experience is more like a feeling than it is of the intellect (ineffability); (2) while not of the intellect, it is a font of knowledge akin to insight or awareness or some sort of illumination (noetic quality); (3) it is fleeting, usually lasting no more than seconds or a minute at most (transiency); and (4) one feels swept up and held by a superior power (passivity).[2]

Others have suggested additional markers: a sense of oneness with all that is, for instance, or that it serves as a springboard to service in the larger community. Like the story of Mary Magdalen, it is confusing at first and it takes time to discern.

1. Stanley Kunitz, *The Collected Poems* (New York: W. W. Norton, 2000), 141; Bill Moyers, *The Language of Life* (New York: Doubleday, 1995), 243–44.

2. William James, *The Varieties of Religious Experience: A Study in Human Nature* (New York: Modern Library, 1929), 371–72.

Tuesday of the Octave of Easter

God's Story Proclaimed

ACTS 2:36-41
Repent and be baptized, every one of you, in the name of Jesus Christ.

To the Jewish People

Unfortunately, the compilers of the Lectionary chose to insert this phrase, "to the Jewish people," thus abbreviating the more inclusive inspired text that had earlier described the crowd as "you who are Jews, indeed all of you staying in Jerusalem" (v. 14). The end result is to suggest falsely an initial sharp dichotomy between the early disciples of Jesus (who in fact were also entirely Jewish) and their audience, "children of Israel" (v. 22). This narrowed audience can also contribute a falsely anti-Semitic tone to the daily readings of the Easter season each year. After the recognition of the horrors of the Nazi holocaust, we Christians have come to understand our own sad historical contribution to that disaster by the subtle teaching of contempt for Judaism. Starting with the annual Passover celebration, we should use every occasion available during Eastertide as an opportunity to rejoice in the Jewish roots of our faith and our religious heritage and to correct false impressions. Vatican II's Declaration on the Relations of the Church to Non-Christian Religions, *Nostra aetate* (October 28, 1965), makes it clear that "neither all Jews indiscriminately at that time, nor Jews today, can be charged with the crimes committed" during Christ's passion (4).

God's Story Made Present

God's spirit of wisdom is sown in the hearts of all people. God's choice of the Jewish people as his primary instrument for the world's salvation is "irrevocable" (Rom 11:29). Thus they should always and everywhere be held in reverence as brothers and sisters to Christians of every age. As Karen Sue Smith reflects in *America,* Jewish artist Marc Chagall "always . . . assumes the Jewishness of Jesus":

> The Jewishness of Jesus has seldom been rendered more clearly in art than in the crucifixion scenes of Marc Chagall. . . . With this visual vocabulary, the artist connected his own interior world to Western culture and Jewish history. "Perhaps I could have painted another Jewish prophet," Chagall admitted, "but after two thousand years mankind has become attached to the figure of Jesus."

> There is more to it than that, however. Chagall was attached not to the figures of Jesus, but specifically to Jesus dying on the cross. He saw the crucifixion not only as the martyrdom of a Jew, but as Jew with whom he could identify personally. "For me, Christ has always symbolized the true type of the Jewish martyr. . . ."[1]

The Exaltation of Jesus as Lord and Christ

A key element of the Easter proclamation is not only the fact of the resurrection of Jesus from the dead but also the double announcement that Jesus has been formally acclaimed by God as Lord (*kurios*) and Messiah (*Christos*) (v. 36)—that is, both mysteriously sharing his Father's divinity (hence the title "Lord") and embodying once and for all times the royal anointed mission of the kingly son of David. Titles reveal reality and reality seeks its correct title. Jesus is thus "lifted up," not only spatially to the heavens in some mysterious fashion but also in his profound fundamental importance for the salvation of the whole world. The famous hymn quoted in Paul's letter to the Philippians proclaims the same truth—namely, that "God greatly exalted him and bestowed on him the name that is above every name" (Phil 2:9f). Christians are also lifted up from sin by God's forgiveness (v. 38), by God's invitation to forsake their corrupt generation (v. 40), and by the promise of the gift of the Spirit.

God lifts us up to life. Part of the human experience is that of feeling downtrodden, a sense of being lost or misunderstood. Out of such depths we are lifted up by the presence of God. Profound forgiveness overwhelms us. We are vindicated by the events of life—or perhaps simply by the gospel. We are drawn out of isolation and back into a sense of belonging. We come to realize that all such experiences are beyond our own doing; they are moments of being lifted up by God.

The First Required Response: Repentance

At the beginning of the public ministry of Jesus, both Mark (1:15) and Matthew (4:17) had mentioned his messianic invitation to repentance (*metanoia*)—namely, to changing one's mind about God. When the crowd at Pentecost asked, "What are we to do?" Peter repeated that same invitation in this reading (v. 38), and described how God is at work in the salvation of the world. Curiously, that summons is absent from Luke's gospel account of the early ministry of Jesus, perhaps so that the same call might first be placed on the lips of Peter here at Pentecost (v. 38). Peter's invitation now also includes a call to baptized membership in the early community of disciples. By God's grace, the community of believers has become the Body of Christ in our age. Although repentance has been proclaimed with special urgency at unique moments in the history of the world's salvation, a basic willingness to change our minds about how God works is a lifelong and never-ending response to God's grace in our world. A true disciple is continually surprised by God and eagerly open to something more than what we already possess.

God's Story Made Present

God has sewn human longings deep in the human spirit. In one way or another, the question of "What are we to do?" is echoed in the deep hungers we have for "more" than what life already is. Each

of us continually finds ourselves drawn to places where that "more" might be found.

On Thursday nights throughout the summer the city of Milwaukee sponsors "Jazz in the Park" in Cathedral Square. Folks come from all directions: from the north and the south and the east and the west, by car and by bike, by bus and by foot. Blacks and Anglos, Latinos and Asians all come, a sort of gathering of the nations. Couples holding hands come, and couples who seem to have given up doing so. Young adults scatter themselves upon blankets amid cheese and wine and laughter. Oldsters bring tables and candles and glass goblets and gingham-checkered picnic baskets. For some the music is why they come, so that their souls might be stirred or distracted from the day's burdens. For others, it seems, the music is but the occasion—to meet or make friends or simply to be a part of something bigger than themselves. Yet each comes in search of something more, hoping that they might pass through the door that opens into that something, if only for a summer evening. By the end of it all, at best, folks head home having enjoyed themselves.

The search for that "something more," however, is an ongoing search, a heartfelt quest for the ultimate answer that fulfills our deepest longings. Perhaps that is why that crowd of folks from who-knows-where came to listen to Peter. It was surely something more that Peter offered to those who gathered on that first Pentecost. And that hunger still rings true for those who call themselves disciples of the Lord Jesus today.

The Second Required Response: Baptism

Throughout all of Acts, people enter the community of disciples through the ritual of baptism (v. 38). Only by going down into the sacred waters of the death of Jesus and rising to new life in the Spirit can they truly become disciples of the risen Lord and sharers in his mission. Even Paul was baptized (9:18) in order to share initial membership in the final age and thus to be divinely empowered as a herald of the Gospel. By sacramentally sharing the Lord's death and resurrection through our own baptism, we discover the surprise that death is part of the package and that our death is but a preliminary requirement if we are to enter the fullness of life. The reading notes that some "three thousand persons" accepted Peter's invitation and were baptized that first Pentecost day (v. 41). The annual baptism of new members at the parish's Easter Vigil celebration illustrates the perennial relevance of this apostolic admonition. Easter is always celebrated by baptisms as needed and by the entire assembly's renewal of their baptismal vows. Baptism and the Lord's paschal mystery are intrinsically united.

Easter is God's promise of something more to come. The anniversary date of our baptism is a "little Easter" for each of us. There is life to come even after a loved one dies. There is life to come even beyond the empty nest. There is life to come in the face of losing a job or failing a course in school.

Two "First Fruits"

With singular focus and great clarity, Peter proclaims that the initial fruits of such repentance and baptism are (1) the forgiveness of sin and (2) the gift of the Holy Spirit (v. 38). All who gather each year for the celebration of the Eucharist during Easter week continue to rejoice in the gifts that we first received at the time of our own baptism, whenever and wherever that may have occurred. Baptism is both a historical event and a lifelong process. Living with a profound constant sense of God's forgiveness and with the presence of God's life-giving Spirit is the mark of a true disciple of Jesus. One gift leads to the other. Every Christian by definition is a sinner (as Pope Francis insisted so dramatically shortly after his

election) but is forgiven and revitalized in Christ through the gift of the Holy Spirit in baptism.

God's Story Made Present

God's forgiveness ushers in a new presence of the Spirit into our lives. People of faith live with a different spirit that shows itself at various times. While the presence of the Spirit cannot be proven, it is also something that cannot be denied. The psychologist Carl Jung had his own issues with formal religion, but his writings recognize something at work in the human spirit beyond simply human instinct.

Life has always seemed to me like a plant that lives on its rhizome. Its true life is invisible, hidden in the rhizome. The part that appears above ground lasts only a single summer. Then it withers away—an ephemeral apparition. When we think of the unending growth and decay of life and civilization, we cannot escape the impression of absolute nullity. Yet I have never lost a sense of something that lives and endures underneath the eternal flux. What we see is the blossom, which passes. The rhizome remains.[2]

ANTIPHON—PSALM 33:5B
*The earth is full of the goodness of the Lord.
(or: Alleluia)*

Psalm 33:4-5, 18-19, 20, 22

It is very possible that Psalm 33 was used for Israel's festive renewal of the covenant in the temple each new year, accompanied by music and song (v. 2). For Christians the annual celebration of Christ's resurrection always marks a sort of new covenantal beginning and a fresh start for all of creation. In particular, the psalm's reference to deliverance from death and preservation from (eucharistic?) famine (v. 19), as well as Israel's hopeful waiting for God's *hesed* (faithfulness, v. 22) makes this psalm response perfect for Easter week. One should not forget that this unique type of faithfulness (the word in Hebrew is *hesed*, translated in the lectionary as "kindness," and thrice repeated in vv. 5, 18, and 22) is obligatory for all covenant members toward each other—so even God is somehow bound by his own promise to care for his people! We celebrate God's gift of mutuality in a special way each Easter through our baptismal share in Christ's paschal mystery. Moreover, each Easter and Pentecost the entire church is created anew.

The Refrain

The Lectionary refrain is taken from the psalm response (v. 5) as recited by the entire congregation today. In this case, however, the phrase is poorly translated into English and does not reflect the richness of the actual Hebrew text. Once again, the original Hebrew wording insists that it is *hesed* or God's covenantal kindness or mercy that fills the earth! Jerome's Latin Vulgate used *Misericordia*, which is much more precise than "goodness." The 1970 version of the New American Bible offered "kindness," and the 1992 version of that Psalter suggested "mercy." Our God is not only good but also faithful! There is obviously still more careful work to be done in sharing more clearly the fullness of the original meaning of this inspired text.

GOSPEL ACCLAMATION—PSALM 118:24
The very day in which Christ rose from the dead was the day when God intervened so dramatically in the life of Mary Magdalen and in all of human history.

JOHN 20:11-18
I have seen the Lord, and he said these things to me.

Lectionary note: John's gospel account of the resurrection begins with Mary's shocking discovery of the empty tomb and her hasty report back to the disciples (v. 1). In a second scene, Peter and John then rush out like Easter joggers to verify her startling experience, although John (this "beloved disciple" may symbolically represent every disciple of all centuries since each person is also uniquely beloved) seems to perceive the full truth of

what had happened, even from the beginning (vv. 3-10).

Mary Magdalen, Healed for Witness

In the Lectionary version of this text, the name of Magdalen has been transferred from v. 18 to the opening v. 11 in order to make very clear the identity of this early witness to the Lord's resurrection. Readers of the gospel will often feel a similar need to identify more specifically a figure when the gospel text itself uses the generic "he" or "she." Mary was a devoted follower and perhaps close personal friend of Jesus during his earthly ministry. Luke identified her as one of the generous wealthy patronesses of the Twelve during their public ministry in Galilee (8:2), adding that Jesus had cast out some seven evil spirits from her—possibly referring to a deep depression or some other emotional or psychological affliction. Her friendship with Jesus had healed her and prepared her to serve as the first witness to his resurrection. This same Mary is presented in the Easter Sunday liturgy each year—and again on Easter Tuesday—as a unique witness figure in the resurrection story. Consequently, the church's liturgy suggests that she is the primary example against whom Christian people of all successive ages will be measured. Any healing we might experience in our own lives is given and destined for witness.

Although John's gospel may be a bit playful in reporting this confusion of identities, the dialogue between Mary and the gardener (v. 15) also serves to suggest the deeper truth that the risen Lord can indeed now be mysteriously present in anyone and everyone—even a casual cemetery worker who happened to be nearby! This is the same gospel that contains the discourse of Jesus about the vine and the branches (John 15:1-10), underscoring the life-giving relationship between Jesus and every baptized disciple. In fact, virtually every person in John's gospel can represent an entire class of believers. Mary herself serves as a reminder and symbol for the many women who were major witnesses to the Lord's resurrection among the first generation of Christian disciples. Amateur gardeners may well be among the daily Mass crowd in any parish, but everyone is a witness to the work of God in his or her own life.

God's Story Made Present

God uses each of us as a measuring stick of faith. At some point in our lives each of us finds ourselves compelled to live out our faith beyond merely saying "I am a believer." It may mean we stand alone, but then alone we must stand. Yet out of our personal convictions we profess what God calls us to do because "I have seen the Lord."

In George Bernard Shaw's play *Saint Joan* there is a scene between Joan and Captain Robert de Baudricour, a military squire, over how it is that Joan knows what God wants of her. It is Robert who challenges her, and so she explains, "I hear voices telling me what to do. They come from God." Robert rebuts and insists, "They come from your imagination." "Of course," replies Joan. "That is how messages of God come to us."

Stop Holding On

Although Peter and John ran stumbling in haste to see the empty tomb (20:1-10), as the Gospel of John tells the story it was Mary of Magdala who was graced with the first encounter with Jesus newly risen! Much has been made of the admonition of Jesus not to cling to an earlier pre-resurrection relationship (v. 17). After all, it is the return of the risen Jesus to his Father that completes his redemptive mission and inaugurates the final age of human history. Only then can the larger world's destiny begin to unfold. By baptism all Christians are invited into that last age of human history. No one is allowed to cling to the past if it prevents and precludes receiving the fuller and better gift of sharing in Christ's extraor-

dinary future existence in the next age. Religious experiences should not be kept personally hoarded and frozen, but rather used as springboards to our apostolic activity and service within the larger community. At the same time, our own personal experiences of God cannot be forced upon others as if it were now somehow their obligation or duty.

Personal faith evolves and deepens with new insights and new challenges and new surrenders. That new gift may call for letting go of past faith practices in order that they may be replaced with new ones. We not only cling to people but also to ways of living faith. Each new pastor offers new ways of being a parish. Each new pastoral assignment offers new ways of being a priest. Each new pope offers new ways of being church. Always there is a letting go.

God's Story Made Present

God's story belongs to the entire human community. In recent years many have given their own testimony to the fact that life does not end in death. Quite publicly they have told of their own experiences of consciousness though proclaimed clinically dead. For them it has been the realization that death ends in life. Among them are:

Anita Moorjani, *Dying to Be Me: My Journey from Cancer, to Near Death, to True Healing* (Carlsbad, CA: Hay House, 2012)

Eben Alexander, *Proof of Heaven: A Neurosurgeon's Journey into the Afterlife* (New York: Simon & Schuster, 2012)

Don Piper and Cecil Murphey, *90 Minutes in Heaven: A True Story of Death and Life* (Grand Rapids, MI: Revell, 2004)

Todd Burpo and Lynn Vincent, *Heaven is for Real: A Little Boy's Astounding Story of His Trip to Heaven and Back* (Nashville: Thomas Nelson, 2010)

Each tells his or her own story of experiencing life beyond death. While their stories are ones of resuscitation and not of resurrection, they are nevertheless personal experiences of life beyond the realms of what appears as death.

God Shining through Mystery

First there was the alarming experience of the empty tomb (v. 12), and then there was an unexpected encounter with the risen Jesus as Mary turned away in her grief (v. 15). The God of Israel always seemed to have preferred the surprise of a burning bush at Sinai (Exod 3:2), the fright of a thundering mountain (Exod 19:16), and the deafening silence of Elijah's Mount Horeb (1 Kgs 19:12). Although God can use any aspect of material creation to signal his presence, nothing created can ever fully contain the mystery of God's being. Creation both reveals and hides. Even the risen Lord comes disguised as a gardener (John 20:15), a fellow traveler to Emmaus (Luke 24:15), or a stranger cooking breakfast by the lakeshore (John 21:4). Each of the disciples tells the story of an encounter with a risen One but invariably meets with an element of doubtful skepticism (Luke 24:11; Mark 16:11-14). Somehow every person's story provided additional clues for someone else and enabled others to have a sense of what to look for. There is both a personal and a communal aspect to every account of meeting the risen Lord.

God's Story Made Present

God is known amid the uncertainty of mystery. How and when we come upon the risen Christ is always clothed in uncertainty and wonder. The Polish poet Czesław Miłosz writes:

> Epiphany is an unveiling of reality. What in Greek was called *epiphaneia* meant the appearance, the arrival, of a divinity among mortals or its recognition under a familiar shape of man or woman. Epiphany thus interrupts the everyday flow of time and enters as one privileged moment when we intuitively grasp a deeper, more essential reality hidden in things or persons.
>
> A polytheistic antiquity saw epiphanies at every step, for streams and woods were inhabited by dryads and nymphs, while the commanding gods looked and behaved like humans, were endowed with speech, could, though with difficulty, be distinguished from mortals, and often walked the earth. Not rarely, they would visit households and were recognized by hosts. The Book of Genesis tells about a visit paid by God to Abraham, in the guise of three travelers. Later on, the epiphany as appearance, the arrival of Christ, occupies an important place in the New Testament.[3]

Tuesday of the Octave of Easter

1. Karen Sue Smith, "Child, Martyr, Everyman," *America* (March 3, 2014): 26.

2. C. G. Jung, *Memories, Dreams, Reflections,* edited by Aniela Jaffé, translated by Richard and Clara Winston (New York: Vintage, 1989), 4.

3. Czesław Miłosz, in *A Book of Luminous Things: An International Anthology of Poetry,* edited by Czesław Miłosz (New York: Harcourt Brace, 1996), 3.

Wednesday of the Octave of Easter

God's Story Proclaimed

ACTS 3:1-10

What I do have I give you: in the name of the Lord Jesus, rise and walk.

Praying in the Temple

In Jerusalem the temple ritual included more than the solemn sacrifice of animals as prescribed by the law of Moses. People also gathered regularly each day for prayer in the section of the temple called the Court of Israel. The priest Zachary took his turn and presided, for example, over the offering of incense (Luke 1:10). It was a short walk from the portion of the old city inhabited by the early followers of "the Way" (as Christianity was first named) to the temple for the public singing of psalms, presumably a devotion scheduled seven times each day (Ps 119:164). Apparently Peter and John remained members of the temple prayer community and joined their "third hour" morning service (v. 1). Eventually this practice inspired the church's practice of the Liturgy of the Hours. Retaining the custom of daily communal prayer in contemporary Catholic parish life unites us with the early Christian community, and echoes the practices of Jewish piety at the time of Jesus. In an earlier age, Sunday afternoon Vespers was part of parish life, and even today that type of prayer often marks the Advent or Lenten seasons.

In prayer God gives strength for the journey. For many folks the practice of participating in daily Eucharist seems to bring a wholeness to their daily living, offering a focus and fresh direction to that day's tasks. Without it they seem themselves to "limp" through the day. With it they are able to stand and confront difficulties, walk with those who may be contrary, and be amazed at how divisions may be healed.

The Beggar Lame from Birth

In the language and metaphor of Judaism, "walking" referred to one's entire moral life—perhaps like "walking the talk" in contemporary jargon. The psalms even offer a blessing for those who do not "walk in the counsel of the wicked, nor stand in the way of sinners" (Ps 1:1). The more pious Pharisees at the time of Jesus wore a garment with tassels so that the bouncing fringes might remind them that every step throughout the day should be a response to God's will (see Matt 23:5, as well as the story of the woman with the hemorrhage who touched the tassels of the cloak of Jesus in Luke 8:44). With these tassels, the Pharisees kept the need for obedience in mind as they fulfilled the various practices that made up their daily religious and family duties. Thus lameness was easily a symbol for a life less moral than it should be, and it is thus an impairment that both Jesus in the gospels and his disciples in Acts cured. By describing this first apostolic cure after the resurrection as curing the lame, Acts was able to illustrate the continuity between the public ministry of Jesus and the religious leadership of his apostles after the resurrection. The very notion of disciple as a (walking) "follower" (Mark 1:16-20) sets the pattern for all of life.

God's Story Made Present

God does cure our limping lives. From the spirit of the risen Lord springs a new wholeness to life. God's loving presence uses the gift of faithful friends, as well as medical treatment, to bring us to greater wholeness. Hospital patients who have someone who loves them and to whom they can go home tend to heal more quickly. In much the same way even complaining about our illnesses to family or friends seems to relieve the pain, if only temporarily.

Pat had quit drinking thirty years before, yet she would always remind anyone listening to her story that she was a recovering alcoholic with the emphasis on the recovering. It was a lifelong journey for her as anyone who suffers from addiction will attest. On more than one occasion she would comment on how she would never wish that disease on her worst enemy, but then she would also go on to say that what she had learned through recovery had been so life-giving that she would never want to live without that wisdom. It had become a grace. Pat had certainly limped through a portion of her life, but once she began to walk the path of sobriety, she did so with determination born of faith in how God had raised her up. She would insist her strength was from God. It was at that point in her life that she became a believer and a follower.

**Wednesday
of the
Octave
of Easter**

attraction to the monotheism and moral code of Judaism but were not quite willing to accept the social restrictions of a kosher diet or circumcision. The refrain's invitation to that entire group recognizes that even Gentiles from all nations can share the early Jewish community's joy at Christ's resurrection. The inclusion of this group also serves as a preparation for Christ's final command to "make disciples of all nations" (Matt 28:19). Ironically all these centuries later, it is now we latter-day Gentile "converts" who make the ancient Jewish refrain our own song.

ANTIPHON—PSALM 105:3B

Rejoice, O hearts that seek the Lord. (or: Alleluia)

Psalm 105:1-2, 3-4, 6-7, 8-9

In 1 Chronicles 16:8-22—where the words of Psalm 105 are included and repeated—we learn that David appointed a choir to sing this hymn in the temple. Its musical references celebrate all the wondrous deeds of God (v. 2). The historical gift of the covenant (v. 8) stood out as a major memory whenever Israel rehearsed God's generous goodness and fidelity in song. By choosing this psalm for the church's Easter week liturgy, we now implicitly include the raising of Jesus among those "great deeds" for which we give thanks. In particular, the liturgical use of this psalm as a response to the story of the healing of the lame beggar at the entrance to the temple is also appropriate for our own "limping into leaping" lives. Communal songs are important means for praising God.

The Refrain

The invitation to rejoice (v. 3) as an alternative to the simple repetition of the Alleluia serves nicely to emphasize the entire church's joy at Easter. In Second Temple Judaism and early Christianity, "God seekers" were those Greeks and Romans who felt an

GOSPEL ACCLAMATION—PSALM 118:24

Each day during the Easter Octave we repeat our joy over the way in which God has intervened in human history. We can also experience this weeklong "day" as part of our journey to Emmaus or as one more experience during this week's new eight-day recreation story.

LUKE 24:13-35

They recognized Jesus in the breaking of the bread.

Lectionary note: In Luke's gospel this chapter's first scene recounts how the women's report of their encounter with the fellow in dazzling clothing at the tomb (vv. 1-11) led Peter to check it out himself, much to his eventual amazement (v. 12). Luke then recounts today's story of the trip to Emmaus (vv. 13-35). Later, after the two disciples returned to the Upper Room and recounted their own experience on the way to Emmaus, Jesus himself appears back in Jerusalem by way of personal verification and asks for some food to demonstrate the reality of his resurrection (vv. 36-43). The chapter includes three segments or "acts" in the drama.

People on the Road to Emmaus

The note that one of the travelers was named Cleopas is striking (v. 18). Although the precise spelling occurs

nowhere else in the New Testament as the name of a disciple, some have wondered if this might be a variant form for the name of the husband (Clopas) of Mary who stood under the cross on Calvary (John 19:25). Others have suggested that the two travelers may have in fact been that same married couple. In any case, Luke's account of the journey of these two disciples on Easter Sunday also serves to prepare for all the subsequent missionary travels described later in the Acts of the Apostles. This trip, like so many others throughout life, became an occasion for the deepening of their faith and for an ever greater understanding of the paschal mystery of Christ's mission. They grew as they traveled. Once again, walking is a metaphor for the moral life of the members of a community once called "the Way" (Acts 9:2). Even today among many different national groups there is a common custom of making an "Emmaus" visit to relatives and friends on Easter Monday. Any travel that changes us can be a pilgrimage.

True disciples of Jesus are spurred to be a people on the move, open to changing their ideas regarding how God works in our world. The Congregationalist preacher Henry Ward Beecher is reputed to have said: "There are two things we should give our children: one is *roots*, the other is *wings*." It is important for Christians to be rooted in tradition while being open to the surprises on the journey of life.

God's Story Made Present

The pilgrimage of life is a walk into knowing God. Since medieval times pilgrims and penitents have made the pilgrimage to Santiago de Compostela. With this being the most arduous pilgrimage in Europe, they would gather at monasteries to travel in groups for safety. Walter Lombaert of Belgium tells of a recent journey he made with two youths. For the boys it was a walk into a new life.

In my journey to Santiago, I acted as a guide for two boys who had spent more than six months in state-run education homes in Mol and Ruyselede. I focused primarily on their lives and paid little attention to the cultural aspects of the road, from Jaca over the Pyrenees to Santiago. Personally, I give great value to the influence of a path that has been walked by millions of pilgrims since early medieval times. The people we met along the way gave us great support in creating a climate in which changes and transformations could happen. . . . I can tell that they (the boys) came out of the pilgrimage in another state of mind, as stronger individuals with more self-respect and with a new sense of direction.

Religiousness and the ability for contact with God lay inside ourselves, where pilgrims can truly meet—whatever their beliefs. A pilgrimage really works when it is long enough to make it the "normal life" you are living. It is not an abnormal life from which you then return to normality.[1]

Divine Catechesis:
Explaining Life's Sorrows

The mysterious fellow pilgrim met on the way to Emmaus took the occasion to listen carefully to the prior religious experience of the two travelers, sad and sorrowful as it was (vv. 18-24). This type of listening is also a significant element for the entire contemporary restoration of the Ritual of Christian Initiation of Adults (RCIA). The world's salvation history includes our own stories as an integral portion of the larger story. The stranger then responded by explaining those same terrible things, but interpreted in the light of the Scriptures (vv. 25-27). Instead of interpreting the Scriptures, Jesus explains our lives in the light of those Scriptures! The great mystery and surprise for the disciples was the *dei pathein* ("had to suffer," v. 26) of Jesus as a first step in order for his exaltation to occur. This theme of the "paschal imperative" in Luke serves to repeat and reemphasize the teaching of Jesus as found in his triple passion predictions (Luke 9:22; 9:44; 18:31-34). The fact that this teaching was repeated three times in the gospel (the customary manner of expressing the superlative in Hebrew) underscores the importance of such sorrow in the salvation of the world.

God grows renewed faith in us as we struggle on the journey, not because God injects suffering into our lives, but because any new transformation means leaving something of the past behind so that something new may break forth. It may be formerly satisfying methods of prayer that are set aside in order to receive new ways that enrich us more deeply. Past understandings of who God is unfold into new ways of believing the presence of God.

Sacramental Intimations

The mysterious fellow traveler offered an extensive explanation of the Messiah's life and mission as illustrated through the invocation of the Scriptures (v. 27). The fact that this was followed by the pause of these early disciples to break bread at the inn (v. 30) suggests that this combined ritual of Scripture and eucharistic meal was already familiar in early Christian gatherings. These two actions provided a "eucharistic" template for this account. From the very beginning faithful disciples of Jesus have gathered to break the Word as well as the Bread (see Acts 2:42). The phrase "breaking of the Bread" in fact quickly became a name for the Eucharist. One's life pilgrimage, when understood in the light of faith, inevitably leads to the celebration of the Eucharist, which in turn further illuminates the rest of the journey we share as members of God's people!

God's Story Made Present

God feeds our deepest hungers through the Eucharist. Whenever we gather, there is the hope that perhaps something will be said that will bring light to our lives in a way we had not seen before. Frederick Buechner described it in this way:

In the front pews the old ladies turn up their hearing aids, and a young lady slips her six year old a Lifesaver and a Magic Marker. A college sophomore home for vacation, who is there because he was dragged there, slumps forward with his chin in his hand. The vice-president of a bank who twice that week has seriously contemplated suicide places his hymnal in the rack. A pregnant girl feels the life stir inside her. A high-school math teacher, who for twenty years has managed to keep his homosexuality a secret for the most part even from himself, creases his order of service down the center with his thumbnail and tucks it under his knee. . . . The preacher pulls the little cord that turns on the lectern light and deals out his note cards like a riverboat gambler. The stakes have never been higher. Two minutes from now he may have lost his listeners completely to their own thoughts, but at this minute he has them in the palm of his hand. The silence in the shabby church is deafening because everybody is listening to it. Everybody is listening including even himself. Everybody knows the kind of things he has told them before and not told them, but who knows what this time, out of the silence, he will tell them?[2]

Recognized in the Breaking

The bread of the ancient Near East, like that of similar contemporary cultures, was typically a flat round loaf baked on a stone oven. When fresh, they were torn and dipped into sauces and gravies, but they quickly hardened and had to be broken when used. The travelers to Emmaus suddenly recognized the true identity of their new acquaintance from the way he broke the bread at the end of the day (v. 30)—namely, long after its daily baking at dawn. Perhaps Jesus had a long and uniquely familiar practice of breaking bread (v. 35). Perhaps early on he saw that gesture as symbolic of his own destiny to be broken and given away for the world's salvation. In any case his characteristic gestures suddenly revealed his identity, much to the astonishment of the two fellow travelers! The moment that they knew who he was, he disappeared: "Mission accomplished."

**Wednesday
of the
Octave
of Easter**

Whenever we break open our lives, the Lord Jesus becomes enfleshed. If the divine presence revealed by Jesus in the breaking of the bread reveals his own self being broken open for others, and if he commanded us to "do this in remembrance of me," then it is not only the breaking of bread that we are commanded to do but also the breaking open of our own selves. One reflects the other. It happens in going where we do not want to go, in forgiving even when it is not recognized or appreciated, in being faithful to commitments that have lost their luster, in being willing to lose rather than to compromise.

1. Jennifer Westwood, *Sacred Journeys: An Illustrated Guide to Pilgrimages around the World* (New York: Henry Holt, 1997), 70.

2. Frederick Buechner, *Telling the Truth: The Gospel as Tragedy, Comedy, and Fairytale* (New York: Harper & Row, 1977), 22–23.

Thursday of the Octave of Easter

ACTS 3:11-26
The author of Life you put to death, but God raised him from the dead.

Children of Israel

Here in the temple (v. 11) Peter can rightfully address the crowd as "children of Israel" (v. 12) with a sharper focus than was appropriate earlier from the Upper Room where the crowd was more inclusively universal (2:14). The pattern of Acts is that Israel should be addressed first with the announcement of salvation through Jesus the risen Lord. What better place than in the temple? The Jewish Peter invokes his bond of solidarity with those for whom God is "the God of our fathers" (v. 13). As a result of God's plan for the world, the children of Israel are members of a single extended family. The historical joys and heartaches of each person, therefore, belong to everyone. By God's providence the Jewish nation must also be included whenever we Christians explore our own family tree of faith and list our ancestors in faith as well. "I handed on to you," says Paul, "what I also received" (1 Cor 11:23; 15:3). Paul had been blessed by his own ancestry in faith, and he shared that same heritage of faith with his converts as he traveled. By God's generous goodness, Israel belongs to all of us, and we somehow belong to Israel.

God brings us to faith through one another. Genealogy has become both a hobby and a business as many eagerly seek out their ancestry. The reality, however, is that it becomes difficult and often impossible to know more than names, dates, and perhaps professions. Even more difficult is it to learn someone's faith history. Though we may discover religious backgrounds, how our ancestors lived out their faith is often lost unless we are fortunate to have letters or diaries that reveal such information. Yet the reality is that for the most part we are people of faith

because those before us were people of faith and sought to pass that on. Though our familial genealogy may not reveal a great deal regarding the faith of our ancestors, we do have the saints of our tradition who in many ways have left us a legacy. In the end we have become people of faith because those before us were.

Wholeness Discovered in Retrospect

Looking backward through all the struggles of Israel over the centuries, Christians have discovered some unexpected clear paths of development. Even when the unfolding ideas of God were not as yet known to the actual Jewish participants at the time, certain elements have become more significant and clearer to those of us who follow Jesus. For us the life and death of Jesus has become the prism for seeing and understanding everything. At the same time, it is imperative that we find a way to witness our Christian convictions while still respecting those who read the same inspired texts of faith differently.

In a world that finds it difficult to recognize the hand of God, *God appears to us in rearview mirrors.* We often see things more clearly in retrospect. We recognize the hand of God in a job loss that brings new and more satisfying employment, in growing older that brings wisdom to our lives, and in the unexpected birth of a child that brings new joy to our days.

Another Call to Repentance

Echoing an invitation from his earlier Pentecost speech (2:38), Peter again calls the crowd in the temple to *metanoia* ("change of mind," v. 19). This summons is repeated by Peter and Paul wherever they travel throughout their known world as messengers of the Good News of Jesus. This invitation is a theme that is woven throughout all of Acts. The same summons is extended to us every day and with special urgency each Easter season. This is in fact a daily lifelong process rather than something accomplished once and for all. The same encouragement had constituted the very first words of Jesus at the beginning of his public ministry (Mark 1:15).

God walks in through new doors of conversion. God constantly calls every human generation from all times and places to a new understanding of how he works in our world. We seek to be tolerant of someone and so come to recognize God's face in their demeanor. We try to look at an issue from the perspective of the other and find that our own wisdom is broadened. We surrender an area of sinfulness and find unexpected peace.

Acting Out of Ignorance

The text does not shy away from a description of the objective sin of the crucifixion, namely, putting to death the author of life (v. 15) as a later and more profound understanding would express it. Peter nevertheless insists that both people and leaders acted out of ignorance (v. 17) and thus became unwitting instruments of God's plan for salvation. The acknowledgment of that same ignorance also undercuts any basis for anti-Semitism in these scriptural passages. Peter requests repentance (*metanoia*)—that is, a change of mind and a willingness to think differently (v. 19; not necessarily limited to contrition for deliberate sin). Peter's attitude of "pastoral kindness" toward the populace in the temple is consistent with the entire Gospel of Luke, which had constantly noted the presence of crowds glorifying God for the works of power done by a second Moses, the great prophet Jesus (v. 22, quoting Deut 18:15). The children of Abraham again become God's means for blessing all the families of the earth (v. 25, quoting Gen 12:3). This passage concludes with Peter's conviction that the risen Lord is being sent to bless the

people of Israel (v. 26). Judaism is constantly presented very positively in these two books of Luke. That conviction was an undercurrent in his appeal to the more sophisticated portions of his society (Luke 1:1-4).

God spins wisdom out of ignorance and even sin. At times reluctantly, we've come to realize how the sexual abuse crisis and the subsequent response by the institutional church eventually has led to greater openness and respectful awareness of those who have suffered so greatly. At other times personal tragedies have become the impetus for courage and strength never before recognized.

ANTIPHON—PSALM 8:2AB
O Lord, our God, how wonderful your name in all the earth! (or: Alleluia)

Psalm 8:2ab, 5, 6-7, 8-9

As a responsorial hymn, Psalm 8 celebrates the majesty and power of God the Creator of the world. With distant echoes from the stories at the beginning of Genesis, the psalm pays special tribute to the unique dignity of human beings amid all God's creatures. In particular, by the fact that the hymn celebrates the glory of the "son of man" (v. 5), it offers an allusion to the title often used by Jesus during his earthly ministry, either to underscore his humanity or to refer to the ancient eschatological figure associated with the end of history (Dan 7:13). Scholars admonish us to be cautious in any effort to render the title "son of man" in more inclusive language lest a reference to the title of Jesus in the prophets or the gospels be obscured as a result. The liturgical use of this psalm as a community response within the Eucharist thus places Peter's temple speech in the even larger context of the world's creation and purpose.

The Refrain

The Scriptures often pay tribute to a person's name as representing the person him- or herself. Over the centuries even God's personal name, YHWH, became increasingly venerated in Israel as sublimely unspeakable; spoken prayers simply used the vowels of the Hebrew word for Lord (*'Adonai*) when referring to God. Today's refrain (v. 2) praises the name and person of God for all the wonders of creation, including by reason of today's Lectionary arrangement, the healing of the lame beggar in the preceding passage. In today's world, this same refrain might easily be invoked by faithful Jews and Christians to counter the way in which God's name is taken so casually. Unfortunately, our contemporary society uses God's sacred name as an expression of surprise, disagreement, disgust, or anger. The ancient commandment not to take the name of God in vain (Exod 20:7; Deut 5:11), though possibly referring initially to the application of God's name to an idol, still remains an obligation for us today.

Gospel Acclamation—Psalm 118:24
Although the same verse from Psalm 118 is used each day throughout the week, it serves to introduce each day a slightly different event in the early church's experience of the risen Lord. Today's "this day" opens the door to Jesus showing his glorious wounds and sharing yet another meal with the folks in the Upper Room.

Luke 24:35-48
Thus it was written that the Christ would suffer and rise from the dead on the third day.

Lectionary note: Immediately after yesterday's account of the risen Lord mysteriously traveling on the journey to Emmaus with his disciples (24:13-35), today's gospel continues with Luke's account of a "third act," or surprise meeting, with him back in the Upper Room. In Luke's gospel that in turn will be followed by a final promise of divine presence in their midst (v. 49) and the concluding description of the ascension (vv. 50-53). Tomorrow's liturgy, however, will return to John's gospel for the story at the lakeshore. The same event of Christ's ascension from Luke's perspective will be repeated from

a different angle later in Acts (1:6-12; see also the readings for the feast of the Ascension).

Christ's Greeting of Peace

The lectionary has decided to repeat the same verse that had served as a conclusion to yesterday's passage as the beginning for today's reading, thus emphasizing the eucharistic implications of the words—namely, the "breaking of the bread" (v. 35). The customary Semitic greeting of *shalom* now moves in this instance beyond mere cultural patterns of politeness to the gospel's more profound theological expression of faith. The Hebrew word itself suggests a restored unity of previously scattered parts. The Lord's death and resurrection have established a new reconciling relationship within the entire created world, heavenly as well as terrestrial. Everything is now put back together again in a new way. Christ's greeting to the people (v. 36) still gathered in the Upper Room thus also serves to announce the cosmic reconciliation achieved through the paschal mystery. Participants in our contemporary Catholic liturgical services should not forget the Easter implications of every exchange of the sign of peace, and its recognition of the new age into which Christ has introduced the world by his redeeming actions. If that common liturgical greeting is always somehow "paschal," it also contains the seed of being sent out on mission to the larger world every time it is used!

The gift of inner peace, namely, "wholeness," is the presence of God sustaining us as we enter into life's struggles. Every liturgical sign of peace transports us again back to the Upper Room and renews our grateful sense of redemption and mission. Spiritual writers remind us that a deep inner sense of peace even in the midst of turmoil and conflict is the fruit of prayerfulness. The preacher can help those in the assembly name that inner peace.

Healed Hands and Feet

Luke's gospel deliberately rejects the early Gnostic heresy that the risen Jesus was merely a ghost (*pneuma*) without flesh and bones (vv. 37, 39). Although John's gospel refers to showing both "hand and side" (20:2, perhaps to echo the outpouring of blood and water of 19:34), Luke's inclusion of feet may well introduce and reinforce the way Easter includes the missionary journeys of Acts. Showing his wounded hands was a literary way of referring to his prior work for the sick and needy during his earthly ministry, and showing his wounded feet, a reminder of the apostolic journeys yet to come. Both have been gloriously healed in the process of resurrection. It would take years, however, together with the inspired teaching of Paul, to fully comprehend the reality of Jesus as the firstborn of the new creation (Col 1:15). The hand we shake at the daily Eucharist's sign of peace can serve as a reminder of the flesh and blood reality of the resurrection in which we already share because of our baptism. Easter is also a *kairos*, a special, "acceptable" time to profess the fullness of our faith in the incarnation. Both Christmas and Easter are parts of God's plan for the full and final salvation of creation.

The Spirit of the risen Lord is made flesh in the flesh of the world. The incarnation is experienced not only in individuals but more and more as well in society as a whole. Recent studies have shown that today more than at any other time in history a person is statistically more likely to die in bed from natural causes. Despite the impressions we receive through the media, the world is less violent today than it has ever been. In part it is because of the growing distribution of wealth—there are more people who have more to lose if they choose to do battle. In part, too, it is because we employ others to protect ourselves, such as police and military forces. And in part it is because of the growing number of democracies in which one person cannot build up a lifetime legacy of power and wealth on the back of an entire nation. Thus nations, too, are much more cautious about going to war.

Resurrection, not Revivification

Although Luke clearly presents Jesus as risen bodily from the dead, this is not simply a return to life in this age as John's gospel had described the raising of Lazarus who needed help in removing his shroud (11:1-44). Now Jesus passes through locked doors and is no longer bound by geography, appearing first in Jerusalem and then in Galilee. The gospels insist that Jesus has risen to the next age, as also illustrated, for example, by the admonition of Jesus to Mary Magdalen not to hold on to him (John 20:17) since he must return to his Father. His death and resurrection was not simply for himself but was a necessary prelude to the universal proclamation of the grace of repentance and the gift of forgiveness (v. 47). He becomes a man for others at still a deeper level than ever. Although still wondrously present in our midst, Jesus already embodies the qualities of life in the next age, which he graciously and generously shares with us even here and now, albeit in rudimentary fashion, through our baptism.

In baptism we die to self, and God raises us to the next age. The individual who confronts addiction becomes a new person, one who reflects a new becoming. Teenagers move from preoccupations about themselves and grow into caring adults willing to sacrifice their own wants. Young couples become parents, and suddenly there is someone immensely more important than their own comings and goings. In myriad ways societies are being forced to confront their racism and injustice and intuitional violence. Again and again our lives give witness to a new age that is dawning.

Everything Written in the Law, Prophets, and Psalms

The sages remind us that life is lived forward but understood backward. Perhaps only in the light of their belief in the resurrection of Jesus, were the apostles able to trace so many different earlier lines of Israel's faith and then to understand how everything finally converged in the person and mission of Jesus. They called Jesus "servant" (Acts 4:27), then "Lord" and "Christ" (Acts 11:17) who "had to suffer and rise" (v. 46). Luke's gospel was not written until the 80s. That span of time gave the early church about half a century to discover and explore the clues that had been scattered throughout the pages of the earlier Scriptures of Israel. A new clarity and confidence comes eventually from life lived in faithful and trusting patience. Looking backward increases our gratitude as well as our understanding. "All things work for the good of those who love God" (Rom 8:28), even the tougher things of life when viewed in retrospect.

God's Story Made Present

ACTS 3:11-26 AND LUKE 24:35-48

God is recognized in the rearview mirrors of life. God's gift of faith enables us to trace wonderful patterns of divine goodness in the way our own lives unfold.

August died at the age of eighty after years of working in the lumberyard at Panzer Lumber Company in Sheboygan, WI.

Though to many his life didn't seem to have a lot to show for it all, there was a wholeness to it all. He was at peace and pretty much lived life as it came along—even the dying part. At its end his life seemed fairly worn and frayed. When he surveyed his smattering of the world, he did it with a shuffle; he insisted on cooking his own meals, even though those meals came mostly from cans. He never bothered owning a phone because there was always a neighbor around who did, he said. Why any of that would make his life seem whole made little sense, except that it did to those who knew him.

There have been others, too—women and men who at some point in their lives seemed to have it all together. No regrets, they would say, even while admitting that there were portions of their living that were less than exemplary. Still for them it had all become one in some satisfying and worthwhile way.

Erik Erickson, the psychologist who offered much toward understanding the process of human growth into adulthood and maturity, noted that each stage of life has its own task. The final stage, he says, is integration, which is another way of saying that the challenge is to put all the pieces together in a way that makes sense. In some ways it's like putting together a jigsaw puzzle—if we stay at it long enough. It is as we come to faith in retrospect that we recognize the hand of God in the events of life.

Friday of the Octave of Easter

God's Story Proclaimed

ACTS 4:1-12
There is no salvation through anyone else.

Imprisonment for Faith in the Risen Jesus

It was not the mere reference to resurrection as such that resulted in the arrest of Peter and John, because it was already common for all the Pharisees of the day to believe in resurrection (as contrasted with the Sadducees who did not hold that doctrine; see Acts 23:6-8). Rather, it was the announcement of the resurrection *of Jesus* (v. 2) that caused the problem! After all, Jesus had been executed as a political agitator and a serious potential threat to peace. The leaders of that day feared that this teaching of the apostles could stir up the crowds again and foment social unrest, if not actual revolution. They were frightened of the ominous Roman power and its often cruel imperial authority. The city's leadership imprisoned Peter and John for expressing their faith in Jesus as risen and still active in their midst.

God's Story Made Present

The Spirit frees us from death's hold. Like Peter and John, it would seem that the profession of faith in Jesus the risen Lord had its price. In every age there are those rare souls who seem to be able to live by the Spirit of Jesus and for whom bodily death is not the ultimate enemy. They are able to live by a different vision and walk a different path, and when they enter our lives we are no longer the same. Consider the words of Dr. Martin Luther King Jr. on the day after Selma's infamous "Bloody Sunday":

If a man happens to be thirty-six years old, as I happen to be, and some great truth stands before the door of his life, some great opportunity to stand up for that which is right—he's afraid his home will get bombed, he's afraid that he will lose his job, he's afraid that he will get shot or beat down by state troopers—he may go on and live until he is eighty. He's just as dead at thirty-six as he would be at eighty, and the cessation of breathing in his life is merely the belated announcement of an earlier death of the spirit.

Man dies when he refuses to stand up for that which is right. A man dies when he refuses to stand up for justice. A man dies when he refuses to take a stand for that which is true. So we are going to stand up right here amid horses, we're going to stand up right here in Alabama amid the billy clubs, we're going to stand up right here in Alabama amid police dogs if they have them, we're going to stand up amid tear gas, we're going to stand up amid anything that they can muster up—letting the world know we are determined to be free.[1]

The Power Behind the Cure

As the early Christian community's primary spokesperson, Peter made it very clear that the source for the beggar's cure rested in the power of the risen Jesus alone (v. 10). Peter thus confessed that the name of Jesus the Nazorean—as well as the personal authority divinely invested in that name—has salvific power for all the ills and ails of the world. Peter insisted that only by the authority of his Lord could such miraculous cures be accomplished. Just as Peter was humble in acknowledging that he certainly didn't affect the cure by himself, the best of physicians bring the same attitude in their own service to today's sick and suffering. It is God's power, however, that is always ultimately behind all the care and the prescriptions afforded by good medicine today.

Mystery permeates all of life, even science. Effective modern medical treatment continues to offer new medicines and innovative procedures for alleviating human suffering and curing diseases. Competent doctors and experienced nurses serve as key instruments in dealing with human sickness and disease. God's divine power permeates even the most routine exercises of our contemporary medical care and health services. Yet every once in a while we hear of someone being healed though the doctors are confounded over how it could have come about. As much as we try to explain the workings of life, there are those moments when we have to accept the fact that we simply do not know the whys and wherefores. We live with mystery.

Reverence for the Name

Gradually over the centuries the people of Israel learned to deepen their respect for the Divine Name. By the time of Jesus, the priests in the temple in Jerusalem would not even dare to pronounce the personal name of their God aloud. That deep respect is signaled by the practice of printing the word LORD in small caps wherever the name of God (YHWH) is found in the text of the Hebrew Scriptures. That same respect was gradually transferred by early Christians to the name of Jesus, though without the corresponding unwillingness to speak it. Once again, however, we cannot help but be reminded, by way of contrast, of the dishonor given so casually when that same name is used by contemporary individuals to express mere human surprise, pain, or anger! Nothing could be further from the piety and practice of the early church. Even though our social patterns have changed in recent decades, the original goal of once popular parish Holy Name Societies—namely, respect for the sacred name of Jesus—should not be left casually to the quaint dust bin of cultural or devotional history.

Names always matter, and the name of Jesus matters a great deal. Even in daily life, we come alive with a new sense of joy at the mere mention of the name of someone we love dearly. We are changed by the people we love, and their names bring a smile to our hearts. We find a new sense of unity when we join others who feel the same way about God's name.

It happens when we begin and end our liturgical prayer with the sign of the cross reminding ourselves to whom we belong. It marks our common meal prayer. We notice respect for God when we see people sign themselves in a restaurant. We notice expressions of faith at sporting events. It is not only the sign of the cross but the name of God behind that sign that matters.

Jesus as the Sole Source of the World's Salvation

This passage's reference to the "human race" may perhaps be the first biblical reference to the unique role of the name and person of Jesus in the salvation of the whole world (v. 12). It has been the constant teaching of all Christian churches that Jesus alone is the instrument of universal redemption. We all insist that there can be no salvation except through his life-giving death and his redemptive mission, not to condemn us, but to save us (John 3:17). At least implicitly, according to this conviction, Jesus is therefore the source of divine salvation for all the religions of the world. In recent times, however, the question of the salvation of the Jewish people has received more careful attention by the Catholic Church. On the one hand, Catholics (especially since the Holocaust) now recall ever more clearly Paul's teaching that the "gifts and the call" of Judaism remain irrevocable in God's eyes (Rom 11:29). On the other hand, we also remain committed to our belief in the crucial role of Jesus Christ for the salvation of the whole world and all its generations throughout history. Precisely how to reconcile these two truths, however, is the theological and ecumenical challenge of the church today.

By reason of the covenant, God never forgets his people, no matter whomever or wherever they may be. People in prison, even for serious crimes, can experience conversion and a new love for the God who has been so good in spite of their own weakness. Marriages bruised by a spouse's flirting with infidelity are able to grow stronger by the renewed appreciation of enduring love. God's love remains forever.

A Stone Once Rejected Now Becomes the Basis for Everything

Skilled masons know that a carefully placed "keystone" can hold an arch in place for centuries by maintaining the needed tension to defy gravity. A different function is played by a carefully aligned cornerstone at the foundation of a corner angle of walls, providing a solid base for the entire edifice. Israelite leaders were implicitly called stones from which the tower rose strong and straight (Zech 10:4), and the house of David is called a tested cornerstone for Zion (Isa 28:16). The First Epistle of Peter calls Jesus the cornerstone of the Christian community (2:5), though one previously rejected (Ps 118:22). This fundamental architectural image was useful for explaining the importance and the mystery of Christ's crucifixion and subsequent exaltation by God. Peter's speech reflects the way in which the early church wove biblical citations and poetic imagery into the apologetic tapestry of Christian preaching and catechesis.

God's Story Made Present

God builds the church with rejected stones. Solanus Casey (1870–1957) was an American Capuchin friar and priest who was known during his lifetime as a wonderworker and was the first person born in the United States to be declared "venerable" by the Roman Catholic Church. He is now a candidate for beatification. Solanus was known for his great faith, humility, and role as spiritual counselor and intercessor. Baptized Bernard, at the age of twenty-one he expressed an interest in becoming a parish priest, and so he entered St. Francis Seminary in Milwaukee. Students of that time were expected to have a working knowledge of Latin and German. Because of his academic limitations, he was encouraged to join a religious community with the possibility of being ordained a simplex priest— that is, one who could say mass but would not be allowed to preach or hear confessions. Thus he joined the Order of Friars Minor Capuchins in Detroit and was ordained a simplex priest. Throughout his priesthood he served primarily as monastery porter, serving as receptionist and doorkeeper. He became known for his great compassion and wisdom in advising those who came to him, and many considered him instrumental in cures and other blessings they received. Indeed, the stone rejected by the builders has become the cornerstone.

ANTIPHON—PSALM 118:22
The stone rejected by the builders has become the cornerstone. (or: Alleluia)

Psalm 118:1-2, 4, 22-24, 25-27a

This psalm, as noted in the Talmud, was recited antiphonally in the temple liturgies with various portions of the assembly taking their designated parts. The final verses of today's liturgical refrain were sung by pilgrims at the gate (vv. 22-24) who were in turn blessed by the priests of the temple (vv. 25ff). Even God-fearers (v. 4)—that is, those proselytes who were still considering formal membership in the Jewish faith community—had a voice. It seems most appropriate that this psalm, which once reflected a pilgrim's awe at the temple's architectural cornerstones (v. 22), is selected by the Lectionary as a response for the crowds who gathered at the same temple gates when the beggar, cured by Peter, began to leap for joy. Again and again as echoed in this psalm, the pilgrims sang of God's mercy (*hesed*)—that is, God's mutual faithfulness to his covenanted people throughout all ages (v. 1).

The Refrain

While Jerusalem's Basilica of the Holy Sepulchre was being renovated in the late twentieth century, huge blocks of stone were piled in a neighboring courtyard, some quickly rejected for flaws as they awaited the mason's finishing chisel. The very same process of selection had undoubtedly occurred during the time of Solomon's initial building efforts some 2900 years earlier, as well as during Herod's massive renovation at the time of Jesus when actual visitors to the temple would have seen the stones cast off to the side. Moreover, the Christians' subsequent application of the designation of "temple" to the body of the risen Lord (see John 2:21 on the occasion of John's account of the cleansing of the temple) enables this psalm to serve as a powerful hymn during the Easter season. In the first reading Peter cites Psalm 118, referring to Jesus as a stone rejected by human authorities (v. 22), yet serving as the source of salvation for the world. The citation of the psalm in Peter's speech makes verses from that same psalm a perfect liturgical response for the community's response at Mass during Easter week.

GOSPEL ACCLAMATION—PSALM 118:24
The day in which God has acted now even includes an astonishing catch of fish and a lakeshore picnic with the risen Lord!

JOHN 21:1-14
Jesus came over and took the bread and gave it to them, and in like manner the fish.

Lectionary note: Since John's gospel had already offered a concluding invitation and exhortation to faith in Jesus as Messiah and Son of God (20:30), the gospel's twenty-first chapter must be an addition to the original text. Perhaps it represents another inspired portion of Scripture judged helpful for countering an early christological heresy or two. In John's gospel today's passage is then itself followed by the account of Peter's sorrowful renouncement of his earlier triple denial in the high priest's courtyard (18:15-18, 25-27) and the triple reinstatement of his mission to feed the Lord's flock (21:15-19). Finally, the gospel's concluding chapter will end with the

prediction by Jesus of Peter's destiny as contrasted with that of John (vv. 20-22) and with the gospel's second and definitive conclusion (v. 24).

Fishing as Missionary Activity

In his gospel account, Luke's great fish story had included a catch numerous enough to tear the nets, ending in Peter's humble admission of personal sinfulness and the Lord's response, which summoned him to be a fisher of human beings (5:1-11). That was Luke's catechetical way of describing the call of Peter and offering a remote preparation for the missionary activities of Acts. By way of comparison, John's manner of telling the tale retains the great catch in his final chapter and also includes Peter's implicit expression of sorrow for his earlier denial. The 153 large fish (v. 11) are brought to shore by apostles to become part of the eucharistic breakfast, just as new converts to "the Way" were baptized (Acts 2:41). The account proceeds to describe the Lord's triple pastoral invitation for Peter's assistance in feeding the lambs and nourishing the sheep. For John, the event is as much a revelation of Jesus (v. 1) as it is a summons to servant leadership for Peter in two different ways. What had begun as a possible antidote to Peter's personal boredom (v. 3) becomes an account of a significant moment of grace and growth for the entire church. God always seems to have a sense of humor about things. Apparently John felt the need to add this story to his gospel, thus illustrating the enduring double vocation of Peter as roving missionary, fisherman (vv. 3-6), and residential pastor and shepherd (vv. 15-19).

God's Story Made Present

Discipleship entails fishing the entire community. In the 1980s the Archdiocese of Milwaukee was faced with the reality of a declining number of priests to serve in local parishes. In addition, the archdiocese was forced to confront the reality that as demographics changed so did the number of active parishioners in some of its inner-city and rural parishes. In some instances parishes merged with others to form new and more viable faith communities. In other instances parishes were obligated to close their doors. Occasionally a parish protested that while their numbers were small, they nevertheless had sufficient revenue in parish coffers to remain open and provide a salary for a parish priest. Such a solution did not resolve the shortage of available clergy. Consequently criteria were established by which decisions were made as to which parishes would merge or close and which would remain open. One such criterion was whether or not there was sufficient viability in the parish to enliven ministries to the community, both internally and externally. In other words, there is more to a faith community than attending Mass on Sunday. Like Peter, every faith community is moved by God to be both a missionary to the larger civic community, as well as a shepherd to the faith community within.

Eucharistic Overtones

The way John recounts the story, Jesus had already prepared breakfast for his hungry disciples (v. 9) even before they came ashore. On that score he might even be considered the divine patron of every campfire cook! He proceeded, however, to invite an additional contribution from the fishermen themselves (v. 10), perhaps as a signal of the way in which he always welcomes our personal participation, however minimal, in the work of the Gospel. From its earliest years the Christian community used the symbol of a fish for Jesus himself since the Greek word for fish (*ichthus*) could be expanded to make each letter a separate word, representing the ancient confession of faith: ΙΧΘΥΣ, *Jesus Christ, Son of God and Savior*. Thus a meal, comprised of both bread and fish made sacred, signals deeper eucharistic meaning to

the early communities and their gatherings—and to us. The gospel accounts of the multiplication of loaves and fishes conveys the same message (see, for example, Mark 6:34-44).

God energizes us in eucharist. Our family meals generally call us from our daily work to be refreshed at the table. They seldom are tinged with the impetus to go out to work. Though our tradition seems to emphasize being sent out from the eucharistic meal and into life, this gospel seems to reverse that order and calls us from life and its labors into the Eucharist. It is at the meal that we come to understand our lives, why we labor, and how we find ourselves grateful for the persistence and faithfulness to the tasks that are necessary.

Initially Empty Nets

Even after a long night of hard work by experienced fishermen, their labor remained fruitless and their nets discouragingly empty (v. 3). It was only at the word of Jesus and his playful invitation to look to the other side of the boat (v. 6, something not particularly welcome by tired, unsuccessful fisherman) that they found abundance. One cannot help but recall the events during the public ministry of Jesus when the disciples wanted to dismiss the crowds because they had only a woeful bit of food in the shape of a mere five loaves and two fish for over five thousand people (Mark 6:38). The word of Jesus made the difference. Even earlier in history the empty coffers of the people of Israel, wandering in the barren desert, had been filled and fed by manna and heavenly quail by the word of Moses (Exod 16:1-12). The starving widow had only a tiny jug of oil and a handful of flour before Elijah's word brought enduring nourishment throughout the terrible drought (1 Kgs 17:7-16).

Like a fisherman, God provides a catch of abundance out of emptiness. Nevertheless, God's plans always seem to include surprising developments quite contrary to the world's expectations. The person serving time in prison, perhaps guilty of a heinous crime, comes to goodness and faith. Street people live their lives with great generosity for one another. The troubled teenager grows up to be a model spouse and parent. The same is echoed in the life of Saint Camillus de Lellis who, once addicted to gambling, gambled on God and gave his life away to care for the sick.

Friday of the Octave of Easter

1. Martin Luther King Jr., speech at Brown Chapel AME Church, Selma, AL, March 8, 1965.

Saturday of the Octave of Easter

God's Story Proclaimed

ACTS 4:13-21

It is impossible for us not to speak about what we have seen and heard.

Apostolic Boldness

Immediately after the resurrection and certainly after the gift of the Spirit at Pentecost, the apostles seem to be different, somehow newly changed by their encounter with the risen Jesus. They are now described as marked by the quality of *parrēsia* (v. 13)—that is, boldness, frankness, courage, and confidence. The first use of the word had already been found in Peter's address on Pentecost (2:29), but even that initial characteristic of Peter reflected the style of the personal words of Jesus at the Last Supper as noted by the surprised apostles at that table (John 16:29). True friends and companions of Jesus are recognized for their candor in service to the truth. Like them we are similarly called to be respectful but also courageously honest in bearing witness to our beliefs. "Therefore," as the Epistle to the Hebrews reminds us, "do not throw away your confidence (*parrēsia*); it will have great recompense" (10:35).

The Spirit translates fear into boldness. Our boldness as baptized disciples of Jesus is a reflection and echo of God's interventions in our world and makes us "apostolic." Resurrection speech is honest and frank. Whether we agree with their methods or not, those who protest nuclear facilities to the point of imprisonment and those who protest the presence of abortion clinics do live out their convictions with apostolic boldness.

Futile Human Prudence and Caution

The leaders of the temple and the prominent persons of Jerusalem felt the need to admonish Peter and John to greater caution (v. 17). To them it seemed more prudent not to speak in the name of the recently crucified disturber of the peace lest the ire of Roman authority come down upon the city in a more brutal, comprehensive, and ruthless fashion. Peter and John's reply in unison stands as a perennial acknowledgment of the duty to obey God rather than any human authority that acts contrary to God's will (v. 19). They offered the first Christian example of the imperative of rightly formed conscience; that same attitude therefore also is apostolic and paschal. Their clear expression so won the populace that the leadership in Jerusalem was not even able to punish those who spoke so boldly (v. 21). In Acts that same forthrightness will accompany the disciples all the way to Paul's bold teaching in Rome (28:31), no matter what forces of opposition they encountered as they traveled and proclaimed the Good News of Jesus, the risen Lord and Savior.

God's Story Made Present

God's Spirit moves the human heart to a right-formed conscience. Each person who seeks to follow Jesus has received a portion of Spirit. Not every voice is the Spirit's echo, yet it might be.

Thomas Aquinas once wrote, "Conscience is more to be obeyed than authority imposed from the outside. By following a right conscience you not only do not incur sin but are also immune from sin, whatever superiors may say to the contrary. To act against one's conscience and to disobey a superior can both be sinful. Of the two the first is the worse since the dictate of conscience is more binding than the decree of external authority."[1]

And Joseph Ratzinger (later Benedict XVI) once wrote, "Over the pope as expression of the binding claims of ecclesiastical authority, there stands one's own conscience which must be obeyed before all else, even if necessary against the requirement of ecclesiastical authority. The emphasis on the individual, whose conscience confronts him with a supreme and ultimate tribunal, and one which in the last resort is beyond the claim of external social groups, even the official church, also establishes a principle in opposition to increasing totalitarianism."[2]

ANTIPHON—PSALM 118:21A
I will give thanks to you for you have answered me. (or: Alleluia)

Psalm 118:1, 14-15ab, 16-18, 19-21

The very same psalm that had been used as the response to yesterday's first reading, albeit with a different refrain and new verses, is used again today. On both occasions the psalm begins with an expression of gratitude for God's enduring mercy (*hesed*), or covenantal faithfulness (v. 1). It is precisely that divine quality of fidelity to us human beings that explains the redeeming death of Jesus "for us and our salvation" (Nicene Creed). Psalm 118 is not only a hymn of thanksgiving (v. 1) but an entire liturgy with antiphonal verses celebrating the fact that God has not delivered his faithful servant to death (v. 18), but rather opened the temple gates to all the "just" (v. 20)—that is, to those who live in right relationship to the entire world. In particular, the psalm acknowledges that all "strength and courage" such as that exhibited by Peter and John come from God who is the "savior" of his servants (v. 14). Anyone entering the Temple Mount in Jerusalem today will see an iron box fixed to the stone wall and labeled—not "charity," as we might expect—but *tzedeqah* (justice). Those who come to pray are invited to make a donation toward a world more fully imbued with God's justice.

Gratitude

The refrain (v. 21) places an expression of gratitude on the lips of the entire eucharistic assembly and specifies that the motive is twofold. First of all, the congregation is invited to give thanks for God's enduring goodness (v. 1) and mercy—that is, *hesed* or reciprocal covenantal kindness. At the end of this psalm response, however, the additional motive is

God's positive response to prayer and God's gift of salvation from whatever difficulty that has recently been experienced (v. 21). God's response, whatever it may be, is also a source for thanksgiving. The use of these sentiments at the end of the first week of Easter continues the church's jubilant cry of thanks for the resurrection of Christ and for everything that event entails for his faithful people. How can one not be grateful for this radical change in the history of our world? The Eucharist is one way of grateful response.

GOSPEL ACCLAMATION—PSALM 118:24
In summary fashion we are reminded that the day that the Lord had made included the appearances of the risen Lord to Mary, to the two on their way to Emmaus, and the incredulous Eleven in the Upper Room.

MARK 16:9-15
Go unto the whole world and proclaim the Gospel to every creature.

Lectionary note: Just as yesterday's gospel passage was taken from an addition to John's gospel, so also today's text comes from inspired verses added to Mark lest that gospel conclude with the downbeat note of the women's fearfulness and silence (16:8), which could then signal the lack of the very gift of courage described in our first reading from Acts. The entire first week after Easter has provided a rich sampling of resurrection stories selected from the various gospels. The week now concludes liturgically with Christ's command that the disciples proclaim the Good News of the resurrection to "every creature" (v. 15). A remarkable cosmic element of land and water, plants and animals are thus included among the gospel's recipients in a wonderful echo of the first chapter of Genesis. Curiously, not mentioned in this liturgical reading are any of Mark's subsequent references to baptism (v. 16), the remarkable signs that might accompany their message (v. 17), or the ascension (v.

19). Perhaps the composers of the Lectionary did not wish to dilute the great commission or to offer a distracting reference to the ascension until it could be properly celebrated liturgically about forty days later.

The Mystery of Belief and Unbelief

Although these verses have been declared inspired by the church's early authorities, they do not appear in all the ancient manuscripts. Careful study suggests that the verses are in fact a compilation of references from the other gospels to complete the story and to avoid having Mark's gospel end with frightened silent women witnesses (v. 8). Thus we are told again of the appearance to Mary the Magdalen (from whom the seven demons of depression had once been driven, v. 9; see also Luke 8:2), who in turn announced the Good News to his mourning yet somehow skeptical disciples (v. 10). The travelers to Emmaus (Luke 24:35) believed, but those back in the Upper Room to whom they reported their experience did not (v. 13).

The theme of unbelief is realistically acknowledged in several of the resurrection narratives. In fact throughout Mark's entire gospel, the disciples were often hard-hearted and hesitant to believe (8:17-21). This summary includes that same response of disbelief repeatedly given to the report of Mary (v. 11), and to the two disciples who had come running back from Emmaus (v. 13; see also Luke 24:13-35). John's gospel includes the same reluctance, personified in Thomas who had been absent from the Upper Room on Easter Sunday (John 20:24-29). The certitude of our faith has been called "moral" because it differs from mathematical or scientific human conclusions, and thus it allows the individual to give a personal response to the news of the resurrection that remains free. Our faith, from the very beginning and even after all these years, is reasonable but not compelled. The act of personal faith leaves us free to respond positively or negatively to the witness of others. Even their faith does not force our minds, but rather offers an example for us as we make our own decisions for or against the Gospel. Absolute proof beyond all doubt is not given to us, but the assent of faith makes sense to inquiring minds and allows an intelligent and discerning Christian to enter God's new world of justice and peace. We believe, moreover, that faith itself is a gift from God that enhances our human nature.

God's Story Made Present

It is God who brings us to faith, not we ourselves. How is it that disbelief moves to belief? When it does take place we can find ourselves simply sitting back in awe. The following is an account of a parish minister who worked with high school youth.

Too often I have watched a shift take place in the psyche of high school youth during Christmas vacation of their junior year. Most regularly that truth particularly seems to play out in their preparation for celebrating the sacrament of confirmation. Prior to Christmas vacation it seems difficult, if not impossible, to engage them in any group discussion of what they believe about God or Church or Jesus or anything else they might hold in faith. I am not suggesting that they do not have faith. I have simply found them reluctant to share it, particularly in a group. After Christmas vacation, however, they seem to return somehow more mature, more willing to risk telling you and one another who they are and what they believe. I have no idea why it happens over Christmas vacation. I only know that it does happen. If it happened to the Eleven, why should it not still take place in our own day?

1. St. Thomas Aquinas, *De Veritate*, q. 17, a. 5.

2. Joseph Ratzinger, commentary on the Pastoral Constitution on the Church in the Modern World, in *Commentary on the Documents of Vatican II*, vol. 5, edited by Herbert Vorgrimler (New York: Herder and Herder, 1967), 134.

Second Week of Easter

Monday of the Second Week of Easter

God's Story Proclaimed

ACTS 4:23-31

As they prayed, they were all filled with the Holy Spirit and continued to speak the word of God with boldness.

Community Prayer

When Luke praised the idyllic communal life of the early Christian community immediately after Pentecost (Acts 2:42-47), he noted that they devoted themselves to prayer (v. 42), always praising God (v. 47). Inspired by the Holy Spirit (Rom 8:26), communal prayer and care for the needy were essential elements in their experience and identity. In today's reading we have an example of that prayer. The report of the experience of Peter's and John's arrest and their interrogation before the Sanhedrin (4:1-22) elicited the community's prayer of gratitude for the apostles' deliverance (vv. 24-30). This prayer as offered by Luke can serve as a possible model for our own Christian community prayer: (1) the invocation of God with titles appropriate to divine majesty (v. 24); (2) a citation from the Scriptures (in this case Ps 2 as repeated in the antiphon) that illumines and interprets their experience of persecution by authorities (v. 25); (3) a descriptive reference to some current event, such as the rejection of Jesus by Pilate and Herod in this case, but always placed in the broader context of God's plan for the world's salvation (v. 27); (4) a petition for divine protection and boldness of spirit (v. 29); and (5) some reference to their prayer and work as accomplished through the mediation / name of Jesus (v. 30). The prayer understands that the persecution by ancient nations has been renewed in their own time in the shape of the hostility of the Sanhedrin toward Jesus. Historic Assyrian and Babylonian enemies had come back to life in the form of their own civil authorities! Their prayer is a rare mixture of desperation and confidence because of Jesus.

God brings us to where we should be. In prayer God's Spirit fills us with power. People find the courage to stand alone. Others find peace in surrendering to realities beyond their control. Still others pray to uncover necessary wisdom. In the end, prayer is an expression of dependence upon God and a means of entrusting the future of our spirits' needs to God. That can be bold and risky business, but such is the nature of faith. American poet Mary Oliver recognizes that as well and often returns to that idea in her poetry, noting "How everything turns out one way or another." In her own way she understands the ways of God and is willing to surrender to it. "I won't call it good or bad, just / one way or another."[1]

Home Office Reports

With surprising regularity Luke described the way individual apostles repeatedly returned to the Christian community in Jerusalem or Antioch in order to report the successes of their early missionary efforts. This had been done earlier when the Seventy-two returned from their mission prior to the resurrection (Luke 10:17-20). The same practice is found in Acts. As noted at the beginning of this reading (v. 23), Peter and John quickly reported their experience before the Sanhedrin to the larger community. The reading is about community prayer, but prayer inspired by the testimony of Peter and John. Similarly, the work of Phillip in Samaria was reported to the apostles (8:14) who then sent Peter and John so that the Samaritans might receive the gift of the Spirit. The news of the evangelization of the name of Jesus to Greeks in Antioch reached the ears of the church in Jerusalem (11:22), which then sent Barnabas to serve as a resident teacher in their midst. Paul and Barnabas also reported the results of their first great missionary journey to the community at Antioch—namely, "what God had done with them, and how he had opened the door of faith to the Gentiles" (14:27). The purpose of these visits and reports was not merely good communication on the part of the first apostles but an expression of their belief that all the religious experience of Christians somehow belongs to the whole church, which retains the responsibility of judging its conformity to the Gospel they had received from the Lord at the time of the Great Commission (Mark 16:15; Matt 28:19; Acts 1:7). The reports inspired grateful prayer and further action; they are an important part of the bigger picture.

Monday of the Second Week of Easter

It is through the community that the Spirit gives approval to the works of the Gospel. Throughout the ages, "lone ranger" ministry without community accountability has continued to be problematic. With the advent of pastoral councils an attitude of mutual discernment has been required and facilitated between parochial leaders and the community of faith. Each has their own wisdom to offer in the process of decision making. Leaders are expected to bring a vision of church beyond the local community, and the local faith community is expected to ground decisions in the day-to-day ministries they perform. Each is in need of the other.

Your Holy Servant Jesus

Among the earliest keys to the church's understanding of the life and mission of Jesus of Nazareth were the five great Servant Songs of Isaiah (42:1-9; 49:1-7; 50:4-7; 52:13–53:12; 61:1-3). Although Jewish piety had traditionally viewed those songs as words of divine encouragement for the entire people of Israel, especially in times of dire persecution, early Christians quickly perceived a deeper and fuller meaning when applied to the ministry of Jesus himself. It is true that all faithful people of Israel, and in particular the prophets, had been called servants of God. In fact the psalms are filled with the use of that title. Jesus, however, became recognized by his disciples after the resurrection as God's servant *par excellence.* Early on he was given that title as we hear twice in this brief prayer (vv. 27, 30). In ancient Israel high government posts were held by individuals who gloried in the title of "servant," a practice that continues in modern nations who are served by a minister of finance, minister of the interior, and a prime minister. The bishop of Rome likewise is described as the "servant of the servants of God." Curiously, a study of Paul's epistles in the New Testament suggests that the title was quickly replaced by others such as Lord (*kurios*). Perhaps the move from Semitic culture to the more universal Hellenistic world rendered "servant" language less understandable to those whom they now attempted to evangelize.

God-inspired leadership is always leadership by serving. We can learn to like our bailiwicks, even become protective of our bailiwicks. The wisdom of many vowed religious communities returns their leaders to the ranks of the regulars in a community lest anyone become possessive of their roles or their approaches to common challenges of the day. It's a good practice to assure that service remains service and not power or control. In another context, our nation limits the terms of presidents. To the extent that all public officials must periodically run to be reelected attests that they, too, have terms limited and defined by serving the true needs of the time.

Apostolic Boldness

Already during Luke's description of the Pentecost event, we see signs of the spirit of boldness that characterized Peter's first efforts at Christian preaching. The high priests who later interrogated Peter and John after the healing of the lame beggar were astonished by that same boldness (Acts 4:13 in Greek: *parrēsia*) in those uneducated men. The word itself means frankness, candor, and forthrightness. It was understood to be a special characteristic given by the Holy Spirit and associated with the witness of the apostles. In the prayer as reported in this morning's first reading, we hear of the early Christian church's prayer for the gift of boldness in their preachers (v. 29) and the way in which the same community then spoke so boldly as a sign that their prayer had been heard by God (v. 31). In different ways the entire Christian community gave ample evidence of having received that gift from God's Spirit of truth and love.

God's Story Made Present

The Spirit's power rumbles in our depths. In the 1989 film *Field of Dreams,* Ray Kinsella builds a baseball field in the middle of his Iowa cornfield. He believes that if he builds it, they will come to play ball and to live the dream, as the voice he had heard told him. So he builds the baseball field, and they do come—Shoeless Joe Jackson and the old-time players from the Chicago Black Sox, those White Sox players banned from the game for throwing the 1919 World Series—and they play.

It is Terence Mann, Ray's friend from the East, who sees them play on Ray's field and decides to return with them to the place from whence they came, to the place where those who have died play baseball day in and day out. Terence Mann chooses to approach death not as a problem to avoid but as a mystery into new life. So as all the old-timers walk from the baseball field back into the field of eight-foot-high cornstalks, back into the death from which they came, Terence Mann walks into that field of corn as well—into death, simply because he believes it to be the life for which he longs.

If it is true that there are such individuals in real life like Ray Kinsella and Terence Mann who march to the beat of a different drum, even more so do believers in the Lord Jesus march to the beat of the Holy Spirit. Why we lift up our voices in disagreement with injustice, why we choose to walk a path of care for those who are lost, why we live contrary to the norm—it all comes from the Spirit that beats its rhythm in our hearts.

Pentecost Renewed

When Luke described the great event of Pentecost, he made a point of insisting that they had experienced "a noise *like* a strong driving wind which filled the house" (Acts 2:2, italics added) and "tongues *as if* of fire which parted and came to rest on each one of them" (v. 3, italics added). The text doesn't really say that there *was* wind and fire, but it desperately tries to find frail human examples of the deeper reality occasioned by the powerful impact of a new presence of God's life-giving Spirit in their midst. To the community of the Upper Room, still deeply troubled by the guilt and shame of having fled, or even worse, of having actually denied their Lord and Master at the time of his crucifixion, came an astonishingly renewed unity and vitality; human words failed them, yet some explanation had to be offered for that transforming experience. We call it Pentecost because it occurred at the time of the ancient Jewish festival of the same name. Apparently, at least in this account described in Acts, other early Christian communities also experienced similar powerful moments of new vitality, spiritual energy, and transforming charity, which they quickly ascribed to the power of the Holy Spirit. We hear of the first of these events in today's reading. Struggling for words, they reported that the place seemed to shake as they were filled with the Holy Spirit and spoke with astonishing new boldness (v. 31). The Christian Pentecost was a foundational event in the life of the early church. However it be described, it was also one of God's gifts to other early communities of faith. God had heard their prayer and blessed them with a renewed gift of the life-giving Spirit.

The Holy Spirit unsettles and refashions the entire Christian church. In recent times the church has been refashioned by the initiatives of St. John XXIII, St. John Paul II, and Pope Francis.

> **Monday of the Second Week of Easter**

Ecumenism offers another example of being refashioned by the presence of the Spirit. Even the acknowledgment of sin is used by the Spirit to reshape the church—as in the recent revelations of sexual abuse. Just because something may be unsettling does not mean it is necessarily not of the Spirit. In fact, it may be *precisely* that.

**Monday
of the
Second Week
of Easter**

ANTIPHON—PSALM 2:11D
Blessed are all who take refuge in the Lord. (or: Alleluia)

Psalm 2:1-3, 4-7a, 7b-9

Most scholars see this psalm as a hymn associated with the ritual enthronement of a new king in Jerusalem. The words are based on the human reality that the death of a king often offered a unique window of opportunity for a captive nation to cast off chains of bondage and reassert its freedom. The first task of a new ruler in the ancient world, therefore, was to insist on his authority and to rein in all potential rebels. The psalm acknowledges such resistance against the Lord and his anointed (v. 2) but quickly reports divine dismissal of their futile efforts (v. 4) and the reassertion of God's angry support for the newly anointed ruler (v. 5). The words of the Lord form an oracle of divine adoption for the new king (v. 7). When applied to Jesus, newly risen and triumphant over the feeble political powers of Rome and Jerusalem, these same words pay tribute to a divine Sonship that breaks military power like cheap crockery (v. 9).

The Refrain

The verse from Psalm 2 selected as the antiphonal refrain to the congregation's response to the day's first reading (v. 11) is not included in the liturgical text. It serves, however, as the perfect description of that bold early Christian response to the Sanhedrin's effort to suppress their faith in Jesus newly risen and triumphant over all merely human authority. As if in reply to their humble and prayerful expression of dependence, God has chosen to protect them against futile human op-position. They did indeed take successful refuge in the Lord alone.

GOSPEL ACCLAMATION—COLOSSIANS 3:1
Echoing the way in which the first reading spoke of the community, this citation now adds the fact that the community's prayerful experience is somehow also "raised" with Christ.

The Gospel of John

Written in its final form toward the end of the first century some sixty years after the resurrection, this gospel gives evidence of a matured faith in Jesus as fully divine. It also reflects some of the later disputes that began to mar the relationship between early Christian followers of Jesus and their Jewish neighbors.

JOHN 3:1-8
No one can enter the Kingdom of God without being born of water and Spirit.

Lectionary note: For the first four days of this week the gospel readings are taken from successive sections of the third chapter of John's gospel with its reflections on the meaning of "being born again." This decision of the Lectionary is most appropriate in the light of the annual ritual of the Easter Vigil, which celebrates the baptism of new converts to Christian faith. Through that sacrament they share in the graces of the Lord's redemptive death and resurrection; they receive the gift of membership in the church as well as a new beginning and a new type of life.

Darkness at dawn

The biblical assessment of darkness is essentially mixed and surprisingly often positive. Although John's passion narrative began with the ominous note of nighttime (13:30) as Judas took the morsel dipped in paschal sauce and went off to begin the betrayal, most references are more positive. Even that gesture may have signaled something ultimately luminous! The book of Genesis begins with a brief reference to a world "without form or shape" (*tohu wabohu*), totally covered by darkness (1:2). It was a darkness, however, charged with the potential of a world coming into orderly existence under God's command and ultimately judged "very good indeed" (v. 31). Darkness also covered the Red Sea when Israel prepared to cross its waves in their flight from Pharaoh's army (Exod 14:20). These classic biblical prototypes were perfect examples of the proverbial "darkness before the dawn" and were moments of potential grace. They should be kept in mind as we begin John's story of the visit of Nicodemus who came "at night" (v. 2). The entire pericope is about this leader's darkness open to the light of greater truth represented by Jesus who was recognized by John's gospel as "a light shining in the darkness" (John 1:5) and who was himself "the light of the world" (8:12).

God's Story Made Present

God spins darkness into new grace and fresh starts in our life. Just as the night surrounds the blessing of the Easter candle at the annual Vigil celebration, thus it is in the darkness that God is recognized. In 1931 Arthur Schwartz and Howard Dietz teamed up to write a song entitled "Dancing in the Dark." Since then it has been recorded by multiple artists, including Ella Fitzgerald, Frank Sinatra, Bing Crosby, Tony Bennett, Diana Krall, and many more. The song is not about dancing but about living, about stumbling our way through life as we grope for meaning:

> Dancing in the dark till the tune ends
> We're dancing in the dark and it soon ends
> We're waltzing in the wonder of why we're here
> Time hurries by, we're here and gone

Nicodemus the Seeker

It may be helpful to recall the literary background immediately prior to this story of the nighttime visit of Nicodemus. Jesus had just completed the cleansing of the temple (2:13-22), which the Gospel of John places as a prelude to the public ministry of Jesus. Although the Synoptic Gospels

present that episode as a final act of Jesus' courageous personal confrontation with the authorities in Jerusalem just before his arrest (almost a blast of light before the darkness), John prefers to depict the event in the temple at the very beginning of his ministry, thus gradually introducing Jesus as an alternative and luminously new means of access to the Father. John's gospel then pauses for a thoughtful if brief reflection on the frailty of human testimony and allegiance, even among the new disciples of Jesus (2:23-25). Only then does the figure of Nicodemus appear (3:1-21). Often Nicodemus's nighttime visit (v. 2) is viewed as cowardly and overly fearful of peer pressure or social stigma for giving any credence to Jesus. An alternative explanation, however, might simply be the tentativeness of his initial serious query and a genuine desire on his part for the leisure of thoughtful consideration worthy of the claims that Jesus is beginning to make. The remarkable signs of God's intervention in events such as the transformation of water into wine at Cana (2:1-11) and the cleansing of the temple signaled something that needed further personal inquiry. Perhaps the darkness was not cowardly cover but first steps toward the light. Nicodemus, a "leader of the Jews" (v. 1), responded to the grace with polite respect. His personal approach serves to prepare for the entire section's final statement regarding truth, which comes to light and can be clearly seen (v. 21). Nicodemus enables Jesus to shine like the morning star just before dawn. Nicodemus represents every disciple at the beginning of a faith journey.

Just a few years later this same Nicodemus will return to the pages of John's gospel with a more mature faith and bringing a hundred pounds of precious myrrh and aloes for the burial of the body of the Lord he had come to know and believe (19:39).

God begins us on a journey to faith in the midst of doubt and uncertainty. Knowing that our first steps toward full faith can be tentative, God invites each of us to seek ever more knowledge of Jesus and his mission. It is in the dark of night that we see the distant and faint glimmer of starlight. The first questions of teenagers prior to confirmation or those of converts often open vast new vistas of light. Naming our doubts can also serve to name pathways to renewed faith and trust as we explore ways in which God's Spirit gives birth to renewed faith.

Monday of the Second Week of Easter

Born from Above

One of the striking literary characteristics of John's gospel is the manner in which the same word, phrase, or concept is repeated and offers ever more profound meanings. Each usage gradually deepens and leads to the next. "Born from above" (v. 3) is a perfect example. The basic human concept of "birth" is stated eight times within these eight verses, each slightly different and more revealing of the fuller teaching of Jesus. Human existence, marvelous yet completely natural in its origins, is thus contrasted with an existence different from and transcending our daily world. Just as people can see the physical effects of trees bending and feel the evening breezes without knowing the source of the wind (v. 8), so the true and ultimate source of the fuller life described by Jesus remains mysterious and beyond human understanding. The results, however as yet unnamed, will be obvious to any bystander. Being "born again" (v. 4), because it is clearly not physical, suggests a fresh start and life on a new level, closer to God's way of existence and not achieved by mere human effort. Almost like a gradually rising helix, the concept of new life is introduced and then gradually clarified until it reaches full membership in God's kingdom (v. 3). Subtle sacramental allusions still dance in the background of this process of becoming children of God in a new way. Eventually qualities such as openness to the heavenly Spirit (14:17), loving one another (13:34), sharing divine life as branches of one vine (15:5), and a willingness to lay down one's life for others (15:13) will be further signs of that new life.

Bit by bit God marks the path ahead. God teases us into a new level of human existence that surpasses and transcends religious life as normally understood. The journey of life could be so much simpler, but that is not the path we have been given, nor even the path we have chosen from among the many forks we come upon. We learn our way, coming to wisdom by ways of darkness when choices seem so unsure. In his poem "The Waking" Theodore Roethke muses, "I wake to sleep, and take my waking slow . . . I learn by going where I have to go."[2] He's quite right. Slowly we come to realize what is beautiful and true and wonderful, that too often we've looked in all the wrong places. We do wake up to the fact that we've been asleep, then, and we come to realize what is of value, where love is found, and how the path to goodness sometimes seems to be a spiral that goes round and round.

"I learn by going where I have to go," the poet writes. And is that not how we learn, how we wake up ever so slowly to new light—by going where we have to go? Not where we want to go or think we should go or would daydream our going, but where we *have* to go. And that is how we wake up, too, to how we've been asleep to so much of life.

1. Mary Oliver, "For Example," *Swan* (Boston: Beacon, 2010), 11.

2. Theodore Roethke, "The Waking," *Collected Poems of Theodore Roethke* (New York: Anchor, 1975), 104.

Tuesday of the Second Week of Easter

God's Story Proclaimed

ACTS 4:32-37
The community of believers was of one heart and mind.

A Community of One Mind and Heart in Action

This is the second summary description of the Jerusalem community in the Acts of the Apostles (see also 2:42-47). Both accounts serve as bookends for the account of the healing of the lame beggar and the apostles' first encounter with the Sanhedrin. While the prior text emphasized common prayer and teaching, this passage highlights their unity and their subsequent care for the needy. This pericope states that the multitude (*plēthos*) of believers was one in heart and soul (v. 32), thus from the beginning contrasting their number and their unity. Moreover, in ancient Semitic anatomy the heart was where individuals did their planning and made decisions, which in turn nicely introduced the statement regarding the use of property held in common (v. 35). This is a community united for action. A reader conversant with Jewish piety would immediately recognize the allusion to the great command to love God with all one's heart, being, and strength (Deut 6:5, which Luke adapts to the Greek mentality by adding "mind"; see Luke 10:27) and the corresponding command to love one's neighbor as oneself (Lev 19:18). A community's unity of purpose and action, together with its underlying motivation, becomes evident in its decisions and actions. From their fruit one shall know them. Could any contemporary parish find its "mission statement" in this description?

God's people always look like God when they act in unison. Diversity may be a gift of the Spirit, but never division. When a community rises up together in the face of a natural disaster, when friends gather around those who grieve a loss, when throngs raise their voices in opposition to injustice and oppression, there is always the aura of God in their coming together. A homily might name the points of unity in your specific parish community.

Generosity and Common Property

The Gospel of Luke and its corresponding account in Acts speak of the spread of the message of Jesus to the Roman center of the Gentile world. It was written especially for the affluent and well-educated as evidenced in the double prologues (Luke 1:1-4; Acts 1:1-5). For that reason Luke's gospel repeatedly and uniquely addresses the sin of greed (12:15) and the duty of generosity to the needy (14:13). The same gospel proposes the "Mother Church" in Jerusalem as a model in these matters for all the other communities that would spring into existence as a result of the subsequent apostolic missionary journeys. Paul, Mark, and Barnabas are described later in the book as founding those communities. Jesus himself, as Matthew described his conversation with disciples of John the Baptist, was characterized as curing the sick and preaching the Gospel to the poor (11:2-6). In Luke's theology, a community willing to hold all possessions in common in order to distribute them to the needy was an important sign of evangelical authenticity. This passage helps to set the course for the rest of the story.

God's Story Made Present

When God shares, we share. When a Wisconsin resident had his prayers answered and won a jackpot worth $7.4 million at a local casino, Jacob Lonetree—chairman of the Ho-Chunk Nation—offered some advice to that resident: "There is a certain sense of responsibility that goes with becoming a select member of the community," he said. "When an individual ascends

41

into the realm of financial independence, he has an obligation to society, a call to care for more than himself."

God's Spirit leads us to generosity in unexpected ways. A parish that can only boast of its ability to turn on the lights and pay its bills is not authentically Christian without regular and consistent care for the needy. A homily might name the aspects of parish generosity both within itself and beyond itself.

Tuesday of the Second Week of Easter

Joseph the Son of Encouragement

Today's first reading concludes with a brief description of the generosity of Joseph a.k.a. Barnabas (v. 36). His actions illustrate the previous verses. His charity is so outstanding as to make him a model and patron "saint" for others, apparently both in personal generosity and in religious wisdom. He is singled out here because he would soon be a celebrated catechist in the early Christian community at Antioch to which he would be sent by the apostles (11:22-26). Apparently his personal fidelity to the Gospel and his kindness (v. 23) made him a local legend. In today's reading he is a concrete example of the community's generosity. The same qualities contributed to his nickname of Barnabas ("son of encouragement"). A small select group of leaders including Barnabas and Saul (13:1, 9) were considered teachers and prophets at Antioch. It was from the very same community at Antioch that Paul and Barnabas, after prayer and the laying on of hands, would be sent on their first missionary journey through Asia Minor (13:3). This pair changed the history of the early church and modeled a true team spirit that combined evangelical gentleness (Barnabas) and zeal (Paul). Apparently teaching by encouragement rather than by reprimand was prized at Antioch. The same pedagogical priority was present in first-century Jewish rabbinic circles where the kindness of Rabbi Hillel became the preferred model rather than his more austere contemporary, Rabbi Shamai. In more modern times, St. John XXIII and Pope Francis have employed the same pastoral methodology with much success.

God's Story Made Present

God's kindness spreads to everything it touches. Like honey, it clings and flavors all we do. Long ago I spent an entire summer living with black families in rural Mississippi. I met some wonderful folks there—all generous, welcoming, and gracious. To this day I remember Annie. At least seventy-five years old, she reminded me then of Granny from *Beverly Hillbillies*. She was spry, wispy, and thin as a blade of grass, climbing over barbed-wire farm fences and doing chores in her bib coveralls. She raised chickens, tilled a backyard garden, and swore at life as if she owned it. Once I asked Annie what she did with all the eggs her chickens laid. Sell them? "Lord no," she spun back at me, "I give them away." "But why not sell them?" I asked aloud as I foolishly plodded further into her thinking. "Then you'd have some money for a rainy day." "Heavens, no!" she replied. "I give them away to folks who need them and when those folks have something of whatever I need, why then they give to me."

ANTIPHON—PSALM 93:1

The Lord is king; he is robed in majesty. (or: Alleluia)

Psalm 93:1ab, 1cd-2, 5

Scholars seem fairly united in the conviction that this psalm, together with hymns such as Psalms 47, 97, and 99, was an enthronement hymn used regularly in Jerusalem's annual New Year's covenant renewal ceremony. Although the most ancient origins of the festival were probably in Mesopotamia, the idea of God's kingship found ready resonance with kingship celebrations already present among the people of Israel. Those who returned to Jerusalem from Babylonian exile in 538 BCE were eager to include the same elements into their own worship at home. Poetic references to God wearing clothing such as majesty and splendor (v. 1) and seated on an ancient and stable throne (v. 2) were celebrated joyously, especially after the disappearance of human kings in Second Temple Judaism. In more modern Catholic piety, the feast of Christ the King became more popular as European monarchs claimed increasingly absolute (and unacceptable) authority over the religious life of their citizens in the nineteenth and twentieth centuries.

The Refrain

The refrain (v. 1) would seem to be a communal acclamation at some key moment in the ancient liturgical celebration of YHWH's kingship. We know that such a popular acclamation was the practice, even in the rebellious human coronation of Absalom (2 Sam 15:10). The approval of the people was essential. Since a sentiment of respect for divine kingship or any allusion to it does not seem to be found in the actual words of the first reading from Acts (except possibly the reference to the "resurrection of the Lord Jesus" in v. 33), it would seem that the refrain's real reference is to the Easter triumph of Christ over sin and death. Each congregational repetition of this refrain at morning Mass, therefore, is a new recognition of the risen Lord's glorious authority over all creation.

GOSPEL ACCLAMATION—JOHN 3:14
Departing from the regular pattern of the Lectionary, the liturgy selects the actual final verses of today's pericope, thus alerting the congregation to the high point of what is to follow.

JOHN 3:7B-15
No one has gone up to heaven except the one who has come down from heaven, the Son of Man.

Born of the Spirit

In an unusual decision quite contrary to most other selections for the Lectionary, the church has chosen to repeat the final two verses (vv. 7b-8) of yesterday's gospel and use them again as the introduction to today's reading. That decision can only indicate that the phrases are somehow pivotal to the meaning of each passage. The repetition also illustrates the way the single notion of "born" continues to unfold, develop, and deepen in John's treatment of this theme. By referring to birth "through water and the spirit" (v. 5), John uses human birth and the breaking of water in a mother's womb as an analogue for the spiritual fresh start initiated by baptism as well as the ensuing new life. To be born "from above" (v. 7) and of God's Spirit (v. 8), however, is to become a child of God and to live in a new and different way. Across the world Holy Saturday is an occasion for many being baptized and welcomed into God's family. Each one has a unique story to tell of coming to faith and being "born again"; each arrives with an element of mystery and the unknown movement of God's Spirit. Each now faces a new beginning.

> **God's Story Made Present**
>
> *The wind of the Spirit deepens faith.* A couple of years ago *Newsweek* featured a series of articles on what teens believe about God, sex, race, and the future. One of the articles began with an interview of who they think God is. "Their answers were as individual as the kids themselves. One thought God was like his grandfather: 'He's there, but I never see him.' Another took a harder view, describing 'an evil being who wants to punish me all the time.' Two more opinions followed. Finally, the last teen weighed in: 'I think you're *all* right, because that's what you really believe.' In other words . . . God is whatever works for you. On this all of the youth agreed."[1]
>
> On the one hand, those teens had begun to tell their own stories of coming to faith. Yet, on the other hand, God can't be whatever we want God to be. God is more than putty in our hands waiting to be shaped into what we think God might be. Nevertheless we are all on a journey spurred by the Spirit.

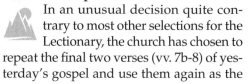

Tuesday of the Second Week of Easter

Teaching and Learning

Just as Nicodemus respected Jesus as a teacher at the beginning of this account yesterday (v. 2), so Jesus now also acknowledges Nicodemus as one who holds the same responsibility in Israel (v. 10). It was a title of great honor and responsibility. Even God was called a teacher (*moreh*, literally, "one who throws ideas out to others") by the prophet Isaiah (30:20). From ancient times the rabbis of Israel were primarily teachers who knew the will of God as expressed in the Torah and who were able to explain its meaning for others. In this case, Jesus chides Nicodemus, teacher from among the Pharisees, for not knowing the deeper implications of God's truth (v. 10), but he also welcomes Nicodemus as one seeking to learn by his asking, "How can this happen?" (v. 9). When Paul listed the various roles exercised by individual Christians as a result of the gift of the Spirit, he noted "teachers" immediately after apostles and prophets (1 Cor 12:28). In the context of contemporary Christian life, parents are the first teachers of their children, and parish catechists help deepen the faith of those with whom they share the teachings of Jesus. As such, they are witnesses to the work of God, as well as instruments and images of that same living God. Teachers can only teach what they have learned. Each of the questions of Nicodemus gives him access to new levels of God's truth.

God brings us to wisdom through the questions we ask. The poet Wallace Stevens once made the observation, "Perhaps the truth depends on a walk around the lake." And so it does. Whether it was Nicodemus who took a walk in the night to see Jesus, Wallace Stevens who takes a walk around the lake, or we ourselves who take a walk around our own questions and doubts, that is the way to wisdom and understanding and the sort of faith by which we get a glimpse of seeing the world with the eyes of God.

Lifted Up to New Life

This is yet another example of the way in which John's gospel plays with images and ideas, first presenting the object as a simple material reality but then suggesting a deeper spiritual significance. To be "born again" is to be "born from above" (that is, obviously not by our own efforts, v. 7) and "lifted up" (v. 15) to a new way of living. At delivery and birth we are lifted up by nurses, doctors, and midwives. Jesus insists that Nicodemus must be "born again from above" (v. 7). Apparently the bronze serpent had once been elevated by Moses as a cure for those who had been bitten by serpents in the desert (Num 21:9) and then artistically represented in the temple. Popular medicine can have some strange remedies. John understands that object and the event it described as a sort of precursor for the healing effected by Jesus when he in turn was lifted up on the cross (v. 14). Both incidents find fulfillment when the risen Jesus is eventually glorified and exalted to the Father in victory forever. Even the humanity of Jesus, the fully human "Son of Man," is lifted up and raised to glory (v. 15). The entire passage is about something very material (and possibly repulsive), serpent or cross as the case may be, changed and "lifted up" to become an instrument of divine action to transform the world. Because Jesus is lifted up, however, so are his disciples.

God lifts us up out of ignorance, sorrow, and sin. The wife and mother whose world has become her children at the exclusions of attentiveness to her husband comes to realize this and is able to find a new balance in her life. The widower lost in grief does move through that grief and into finding satisfaction and meaning in giving time to local charities. The person addicted to pornography comes to realize how it is stifling him, struggles with it, and is able to be freed from its snares. Always there is more going on in our lives than our own efforts.

Belief into Eternal Life

Being born, not by natural human procreation but mysteriously by the Spirit, requires acceptance by faith (v. 12). Such a type of new existence lies beyond mere natural human knowledge or experience. This truth of faith is known on the authority of Jesus the teacher. That same teacher also insists that faith leads to new life at a different level. At the end of this Lectionary passage, John's Jesus adds yet another new idea—namely, "eternal life" (v. 15). The Greek wording of that phrase, however, *zōēn aiōnion*, has its own distinctive nuance. The literal sense is "life of the [next] age." The customary translation of the words as "eternal" merely suggests life that is endless and enduring forever. The basic idea of the Greek, however, is its essential difference from what we experience here and now. Faith does more than remove the ending; it changes everything. We not only see differently; we have different things to see.

God's Story Made Present

Being born again gives life a new set of rules. God's gift of faith changes what and how we see the whole world in which we live and work.

Mark plays backgammon the way children huddle around a Christmas tree or the way bees swarm a hive—as if he can't get enough of it all. According to Mark, backgammon has plateaus of skill and proficiency. As one moves from plateau to plateau one has to unlearn the current level because what once worked no longer does, such that the opposite is now true. In that sense the rules change. We can only take his word for it regarding backgammon, but that is also what happens when one is born again. We are continually forced to reconsider how faith calls us to live.

> **Tuesday of the Second Week of Easter**

1. John Leland, "Searching for a Holy Spirit," *Newsweek* (May 7, 2000), http://www.newsweek.com/searching-holy-spirit-159871.

Wednesday of the Second Week of Easter

God's Story Proclaimed

ACTS 5:17-26

The men whom you put in prison are in the temple area and are teaching the people.

Lectionary note: For some reason the Lectionary chooses to omit the story of the deceptive donation of Ananias and Sapphira (5:1-11), who made a show of generosity but withheld some of their property from the community's common fund for the poor. This was in stark contrast to the immediately preceding tale of the genuine gesture of Joseph called Barnabas (4:36). More puzzling, however, is the fact that the Lectionary also omits the brief account of the miraculous cures accomplished by even the passing shadow of Peter as he walked through the streets of Jerusalem (vv. 12-16), which would have highlighted the continuity between the works of Jesus and those of the apostles after the resurrection.

Divine Deliverance

Somewhat like Peter's later miraculous deliverance from prison after the beginning of persecution by Herod (12:3-18), God's angel intervened to free the apostles in this earlier event (5:19-21). Neither mere human opposition nor iron bars could impede the power of God's word. The powerful words that described and promised "this life" (v. 20) rendered prisons worthless. Note that in this case the angel doesn't command that they simply speak of the resurrection of Jesus, but rather that they proclaim the common life, actions, and whole way of life as people who believe in the risen Lord. The boldness of the apostles could not be cowed or contained, and their entire lives were offered as a motive of credibility for those to whom they gave witness. God continually freed them for their mission of offering witness to the resurrection of Jesus and to the work of God as already previously promised at the time of the ascension (1:8).

God's Story Made Present

The word of God will not be squelched. God breaks any limits imposed on true apostolic witness that human fear or force attempts to impose. It was proclaimed forcefully in Leonard Bernstein's *Mass*—in particular, the "Epistle" movement, which includes the following:

> Go, and lock up your bold men, and hold them in tow.
> You can stifle all adventure, for a century or so.
> Smother hope before it's risen, watch it wizen like a gourd.
> But you *cannot* imprison the Word of the LORD.
> No, you cannot imprison the Word of the LORD.

Civic and faith communities still organize for justice. Volunteers passionately seek to build a better world. The cry of the oppressed refuses to be silenced. And believers do it all in the name of Jesus.

Teaching in the Temple

By way of introduction to the earlier account of the cure of the lame beggar, we were told that Peter and John had gone to the temple at the ninth hour (about three in the afternoon) to pray (3:1). After that cure they had taught the people and proclaimed the resurrection of Jesus (4:2) for which they had been arrested, interrogated, and miraculously released by the angel who ordered them to go back to their place in the temple and "tell people everything about this life" (v. 20). Today's pericope ends with an astonished and exasperated report that the team was back in the temple, "teaching the people" (v. 25)! The apostles prayed, gave witness to the resurrection of Jesus, and taught. Just as the mysterious pilgrim had explained everything, beginning with Moses and the prophets, to the travelers to Emmaus (Luke 24:27), Peter and John are now back in the temple explaining their faith and their new lifestyle to the crowds.

As part of an early baptismal homily Christians were told to "always be ready to give an explanation to anyone who asks you for a reason for your hope" (1 Pet 3:15). We not only proclaim Jesus as risen but also propose reasonable membership in a church. In a sense, the two apostles proclaimed themselves and the life to which they had been called. They stood in the temple courts announcing *who* they were and *why* they were.

God's Story Made Present

When we commit, God moves. The commitments we make matter. What we value, where we put our energies, how we spend our time—they all make a difference beyond what we would anticipate. Peter and John would be bold examples. The following extract, often attributed to the German poet Goethe, notes how a commitment sets into motion an entire series of events:

> Until one is committed, there is hesitancy, the chance to draw back, always ineffectiveness. Concerning all acts of initiative (and creation) there is one elementary truth, the ignorance of which kills countless ideas and splendid plans: that the moment one definitely commits oneself, then Providence moves too. All sorts of things occur to help one that would never otherwise have occurred. A whole stream of events issues from the decision, raising in one's favor all manner of unforeseen incidents and meetings and material assistance which no man could have dreamed would have come his way.
> Whatever you can do,
> Or dream you can, begin it.
> Boldness has genius,
> Power and magic in it.[1]

ANTIPHON—PSALM 34:7
The Lord hears the cry of the poor. (or: Alleluia)

Psalm 34:2-3, 4-5, 6-7, 8-9

Psalm 34 is a Hebrew acrostic—that is, each verse begins with a successive letter of the alphabet. For that reason it may seem somewhat disjointed and generic in its praise for the way God cares for the poor. Because of the reference to "tasting God's goodness" (v. 9), this hymn was often used as a communion song in the early church's celebration of the Eucharist. It is chosen for communal recitation here, however, because it expresses the gratitude of the apostles upon their deliverance from fear (v. 5) and from all distress (v. 7). Moreover, the psalm announces that it is the angel of the Lord who delivers them all (v. 8)!

**Wednesday
of the
Second Week
of Easter**

The Refrain

The notion of "the poor" is one of the classic examples of doctrinal development over the centuries during which the Scriptures of Israel were written, collected, and prayed. Originally, wealth was understood by Israel as a sign of God's favor (Deut 28:8-12) and poverty a mark of special punishment for the wicked (vv. 15-45). Bitter experience over the years, however, clearly showed that evil people did sometimes materially prosper as the prophet lamented (Jer 12:1). Those who completely depended on their God for help and assistance, however, were gradually acknowledged as the beloved poor whom God promised to hear and help (Exod 3:7-10; Zeph 3:12). The refrain is repeated five times in today's liturgy, inviting the congregation to claim areas of their own personal poverty and to rejoice in their having been heard. In God's time and in his way, God hears the cry of the poor and responds to their needs (though not always their wants).

GOSPEL ACCLAMATION—JOHN 3:16
Once again the acclamation takes a significant phrase from today's gospel to highlight its importance and to prepare the congregation to hear its message.

JOHN 3:16-21
God sent his Son that the world might be saved through him.

The World to Be Loved and Saved

The opening verse of this passage is actually quite shocking (v. 16). In contrast to our contemporary image of the "world" (*kosmos*) as a planet luminously floating in space (perhaps spurred by remarkable images from recent space exploration), John sees the world in much more negative terms. Though beautiful, artfully arrayed, and attractive (our modern use of the word *cosmetic*, for instance), the "world" as John saw it was fundamentally hostile and opposed to God's will. Such a world cannot accept the Spirit of truth (14:17) because it is subject to the prince of this world (14:30). At times that world may even be a place of persecution (16:33) and hate toward the disciples of Jesus (17:14) because they do not belong to it (17:16). Against that background (which should be kept in mind throughout the Easter season when passages from John's gospel abound), it is shocking to learn that God even loves the hostile world enough to send his own Son to save it (3:17)! This is a proclamation of good news for everyone, especially those who are both in the world and of it (17:14).

God's love embraces both friends and enemies alike. In *The Road Less Traveled*, M. Scott Peck notices how we humans tend to set up barriers around ourselves in order to protect ourselves from being bruised and hurt. When infatuation grasps us, he notes, we collapse all those protective barriers and let the other enter into every aspect of our living. Eventually, however, hurt again finds its way into our psyches, and one by one we raise up those same barriers. Love, on the other hand, notes Peck, is not about collapsing our barriers but about expanding them in an ever growing circle so that more and more people can enter in. At such times we find ourselves echoing God's way of loving.

Wednesday of the Second Week of Easter

Condemned for Refusal to Believe

In this passage, John seems to be very intent on making a specific theological and pastoral point. God does not condemn us, but rather we condemn ourselves when we freely and deliberately refuse to believe in the name of the "only begotten Son of God" (v. 18). Lurking behind these phrases may well be references to various ancient christological heresies that either refused to ascribe real human flesh and blood to the Son or denied him true divinity. Those who adamantly refuse to believe already here and now exclude themselves from a share in the eternal life of the next age (v. 16). At the same time, the road to belief can be long and arduous for many people. Those who profess atheism may simply be at times rejecting the simplistic and inadequate god of their neighbors. We know that the journey to Emmaus (Luke 24:13-35), as a person's quest for truth about how God really works in our world, may take a lifetime. "God seekers" will be embraced, not condemned by the God who calls each one into being for his mysterious purposes.

God's Story Made Present

The light of God dawns slowly. If God sadly allows us to condemn ourselves, God also allows us to seek and to question. God gives us an intellect and invites us to use it. In *The Experience of God*, David Bentley Hart writes:

> While there has been a great deal of public debate about belief in God in recent years . . . the concept of God around which the arguments have run their seemingly interminable courses has remained strangely obscure the whole time. The more scrutiny one accords these debates, moreover, the more evident it becomes that often the contending parties are not even talking about the same thing; and I would go so far as to say that on most occasions none of them is talking about God in any coherent sense at all.[2]

Truth Comes to Light

From the very first verses of John's gospel, we read of light shining in the darkness (1:5) and of John giving testimony to the light (v. 7). Jesus even dared to proclaim himself as "the light of the world" (8:12) as well as "the way, the truth and the life" (14:6). In his conversation with Nicodemus, Jesus further developed his teachings about those who condemn themselves. Jesus sadly acknowledged the reality of those who prefer darkness because of their evil works (v. 19). Within human experience there exists a vast spectrum of dark works from nocturnal burglaries to carefully disguised evil motives for human actions to domestic abuse artfully hidden from public discovery. We are reminded that those who "live the truth" (v. 21) eventually come to the fullness of light. Even when human beings do the wrong thing for the right reason, God's truth will prevail, and those who try to serve well will be rewarded for their effort and desire.

God includes directions to make life run smoothly. We all realize we can save ourselves a lot of time if we read the directions. Still, most of us do not. Whether it is buying a new car or unpacking a new computer or providing our kitchen with a new appliance, human nature tends to try it out before reading the directions. Only later, if we have problems, do we go to the set of directions. Jesus, the Word of Light, is the one who saves us from the malaise of groping through life. Whenever we live by his Word, life works more smoothly than when we do not or when we fail to reflect upon his wisdom.

> **Wednesday of the Second Week of Easter**

1. Quoted as Goethe's "Until One Is Committed," in *The Rag and Bone Shop of the Heart: A Poetry Anthology,* edited by Robert Bly, James Hillman, and Michael Meade (New York: HarperCollins, 1992), 235. These words belong, however, to William Hutchison Murray's *The Scottish Himalayan Expedition* (London: J. M. Dent & Sons, 1951), where the author attributes the final couplet to Goethe—although the words are from a poor translation of *Faust.* See http://www.goethesociety.org/pages/quotescom.html.

2. David Bentley Hart, *The Experience of God: Being, Consciousness, Bliss* (New Haven, CT: Yale University Press, 2013), 1.

Thursday of the Second Week of Easter

God's Story Proclaimed

ACTS 5:27-33
We are witnesses of these words, as is the Holy Spirit.

Communal Witness

Unfortunately, Western society has become so individualized that we often completely miss the references to community that run through the biblical text. In this case, for example, we should note that the high priest and the Sanhedrin (v. 27) confronted Peter and the apostles (v. 29). Two groups—leaders of Jerusalem and leaders in the early Christian community—faced each other off. It is very easy for us today to overlook the groups standing behind each spokesperson. The problem is compounded by the fact that a "you" in English can be either singular or plural—and our culture inevitably tends to assume the former. Yet the biblical perspective always presumes the social group first and foremost. In Peter's assertion, it is the "we" who are the witnesses (v. 32). The entire community and each member thereof give witness to Christ risen. The individual invariably comes to the biblical foreground only as associated with his or her group. Contemporary religious writers would go so far as to state that the radical individualism of our American society is a spiritual disease. It is contrary to the biblical mind-set, as well as hostile to the authentic Catholic perspective on life.

God chooses entire communities as partners and instruments. The civil rights movement of the 1960s was a major force to further equality among the races. More recently, pro-life efforts have brought about consciousness and defense of the unborn. Both local and national efforts surrounding ecology and the environment have raised their voices in protection of Planet Earth. Communities of faith have sent their own members on mission into distant lands to preach the Gospel.

Obedience to God

Peter confronted the accusation of the high priest by insisting on his duty to obey God rather than any mere human authority, especially if there is ever any contradiction or opposition between the two (v. 29). The primacy of the personal conscience is a fundamental truth in moral decision making, particularly when confirmed by the larger community. Even if we were personally in error on any given issue, our decision to knowingly engage in what we judge to be right or wrong is the final arbiter of the morality of our actions. God judges us on what we happen to think at the time of our decision to act. In that sense we set our own standards for judgment by God. We are, however, promised the gift of God's Spirit as we attempt to make the best decisions possible in any given instance (v. 32). This question evokes the memory of a similar confrontation between the prophet Jeremiah and temple leadership some six hundred years earlier. In that prior struggle, Jeremiah quoted his exasperated God as saying, "I didn't ask you to offer sacrifice; I simply said, 'Listen to my voice!'" (Jer 7:22).

God's Story Made Present

God's heart-to-heart is spirit-to-spirit. The will of God as we understand it remains the final judge of our actions. A guide for our actions is found in the personal motto of St. John XXIII: *obedientia et pax* (obedience and peace).

In his novel *My Name Is Asher Lev* Chaim Potok unfolds the story of young Asher Lev who, for as long as he can remember, has always been driven by a passion to draw and paint. Yet in the community of observant Hasidic Jews in which he lives and for his religiously strict but tolerant father and loving but religiously attentive mother such a passion seems to come from the Other Side, from all that is unholy. In Asher Lev's community of faith creating images flirts with the first of God's commandments that forbids the carving of idols.

What Asher Lev considers a gift is initially tolerated by his father as childhood foolishness. Later it is grudgingly waited upon as something to be outgrown until finally the intent is to bend Asher Lev like a sapling, hoping he will grow toward a different light. Indeed the talent of his young son constantly rasps at the religious values of Asher's father.

The story is told by Asher Lev himself as a memoir of sorts and in the first person singular. Always it is his struggle of sorting from where such a passionate gift would come. If from God, how can it be so contrary to all that one holds? Yet dare one resist if it is of God? If from the Other Side, then how could something so much a part of even a child, of someone created by the Holy One, come from the evil one? Thus much of the novel ricochets back and forth between truths—between the truth of the tradition and the truth of one's own heart, between religiosity and attentiveness to the Spirit, between parental wisdom and one's inner call. Is it the wisdom of the community that is the final word or the wisdom of one's conscience?

Anger versus Truth

The anger of the high priestly party in this tense situation was the result of their frustration with the boldly stubborn apostles (v. 33). Frustration on the edge of full-blown anger was the reason for hauling the apostles back to face the Sanhedrin (v. 27). By way of apostolic response, Peter and the apostles simply gave witness again to the truth (v. 32). The tale becomes a useful occasion to remember that personal anger can either be a gift and grace from God that leads us to blurt out the truth in exasperation or a personal sin that closes us off from the fullness of truth because of the passion of the moment. Anger is a companion or an enemy, an instrument or an obstacle. If we are angry we can always profit from a time-out in order to sort out the true reason for our irritation. Sometimes, for example, we can flare up out of impatient physical tiredness or resentful

self-pity or conviction regarding a very just cause. There may be times when we should be angry. The irritation of the high priestly group in this instance, however, even though it became the occasion for further witness, was not in that latter category.

Seeds of God's truth are sown in the gardens of confrontation. It has been noted that one of the signs of maturity is the ability to live with seeming contradictions, recognizing that truth is somewhere in the tensions between the two. As a nation, for example, we espouse the Republican-championed principle of subsidiarity that states that government is best when carried out closest to those being governed, and we also carry the Democratic banner that espouses the virtues of national government and so seeks to assure equity and universal opportunity. At a more personal level, love demands that we accept one another with warts and foibles and even sins, yet also that we not be complacent but challenge one another to do what is best for both society and neighbor. In faith we profess belief in a God who is just as well as merciful, even though the two so often seem mutually exclusive and incapable of being enfleshed in our own meager lives. The confrontations in our lives can often become doorways to truth and new life.

ANTIPHON—PSALM 34:7
The Lord hears the cry of the poor. (or: Alleluia)

Psalm 34:2, 9, 17-18, 19-20

Although the same refrain is repeated word for word from yesterday's liturgy, the verses actually cited from Psalm 34 for today's congregational response are different. Except for the repetition of the (possibly eucharistic) reference to tasting God's goodness (v. 9), this portion of the psalm focuses its response on God's confrontation of evildoers (v. 17) and his care for the brokenhearted (v. 19). The people gathered for this day's Eucharist are reminded that God hears the just (v. 18) and rescues them from distress, just as he once delivered the apostles from those who attempted to silence their witness.

GOSPEL ACCLAMATION—
JOHN 20:19

Today's liturgy uses an admonition from the appearance of the risen Lord to the skeptical Thomas about the need to believe even what is not seen. This prepares the congregation for the witness of Jesus who testifies to what he has seen and heard.

JOHN 3:31-36
The Father loves the Son and has given everything over to him.

Heavenly Words versus Earthly Speech

Some of the Greek philosophies that were very popular in the first century assumed a vast chasm between heavenly and earthly realities. This passage reflects something of that difference in speaking of what comes "from above" as contrasted with what is merely of the earth (v. 31). (In a different context and with differing language, but with the same perspective, Paul the apostle wrote to the Galatians [5:19-23] and differentiated between the works of the flesh such as immorality, impurity, idolatry, rivalry, jealousy, etc., on the one hand, and the fruits of the Spirit, on the other, such as love, joy, peace, patience, kindness, etc. Each set of behaviors expresses the activities and mentalities of its own world of human existence. The fruits of the Spirit are gifts of God "from above.") In this text John's Jesus speaks of what he knows from having shared life with his heavenly Father prior to the incarnation. Coming from the Father, Jesus can testify to what he has seen and heard (v. 32). In his incarnation, heaven and earth are finally and definitively united once and for all. The "words of God" (v. 34), because of their power and their heavenly origin, are a remarkable gift from God's transforming love. They are spoken by Jesus because he has been sent "from heaven" to speak them. His glorious resurrection seals that unity of heaven and earth forever. Jesus proclaims the heavenly gift of eternal life. At the end of the sixth chapter Peter will ask, "To whom else shall we go? You have the words of eternal life" (6:68). Today's gospel passage, using the same terminology again and again perhaps with deadening effect, concludes and summarizes the entire conversation of Jesus with Nicodemus. The points have been made in spades.

The wisdom of God's Word lifts life to a new height. When we live by the wisdom of the Word, we find greater peace within and among us. There is greater harmony and wholeness to life. People who care about one another and their community thrive. Although those who do not attempt to live by God's Word may find some harmony of life, those who know and live by that word are already lifted up to share "heavenly life"—namely, the life of the next age forever. Because Jesus is the Word of God as announced in the gospel's prologue (1:1), his word is God's word. His word creates, saves, and transforms the entire universe, ourselves included. This is one of the reasons why the traditional symbol for the Gospel of John is the soaring eagle.

Accepting the Testimony of Jesus

On Tuesday earlier this week we learned that the faith of Nicodemus had been limited by his own earthly categories (v. 9) as contrasted with the testimony of Jesus, which was based on his own heavenly experience (v. 11). As a result, Nicodemus remained a person of this earth. This perspective is a perfect example of what scholars call "high Christology"—that is, beginning from above rather than from the basics of human experience as in Mark. Mark's gospel was characterized by persistent human doubt and uncertainty. Today's passage leaps to call that testimony of Jesus "the words of God" (v. 34) and then goes on to speak of human reaction as either refusal meriting God's wrath (v. 36) or acceptance, which leads to a share in eternal life. In accepting the testimony of Jesus, we certify that God is trustworthy (v. 33) and we act accordingly. The words of Jesus actually include the possibility of the gift of eternal life (*zōēn aiōnion*, v. 36). The words of the testimony of Jesus are not his own alone but also the powerful life-giving words of his heavenly Father. Jesus possesses the words of his Father because everything has been handed over to him by his Father. As people of faith we not only proclaim that Jesus possesses and says everything God wants to say to human beings, we accept the invitation and wrap our entire lives around the message.

The gift of Life is discovered anew each day. Each morning the local banker goes into his office, boots up his computer, and makes his way to a site that offers a daily Scripture passage with a brief reflection. A teacher during her lunch break will stay at the quiet of her desk and read a reflection for the day from a book of daily prayer. Each night before he goes to bed a college junior opens his Bible and reads a story from the gospel, then closes the book and spends a minute in quiet thinking about the day just ending. Each in their own way finds the life they lead refreshed by this simple practice.

> **Thursday of the Second Week of Easter**

Friday of the Second Week of Easter

God's Story Proclaimed

ACTS 5:34-42

The apostles went out rejoicing that they had been found worthy to suffer dishonor for the sake of the name.

The Gamaliel Principle

One of the ancient principles for discerning a true prophet was provided by the book of Deuteronomy. It seems simple enough: the words of a true prophet come true, whereas those of a false prophet do not (Deut 18:21). The problem, of course, is the patience and possibly prolonged uncertainty needed for such an assessment. This same test was verified in the case of Jeremiah who predicted the destruction of Jerusalem and a long painful exile in Babylon in contrast to the smoother message of the false prophet Hananiah (Jer 28:1-16). Gamaliel the friendly Pharisee (v. 34) cautioned against any quick punishment for the apostles out of human anger, lest the Sanhedrin end up opposing God (v. 38). He wisely recommended a "wait and see" approach. This was consistent with true prophetic discernment. How long should a community wait? "You will know the final truth," Gamaliel suggested, "when you get there!" Both Gamaliel and Jeremiah were willing to counsel patience.

God waits while we dawdle. God waits for our dawdling over understanding the ways of God. We dawdled over Galileo's question whether the earth orbited the sun. Again we lost our way over the elusive truth behind the practice of indulgences, usury, and slavery, and most recently over evolution. It does seem that it takes us humans some time to figure out the ways of God. In the meantime, God waits. It almost seems necessary for one generation to dawdle over an issue in order for the next generation to recognize the truth God has sown. Parents of teenagers have to discern when to intervene with advice and when to allow their children to learn from their own mistakes.

God's Story Made Present

Sooner or later most of us do come to recognize the hand of God in the midst of life. Bronnie Ware is an Australian nurse who has spent a good number of years caring for people in the end stages of their lives. In time she grew aware of the regrets many had as they approached death, and this awareness led her to write *The Top Five Regrets of the Dying*. Behind those regrets seems to lay a sense that their lives could have had more richness, more meaning. These are the top five she observed:

1. I wish I'd had the courage to live a life true to myself, not the life others expected of me.
2. I wish I hadn't worked so hard.
3. I wish I'd had the courage to express my feelings.
4. I wish I had stayed in touch with my friends.
5. I wish that I had let myself be happier.[1]

Rejoicing after Suffering Dishonor for the Name

Gamaliel asked the leaders of the Sanhedrin to back off and not punish the apostles for continuing to speak of the risen Jesus and in his name. The leadership let them go free but only after administering a beating (v. 40). It almost sounds like a committee compromise. Their black and blue bruises, however, only added to their apostolic sense of accomplishment because they suffered for the truth of God like their divine Master had done. Peter and John rejoiced in the similarity of their experience to the passion of Jesus himself. Suddenly they looked like their risen Lord, scars and all.

God shapes us into his image. Whenever there seems to be an anti-Christian or anti-Catholic bias, we tend to protest vociferously. And yet is that not to be expected (and perhaps tolerated when necessary?) if we are to mirror the Lord Jesus? It may be that at those times we most clearly reflect the Lord Jesus.

ANTIPHON—PSALM 27:4
One thing I seek: to dwell in the house of the Lord. (or: Alleluia)

Psalm 27: 1, 4, 13-14

Scholars tell us that Psalm 27 is a very unique composition that is divided into two very distinctive parts, namely, vv. 1-6 and vv. 7-14. Because they differ so much in sentiment and content, we are sometimes told that the sections did not have the same author. The Lectionary has chosen verse 1 from the first poem of unshakeable human trust in God as an initial communal response because the psalm's speaker (like the mistreated apostles) simply refuses to indulge in fear. The response also includes the refrain of verse 4's dream of visiting the temple again. The remainder of the psalm response, however, comes from the very different second section of the psalm that may well be a prayer of lament from someone in dire need of help. It offers an expression of confidence (v. 13) in the face of enemies, greedy oppressors, and false witnesses (omitted in the Lectionary but presumed known by those familiar with the rest of the poem). The psalm response concludes with a doubly repeated admonition to "wait for the LORD" (v. 14), which nicely reflects the wisdom of Gamaliel! As noted in the commentary on yesterday's gospel passage, Paul contrasted the works of the flesh with the fruits of the Spirit—among which is a long-suffering patience (*makrothumia*; Gal 5:22).

The Refrain

As noted above, the refrain is taken from the first portion of Psalm 27, with its expression of complete faith and trust in God. The phrase (v. 4) indicates the source of such confidence, namely, their association with the abiding presence of the living God in the temple. The words of the refrain, therefore, offer a perfect fit with the prior story because the apostles had been arrested precisely for their stubborn insistence on giving witness in the temple. Moreover, they kept going back because of their commission to speak of the risen Lord Jesus. The congregation of daily participants in a parish weekday Eucharist in our time may well be inspired by that same spirit. We keep coming back for refreshed vision, greater courage, and renewed conviction.

Friday of the Second Week of Easter

GOSPEL ACCLAMATION—MATT 4:4
The Lectionary prepares for John's account of the multiplication of the loaves by a quotation from Deuteronomy 8:3, which was also cited by Jesus when he refused to turn stones into bread simply to satisfy his own hunger after so many days of fasting. His power was for others, not simply for himself.

JOHN 6:1-15
Jesus distributed to those who were reclining as much as they wanted.

Lectionary note: As stated above by way of introduction to Monday's gospel reading, the past four days have been devoted to an extended presentation of the conversation between Jesus and Nicodemus. Today we change and begin our proclamation and prayer over the profound teachings of chapter 6, which weaves its focus between the nourishing Word of God as both the bread of revelation and the bread of the Eucharist.

Exodus Overlay

Those already familiar with the story of the Exodus will immediately recognize the way in which the opening verses of this reading have been patterned on that great foundational event in the history of Israel. A brief list of allusions includes crossing the sea, a large crowd, signs and wonders, ascending a mountain, celebrating the Passover, and feeding the crowd (vv. 1-5).

A review of Exodus 5–24 would help to understand everything that forms the background for these initial five verses of John's introduction to chapter 6. Thus Jesus is deftly proclaimed as a new Moses, liberating his people and initiating them into a new relationship with God. In Exodus Moses had announced the adoption of Israel as God's own family (24:3-8). The words that Jesus will now speak to the hungry crowds have very ancient echoes. John has given the stories of the multiplication of the loaves found in the Synoptic Gospels a clearer and more profound significance. Relationships change and evolve. In this chapter the Lord Jesus proclaims a relationship with God that grows beyond bread as law and into the intimacy of being nourished by God's very presence.

Friday of the Second Week of Easter

As a new Moses, Jesus inaugurates a new way of being fed. One's hunger for God is fed in multiple ways: small group faith sharing, silent retreats, charismatic prayer, centering prayer, Bible study, devotional prayer, and so on. No longer is there a single "right way" to enter into a relationship with our God.

Divine Abundance

The annual harvest cycle in Israel provided grain for their daily baking of the small round loaves (perhaps very much like the pita breads of contemporary Palestine) that constituted their diet. Without the convenience of modern refrigeration or storage, however, the already limited supplies could easily be further threatened by the hungry creatures of the fields. Rats and mice seem to have lived on the edges of human society forever. Although the Israelites perfected the art of clay-lined vats to protect their grain from the previous harvest, supplies were limited and often compromised. To eat and have leftovers was virtually unheard of! In this form of the story, Jesus himself took the loaves, said a (eucharistic) blessing, and did the distributing (v. 11). The miraculous feeding was the work of Jesus alone. The disciples only gathered the fragments at the end (v. 13). They began with only the five barley loaves (the food of the poor) and two fish (v. 9) discovered by Andrew. They finished the banquet with twelve full wicker baskets of bread left untouched by the hungry hands of at least five thousand diners. Such abundance was breathtaking. No wonder they tried to make Jesus a king (v. 15)!

God's Story Made Present

Divine abundance is abundance out of nowhere. Mike shared the following entry from his journal:

God played with me a bit this week, I think. He presented me with challenges and let me pull my way through it on my own. There were other moments of real joy, presented to me in the most casual way . . . like the other night as I waited for a stoplight at the corner of Juneau and Water, there was summer twilight, and people laughing and walking across the street and I suddenly burst out laughing—with joy. . . . I was surprised at how peaceful everyone seemed and I felt that way too. It was as if God were in my car next to me; He clapped his hands once loudly, pointed his finger out the window and said, "See there, there is joy here too, isn't there?" And I laughed because He was right, and because it was so amusing to have God appear out of the blue and tell you to lighten up. It was as if we were buddies on the street together; and I guess we were, which is what made it so remarkable. We need to remember moments like that when things get tense, as they were for me the last couple of days. And so my life unfolds before me on this journey—*yikes!* Where did all that come from?

This is a very good question—where did all that come from? Where did the joy come from? Where did that happening come from? Where did those words come from? Is there another world out there? Abundance that comes from nowhere feels as if it comes from God.

1. Bronnie Ware, *The Top Five Regrets of the Dying* (New York: Hay House, 2012).

Saturday of the Second Week of Easter

God's Story Proclaimed

ACTS 6:1-7
They chose seven men filled with the Holy Spirit.

The Gift of Cultural Diversity

Over the centuries, it has been customary to see this story as the institution of the Christian diaconate, mostly because of its reference to care for poor widows and table ministry. We know from the initial salutation found in Paul's letter to the Philippians that some form of diaconal ministry already existed in the early church (Phil 1:1, with its greetings to overseers [*episkopoi*] and ministers [*diakonoi*]). It is less certain, however, that this story in Acts actually refers to the specific ministry of deacons as we have come to understand them from early Christianity. In subsequent chapters of Acts, Luke does not describe these individuals as continuing their involvement in table ministry, but only speaks of their ministry of the Word. For that reason, Luke probably chose not to use the title "deacon" in this account. More probable is Luke's desire to acknowledge the way early Christianity quickly embraced differing cultural patterns in society, both Jew and Gentile, and stretched itself to embrace them. By recognizing a separate community structure with its own form of sevenfold leadership (v. 7), the apostles gave legitimacy to the cultural diversity inherent among Gentile converts. The Seven are announced as an initial foundation for resolving the Jew–Gentile division in the early church. The fact that all the names of the Seven are Hellenistic (v. 5) suggests the use of their native language and the recognition of their own ethnic customs. The Hellenists shared the apostolic faith in Jesus, but within their own traditions. Diversity need not imply division. A century ago Catholic parishes were clearly divided into Irish, German, Polish, and so on; today the divisions may be Hispanic and Anglo. Everything that blesses legitimate differences and creates unity without demanding uniformity is Good News. Even today there is room for everyone, East and West, at the table. The issue is legitimate and welcome diversity.

God's Story Made Present

God's spirit of service quietly spreads beyond established communities of faith. At the Riverwest Food Pantry local college students from the University of Wisconsin–Milwaukee regularly volunteer time. It is an expectation in the curriculum of many of the university's departments. One student explained that she was required to do twenty hours of community service this semester. Another student reported that her academic major required seventy hours over the course of two years. The food pantry is required to verify to the university the amount of time served. The Spirit's impetus to serve even beyond the faith community itself continues to show its face in civic and national communities.

Feeding the Hungry

From the very beginning, the followers of "the Way" were especially concerned about the hungry poor. Serious hunger could be particularly problematic in the larger cities of the ancient Middle East where people were often separated from family systems of mutual support, and where everyone lived at a distance from the grain-producing regions of the land. All four gospels include stories of some multiplication of loaves by Jesus for the hungry (e.g., Mark 6:34-44; 8:1-9), almost as a privileged sign of the essential work of the Messiah. Without caring for the hungry, any would-be Messiah was not credible. Luke's account of the spread of the early church noted the way they shared food with the needy (2:45; 4:34). The distribution of food to hungry widows without any means of sustenance from their families quickly became a concern of the early community (v. 2). They saw a specific need and addressed it. When some of the Hellenists felt their widows were the objects of discrimination, the apostles appointed seven outstanding leaders to oversee the distribution to all the needy, each in its own cultural setting. The church in Jerusalem became a model for all subsequent groups of Christians. The issue also became a criterion for eventual judgment when the Lord said, "I was hungry and you gave me no food" (Matt 25:42)!

Saturday of the Second Week of Easter

God's true human partners care for the hungry. Even after the lapse of two millennia, modern Catholic parish communities are still judged by the care they extend to the poor, needy, and hungry. Members of contemporary St. Vincent de Paul Societies, parish food pantries, and meal programs are all reminders and extensions of that instinctive primitive Christian impulse. The mark of a fully alive parish may be the number of different ministries it supports and nurtures. Support groups exist for the divorced and those who grieve, for singles and jobless. Religious education programs provide for children with special needs. Liturgical celebrations serve differing ethnic groups. Ministries reach out to teens. Prison ministries and those in need of nursing home care, as well as the homebound. Ministry to those recently married. The list goes on. The reality is that active parishes do stretch themselves to walk with one another, especially those in need.

Prayer and the Ministry of the Word

Often, when suddenly faced with new challenges or demands, we pause in prayer to take stock and assess priorities. In the same fashion, the complaints from the Greek widows of being overlooked or unfairly treated (v. 1) became the occasion for the Twelve to determine their primary responsibilities. They recommitted themselves to their primary duties—namely, "prayer and to the ministry of the word" (v. 4). Both often occurred at the community's regular eucharistic celebration of the breaking of the bread. In so doing they followed the example of Jesus who often slipped away for prayer (Luke 4:42; 11:1), which renewed his energy and sustained his focus on giving witness to the kingdom of God (13:18-20; 14:15-35). As noted at the beginning of virtually every one of his letters, Paul also prayed with and for his communities and taught them in person as well as by letter.

God's Spirit spurs the leaders of faith communities to prayer and teaching. Even amid all the administrative responsibilities that fall upon the shoulders of a contemporary pastor, the two duties of prayer and teaching deserve preeminence and prominence. In fact, everyone in positions of religious community leadership today, ordained and lay alike, is charged to see those same activities as central to the work of the week. These duties are perennial. Interestingly, while everyone looks for a well-oiled and smoothly run community, most complaints come when parishioners do not feel spiritually fed and nourished.

ANTIPHON—PSALM 33:22
Lord, let your mercy be on us, as we place our trust in you. (or: Alleluia)

Psalm 33:1-2, 4-5, 18-19

Psalm 33 has a certain generic character of festivity whose musical accompaniment (v. 2) would make it appropriate for the Covenantal Renewal festival in autumn each new year. No specific event from history can be seen reflected in this psalm's words. The participants in the festival would readily be labeled "just" (v. 1) and "upright" (v. 4), lovers of justice (v. 5) and those who hope for God's covenantal kindness (*hesed*, v. 18). By definition, the just are not only those who have paid their debts, but rather those who live entire lives in right relationship with God's whole world. These are the people invited by this psalm, at least as currently positioned in the Lectionary, to rejoice in the way the early church marshaled its forces to feed the hungry.

The Refrain

The day's refrain (v. 22) is chosen as a response to the first reading's account of restructuring the early community to recognize the needs of the Greeks and to care for their poor and hungry. Those who celebrated the covenant each autumn always renewed their sense of trust in their God. They recognized their obligation to care for needy fellow human members of the covenant. Surprisingly contrary to regular practice, the refrain itself is not mentioned in the portions of the psalm selected for the liturgical response. Because of the variation in English translations, once again it is helpful to note that the original Hebrew behind "mercy" (v. 22) is covenantal kindness (*hesed*). Those who rejoice each year in the covenant know that they themselves have been the recipients of God's covenantal kindness. They are bound together with God and each other in a bond of generosity, respect, and concern.

Gospel Acclamation: Curiously, no specific biblical citation is offered for this introduction. The sentence simply affirms Christ's resurrection, his role in universal creation, and his gift of mercy for all. This collection of random ideas invites us to hear of Jesus walking on water and showing care for his beleaguered apostles in the storm.

JOHN 6:16-21
They saw Jesus, walking on the sea.

God's All-embracing Power

Perhaps by following the account of the multiplication of the bread (vv. 4-14) with this story of walking on water (v. 19), John deftly but clearly demonstrates the universality of the power of Jesus. Both events occur as signs of care and support for his disciples. The power

of Jesus is used for their benefit, not as a form of threat or intimidation. In the Synoptic Gospels the presence of Jesus amid the storm at sea suddenly calmed the winds and waves (Mark 5:35-41). In John's account, however, the boat moves immediately to the shore without any indication of whether the storm abated or not (v. 21). Not only does Jesus have power to multiply food for the hungry, he even shares their experience at sea, guides their history and brings them home. All material creation as well as its unfolding in time remains subject to his will. This is yet another example of the way in which the Father has given everything, even power over material creation, over to his Son (as had been noted in the Lectionary on Thursday earlier this week; see 3:35).

> **Saturday of the Second Week of Easter**

God's Story Made Present

Jesus exercises divine power over time, space, and matter. And so it is that God sustains the events of our lives. Consider the following words attributed to St. Teresa of Ávila:

> May you trust God that you are exactly where you are meant to be.
> May you not forget the infinite possibilities that are born of faith.
> May you use those gifts that you have received, and pass on the love that has been given to you.
> May you be content knowing you are a child of God.
> Let this presence settle into your bones, and allow your soul the freedom to sing, dance, praise and love.
> It is there for each and every one of us.[1]

Controlling Evil Forever

People who spend their lives in the desert often find the power of the sea very frightening. The crashing of waves, the surging of the stormy surf, and the pull of undercurrents were ready symbols of massive power beyond any possible human control. In our own time the annual hurricane season reminds us of the terrible forcefulness of storms at sea. Ancient Canaanite myths of creation often described a warrior god battling the personified sea and forcing its power back within the limits delineated by the shores. Psalm 29 ascribed that same power to the God of Israel by the mere use of his commanding voice (v. 2). The raging of the waters was a persistent symbol for hostile antihuman powers and for all evil. The book of Revelation imagines God finally, once and for all, conquering the sea and rendering it silent, even perchance making it disappear from the face of the earth (21:1). Evil and all its symbols were thus vanquished forever. All these ancient tales and traditions came to mind when early communities listened to this account at their Eucharist and celebrated the sovereign power of their risen Lord who even walked on water if needed to comfort and protect his disciples! Christ walking on the stormy sea was Lord of all, even evil itself.

Saturday of the Second Week of Easter

Without our knowing how, God brings us to the other shore of life.

Much of life is spent crossing from one side of life to the other, from childhood to adulthood, from beginning college to graduation, from giving birth to setting one's offspring free, in other words from one side of the lake to the other. Often enough such crossings assail us with storminess and amid the darkness of uncertainty—the gospel's image of "at night." The promise of the gospel is that the Lord Jesus brings us to the other side with our spirits whole and entire and usually without our knowing how we made it, except that we find ourselves on the distant shore.

In her poem "The Awful Rowing Toward God," Anne Sexton reflects on her own journey of finding God. "And God was there like an island I had not rowed to, / still ignorant of Him." By the time she reaches middle age she comes to recognize that, "I am rowing, I am rowing / though the oarlocks stick and are rusty / and the sea blinks and rolls. . . / though the wind pushes me back."[2] For Anne Sexton her own personal journey was not always smooth. Is it for any of us?

---

1. Quoted in *She Walks in Beauty: A Woman's Journey through Poems,* edited by Caroline Kennedy (New York: Hyperion, 2011), 303. Note, however, that various sources attribute this to St. Teresa of Ávila, St. Thérèse of Lisieux, and even Blessed Teresa of Calcutta.

2. Anne Sexton, "Rowing," *The Complete Poems: Anne Sexton* (Boston: Houghton Mifflin, 1999), 417.

Third Week
of Easter

———

Monday of the Third Week of Easter

God's Story Proclaimed

ACTS 6:8-15

*They could not withstand the wisdom and the
Spirit with which he spoke.*

Speaking with Wisdom and Spirit

When Stephen spoke, his words were remarkably apt for the occasion and insightful. Originally the word "wisdom" (*hokmah* in Hebrew and *sophia* in Greek) signaled the practical ability to do something very well such as the wise artisan Hiram, a bronze worker engaged by Solomon in the building of the temple (1 Kgs 7:14). Solomon prayed for the gift of wisdom (Wis 9:2). That same quality of wisdom was subsequently applied to those who excelled in the use of words and whose knowledge made them respected and valuable counselors at the royal court in Jerusalem. Stephen was recognized as possessing great wisdom because his speech was judged remarkably effective in persuasiveness. Moreover, the Holy Spirit was acknowledged as the ultimate source for his testimony (v. 10). The strength of his conviction as well as the power of his well-chosen words demolished the arguments of his opponents and unfortunately left them angry in their humiliation. A sad reality of the human heart is the tendency to remove, by force if necessary, anything that we are unable to convince; so the members of the Synagogue of Freedmen (v. 9) and the Sanhedrin (v. 12) sought false witnesses (v. 13) to eliminate and silence Stephen's voice, but they could not be successful against the Spirit.

The Spirit continues to unlock the treasure chest of wisdom. Like candy at Halloween or the sizzling spitting heat of a day in July, there can be too much of a good thing. So there may be times when there may be too many different wisdoms 'round and about. Then most of us latch on to one or another piece, decide it's our wisdom and maybe the only wisdom, and then declare everyone else's false. That seems to be how it happens often enough. The Republicans and the Democrats have each proclaimed their doctrine of wisdom, have drawn a line in the sand with howling words, and have blessed it as a truth contrary to the wisdom in anyone else's sandbox. A mother's wisdom often tends to be negotiable, but a father's can be fearsome and final. It would seem one of the tasks of life is to recognize that none of us human beings ever has all of the wisdom if only because God's Spirit continues to reveal new ways in which God is working.

Overcoming Human Fears

The Hellenists (6:1) were very fervent Jews of Greek background and culture who relocated back to Jerusalem in order to live in closer proximity to the temple and the center of Jewish piety. Some, like Stephen, filled "with grace and power" (v. 8), brought a deep and open appreciation for the work of God's Spirit in their lives. Others, like the members of the Synagogue of Freedmen (v. 9), were more attracted to the letter of the law and were often edgy about religious customs or interpretations other than their own. These latter did not easily brook the more charismatic approach to religious practice that characterized Stephen and his associates. They sometimes found errors in faith where none existed, and too quickly denounced their opponents to the religious authorities of the day. At times the differences became bitter. Luke makes an effort to link the trial of Jesus with that of Stephen. Just as Jesus had been accused of blasphemy by the high priest (Mark 14:64), the same charge was transferred by Luke to Acts and is now leveled against Stephen (v. 11). Blasphemy is generally understood as abusive or contemptuous speech against God or sacred things. It is easy to understand how a different approach to the temple could be quickly but erroneously judged offensive and deserving punishment, especially by narrowly legalistic opponents. Eventually the faith of Stephen prevailed, even if his convictions initially cost him his life. The witness of his life therefore remains an inspiration for all subsequent generations of Christians. We can't help but recall that Paul once reminded his colleagues that it is only by hardship that they may enter the kingdom of God (Acts 14:22).

Monday of the Third Week of Easter

God's wisdom overcomes human fears. Sometimes years and even decades are required to sort through thorny questions and to arrive at common understandings. Even the remnants of the fears seem to stay with us as an albatross about our necks. Slavery was certainly such an issue in our history coupled with the economic fears abolition implied. The role of women in society began to unfold with women's suffrage and has not yet arrived at full fruition. Racism is clearly still with us. The church also struggles over issues of sexuality as well as divorce and remarriage—both laced with fears and uncertainties. Always in time God's wisdom rises to the surface.

Garbled Accusations

Biblical background: The accusations against Stephen in fact contain an element of truth, for Jesus did speak about his own body replacing the temple as a means of access to God and claimed to be able to rebuild the temple of his body in three days if it were destroyed (v. 14; see also John 2:21). However, Jesus upheld the law of Moses until everything would be fulfilled (Matt 5:17). Stephen spoke the full truth of the teachings of Jesus, but his accusers neither understood correctly nor quoted accurately. Perhaps this is a perfect example of the way statements can be changed when passed in gossip from one person to another—with the final message becoming radically different from the opinion first confided "in confidence." The careful truth of Stephen's

original statements had been twisted in the process of transmission so as to make them ultimately false. They became the occasion for angry accusations. This story of Stephen and his erroneous accusers should make us more determined than ever to be scrupulously careful when quoting someone else's opinion, and deeply respectful when citing an opinion different from our own.

God's Story Made Present

God's Spirit keeps our speech faithful and true. Given the propensity for human gossiping, perhaps our efforts to speak the truth, to speak it kindly, never to speak the untruth, and always to speak with graciousness are all testimonials to the work of the Spirit in our lives.

Arnold Perrin tells the story of coming to such wisdom while being raised on a farm in Maine. Together he and his father had spent a morning building a hay rack for the back of the family pickup truck. When it was completed his father invited Arnold to take it out to test how it would ride in the back of the pickup. Arnold explained how he was only just beginning to learn how to drive at the time. As he drove through a stone farm gate on the property, he said, he caught the hay rack on the gate post and totally demolished the morning's work.

His father was furious. Tossing the broken pieces back into the truck, his father spent the remainder of the day rebuilding what his son had destroyed. When the second effort was completed his father took the wheel of the truck, and this time he hit the gate post and again destroyed the hay rack. Much later in life Arnold noted that though he had been only fifteen years old at the time, he knew enough of life not to laugh.

The Face of an Angel

The Greek word *angelos* denotes merely a messenger, but when the individual comes from God, the word is often translated "angel" to differentiate ordinary forms of intermediaries from those sent by God. The "angel of the

Lord" appeared to Hagar in the desert (Gen 16:7), prevented Abraham from sacrificing Isaac (Gen 48:16), and spoke from the burning bush (Exod 3:2). This phrase, "the face of an angel," does not seem to be found in any other text of Scripture. Presumably to have the face of an angel is to be transformed by an inner radiance that comes from living in right relationship with God and neighbor. Such radiance establishes personal peace and inner tranquillity in the face of hostility and opposition. Perhaps the author intended an implicit reference to the ancient tale of the radiant face of Moses after conversation with God (Exod 34:29-35) and to the transfiguration of Jesus on Mount Tabor (Luke 9:28-36). True and faithful disciples like Stephen become like their teachers and shining models.

God's peace grounds us amid conflict. The difference between love and infatuation can be difficult to discern. One marker is that when conflict or the difficulties of life arise, love remains and grounds the relationship. Infatuation fades and disappears. It is the same with faith. Amid the conflict of his accusers, Stephen had the face of an angel, which is to say that at his core he was at peace. Deep inner peace becomes the marker of faith. When conflicts arise, the person of faith will be at peace in the midst of it all.

ANTIPHON—PSALM 119:1AB
Blessed are they who follow the law of the Lord! (or: Alleluia)

Psalm 119: 23-24, 26-27, 29-30

Psalm 119 is the longest of the hymns in the Psalter, and by far the most belabored. Comprised of 176 verses, the work struggles to find endless and often tiresome ways to speak about the law (*torah*) and about those who either wisely follow its direction or unfortunately resist its instruction. Each of the twenty-two letters of the Hebrew alphabet initiates its respective eight-verse paragraph. Individual lines may be powerfully insight-

ful and even memorable, but the overall impact of the entire psalm is admittedly tedious and repetitious. Perhaps it originally served as a lesson plan for struggling young scribal students learning how to write. In this responsorial psalm, however, the Lectionary selects two verses that begin with the Hebrew letter *gimmel* (v. 23) and four that begin with the Hebrew letter *daleth* (vv. 26, 29). These lines manage to describe the delight of knowing God's law (v. 24) even amid the power of opponents (v. 23), as well as provide a prayer for deeper understanding (v. 27) and for the avoidance of falsehood (v. 29). These sentiments serve as a response to Stephen's witness.

> Monday
> of the
> Third Week
> of Easter

The Refrain

The verse selected for the antiphon (119:1) sounds remarkably like a blessing composed for those described in the first two verses of Psalm 1. That introduction to the entire Psalter contrasts the faithful with the wicked and recommends careful meditation on God's Torah. This refrain goes a step further to stress the activity that should follow the reflection and that puts the Torah into daily practice. Just as Psalm 1 was composed as a generic introduction, Psalm 119 seems to have the same practical origin and purpose. The refrain's initial counsel is clothed in the literary form of a beatitude.

GOSPEL ACCLAMATION—MATTHEW 4:4
By the choice of the retort of Jesus to the devil who had tempted his hunger with his own divine ability to turn stones into fresh bread (with a quotation from Deut 8:3), the Lectionary accents the bread from heaven as God's revelation that nourishes our life. Later the same phrases will become more eucharistic.

JOHN 6:22-29
Do not work for food that perishes but for food that endures for eternal life.

Working for Food

After the multiplication of the loaves and the attempt of Jesus to escape the crowd's desire to make him a king (vv. 1-15), Jesus sent the twelve away. Then, after a night in prayer, he mysteriously appeared beside their boat to calm a storm on the sea (vv. 16-21). Some of the crowd from the miracle, however, were persistent and finally found him at Capernaum (v. 24) on the other side of the lake where he began to teach. The Lectionary has decided to divide the extended discourse on the Bread of Life into smaller portions and to spread the sixth chapter of the gospel across the entire week. This poses a distinct challenge to homilists because of John's repetitious style. The people who looked for Jesus and even chased after him across the Sea of Galilee wanted food for physical hunger. Jesus begins by acknowledging that they came looking for physical food (v. 26), but he had other gifts in mind. His mission as Teacher and ultimately as Redeemer led him to offer the fullness of a rich human existence. He uses the occasion to encourage them to seek the kind of food that not only sustains daily natural life but "endures for eternal life" (v. 27)—namely, food that leads to life in the next age. This life comes by way of gift from the Son of Man (v. 27), not by personal manual labor or human effort. Living from one harvest to the next was not easy for the ancient world, and the means of preserving food was primarily reduced to drying. The refrigeration and freezing taken for granted today was unimaginable, and the work for daily sustenance very grueling at times. If God's food was gift, it was logical for them to ask what they had to do in order to be in the receiving line (v. 28). Making an act of faith in order to receive the gift is a completely different type of "working."

Monday of the Third Week of Easter

God's Story Made Present

God has sown our lives with hungers. In 1854 when Henry David Thoreau went out to Walden Pond to live a quiet and reflective life, he did not go out to escape life or to preserve life as he knew it, but rather to experience life more fully. He went believing that the future could be more than what he had thus far experienced.

> I went to the woods because I wished to live deliberately, to front only the essential facts of life, and see if I could not learn what it had to teach, and not when I came to die, discover that I had not lived. I did not wish to live what was not life, living is so dear, nor did I wish to practice resignation, unless it was quite necessary. I wanted to live deep and suck out all the marrow of life, to live so sturdily and Spartanlike as to put to rout all that was not life.[1]

While each of us lives with various and sundry hungers, there are those deeper ones that God seems to feed. All of the other hungers seem to be part of our own shallow scavenging.

The Works of God

If the promised nourishment in and for eternal life—namely, the food for the next age—is a gift, then the work to receive that food is God's "effort," not human activity. The only thing demanded of humans is faith in Jesus (v. 29)—which is itself a gift from God. God gives the gift of faith and all the blessings that flow from that gift. Ours is only to freely cooperate with God's generosity, and even that cooperation is the result of the gift of grace. All is grace. The life of a true disciple is filled with profound gratitude.

In faith God brings us to trust. One of the most well-known riddles is found in Greek mythology. According to the story the sphinx guarded the city of Thebes in Greece. Anyone wishing to enter or leave was asked the riddle, "What creature walks on four legs in the morning, two legs at noon, and three legs in the evening?" If they knew the answer, they were allowed to enter or leave the city. If they failed to answer, they forfeited their life and were killed by the sphinx. No one answered correctly until Oedipus came along. The answer was "a human person," one who crawls on all fours in the morning time of one's life, walks on two legs during the middle portion of one's life, and walks with a cane in the end time of one's life. According to the myth, the sphinx was so distraught upon receiving the correct answer that she threw herself off of the wall that protected the city and killed herself.

Sometimes it seems as if life is a riddle, something we spend most of our time trying to figure out, something to make sense of. And just about the time we think we have the answer, we discover the opposite to be true. We think having many things will make us happy, only to realize we were happiest when we had little, when we had a roof over our head and food on our table but little else to cause us worry. We think if only we could control the events of our lives, then the day-to-day affairs would unfold so much more smoothly. Yet it is when we surrender that we come to a deep and trusting peace. That is the work of God.

> **Monday of the Third Week of Easter**

1. Henry David Thoreau, *Walden: Or, Life in the Woods* (New York: Thomas Y. Crowell, 1910), 118.

Tuesday of the Third Week of Easter

God's Story Proclaimed

Acts 7:51–8:1a

Lord Jesus, receive my spirit.

Lectionary note: Today's passage is the passionate peroration that concludes Stephen's speech to the Sanhedrin (6:12). The tone as described is clearly provocative and polemical. Unfortunately, the Lectionary's editorial introduction at the beginning of the liturgical text—namely, "the people, the elders, and the scribes" (v. 51, borrowed from v. 12, which describes the targeted audience of the Synagogue of Freedmen in v. 9)—gives the impression that Stephen indicted all of Israel in his accusations. Such subtleties in the Lectionary have contributed at times to a general sense of anti-Semitic animus in Acts. Contemporary Christian preachers should be especially careful not to add to that popular impression.

The Persecuted Righteous One

In a dramatic fashion the book of Wisdom describes the typical steps by which evil people increasingly harass and systematically persecute the just (2:12-20), and the way God brings final justification and eventual victory to his chosen ones. In that splendid example of ancient rhetoric, their hostile opposition moved from persecution to torture to killing in order to see if his divine Father would truly take care of him (v. 20). These same words were seen by the earliest Christian apologists as predicting the passion of Jesus described in the gospels. That text quickly became a way of understanding the sufferings of the Righteous One (7:52) *par excellence*. The word "righteous" (*tzadik*) was often used in early Jewish literature as a title for the saints of their world. People like Stephen called Jesus "the Righteous One" and proclaimed him as a model for the good and pious Jewish people of Jerusalem, especially when persecuted for their faith. A truly just and righteous person was not merely someone who paid all his bills, but one who was in right relationship with everyone and everything, especially God. Sometimes it takes personal suffering and opposition to become the kind of person God wants us to be. When Stephen applied the title to Jesus (v. 52), even amid the passionate rhetoric of his speech, he provided a frame of reference for the death of Jesus and for all Christians who suffer persecution for their faith. Stephen's vision of the Son of Man in glory at the right hand of God (v. 56) proclaimed his faith in Christ's vindication.

God's Story Made Present

God vindicates his servants, even amid their suffering. It does happen. To Nelson Mandela, imprisoned as if in transparent amber by the unrelenting truth of his convictions. To Rosa Parks, calmly refusing to go not only to the back of the bus but also to the back of life. To a lone and anonymous student remembered forever because he stood in defiance of the military in Tiananmen Square. To say nothing of teenagers daring to choose uncommon mores among their peers, heads of households working in jobs without satisfaction in order to nurture their family, and elderly people reluctantly raising yet a second family of their children's children.

Prayer of Forgiveness

One of the overarching themes of Luke's theology was to show profound continuity between the earthly ministry of Jesus in his gospel and the life of the early church in Acts. The apostles heal and teach as Jesus healed and taught. They all suffered and indeed exhibited the same spirit of submission to the will of the Father. Even on his cross, Luke recalled that Jesus prayed, "Father, forgive them, they know not what they do" (23:34), and ended his life with the words, "Father, into your hands I commend my spirit" (v.

46). Stephen as the first martyr expresses the same sentiments in reverse order—namely, "Lord Jesus, receive my spirit" (v. 59) and "Do not hold this sin against them" (v. 60) before falling asleep in the Lord. The formal witnesses, however, covered their ears because Stephen's attribution of the title Lord to Jesus and his reference to Jesus as the Son of Man in glory (v. 56; see also Luke 22:69; Dan 7:13) seemed like offensive blasphemy. Like Jesus himself, Stephen is proposed as a model for all who would ever suffer persecution throughout the ages.

God's Story Made Present

God turns our hunger for revenge into a hunger for wholeness. Forgiveness is not simply a feeling. As a virtue, it is something we choose, regardless of the kinds of feelings that may accompany that choice.

When her seven-year-old daughter was murdered, Marietta Jaeger Lane felt that the very energy of her life had been stolen from her own existence. She was filled with anger and rage and pain and sorrow and hatred, with the entire spectrum of emotions that only a parent who has ever lived through such violence could know. Yet she chose not to surrender to the desire for revenge. In the end Marietta Jaeger Lane chose a different sort of wisdom.

> I will never pretend or claim that forgiveness is easy. Forgiveness is hard work. It takes daily diligent discipline. It takes prayer and fasting. It counters the way of the world, our own humanness and the work of the powers and principalities. . . . Forgiveness is not forgetting—in fact it is precisely because we *cannot ever forget* what has been done that we *must* learn to forgive, so that we will not remain enslaved to a past. . . . Forgiveness is the only way we can set ourselves free.[1]

Saul Consenting

The passage ends with the brief and poignant comment that Saul watched over the garments of those who participated in the stoning of Stephen. Such was the punishment required by the law for the sin of blasphemy (Lev 24:10-16). At the time Saul obviously still shared the mindset of the rigorous Hellenist Synagogue of Freedmen (6:9) who were at times "more Jewish than the Jews." As someone committed to his own narrow notion of the Torah and the entire Jewish tradition, Saul also saw in Stephen's words something offensive to the name of God. This incident prepares the reader for Saul's zealous persecution of early Christians (9:1) and serves as a subtle but dramatic contrast to his subsequent conversion. As described by Luke, however, in the full drama of Acts, Paul eventually became a dramatic model for everyone who eventually responds to the grace of lifelong conversion. Here we only have the advertising image of the "before," which still required its "after" complement. Before that can happen, however, the word of God sometimes first describes and proclaims the sinner. God had much work to do! Stephen's prayer of forgiveness, therefore, was also implicitly for Saul (v. 60). Eventually his prayer was granted. Once again, it is important to avoid giving the impression that Judaism itself is narrow, negative, and self-righteous. Stephen as one type of Hellenistic Jew was anything but! Nothing could be further from the truth about Judaism, just as Christianity can never be equated with any of its extreme fringes.

God's Story Made Present

God plants seeds of conversion that sprout in their own time. Kathleen Norris is an American spiritual writer who lived for many years in Lemmon, SD. She would go to parochial schools there as an artist-in-residence and teach children how to write poetry using the psalms as a model. This is how she describes one such occasion in her book *Amazing Grace.*

Children who are picked on by their big brothers and sisters can be remarkably adept when it comes to writing cursing psalms, and I believe that the writing process offers them a safe haven in which to work through their desires for vengeance in a healthy way. Once a little boy wrote a poem called "The Monster Who Was Sorry." He began by admitting that he hates it when his father yells at him: his response in the poem is to throw his sister down the stairs, and then to wreck his room, and finally to wreck the whole town. The poem concludes: "Then I sit in my messy house and say to myself, 'I shouldn't have done all that.' "[2]

Tuesday of the Third Week of Easter

ANTIPHON—PSALM 31:6A
Into your hands, O Lord, I commend my spirit. (or: Alleluia)

Psalm 31:3cd-4, 6, 7b, 8a, 17, 21ab

Psalm 31 is a classic example of traditional lamentation and thanksgiving for God's support and deliverance. In this response, the Lectionary is very deliberate to avoid any description of suffering or hint of recrimination against those who had been the cause for humiliation. God is praised as a rock of refuge (v. 3) and a fortress of safety (v. 4). The individual singing or reciting this prayer is filled with confidence in God's mercy (*hesed*, literally, "covenantal kindness"). Although later translated as "kindness," the same Hebrew word is found in the response (v. 17). Such "mercy," because it is covenantal in character, is more than mere compassion. This type of mercy is the duty of members to care for each other. All the verses cited in the responsorial psalm could easily form the extended prayer of Stephen as described in the first reading since they exhibit the same qualities of confidence and trust.

The Refrain

To commend one's vital principle or "spirit" into God's hands (v. 6), as does Stephen at the time of his martyrdom, is to return that spirit to the very God who initially called it into existence. The antiphon celebrates the fact that the

God of creation is also the God of providential care for every creature. The psalmist offers himself to the same divine hands that had molded Adam from the clay of the earth (Gen 2:7). The refrain represents the very words of the prayer of Jesus on the cross (Luke 23:46) and echoes the sentiments of Stephen at his death. The same words could well be the prayer of every disciple at the time of his falling asleep each evening or finally passing from this world to the next.

GOSPEL ACCLAMATION—JOHN 6:35
Once again, the Lectionary has chosen to introduce the gospel passage by reciting its final verse, giving an initial hint as to what is judged most important in the following pericope.

JOHN 6:30-35
It was not Moses, but my Father who gives you the true bread from heaven.

Signs

The actual text of John's gospel simply says, "they said to him" (v. 30), but the Lectionary, like many lectors at times, wisely clarifies the personal antecedents in order to bring the liturgical congregation into immediate contact with the actual participants in the conversation. Jesus had just encouraged the crowd to work for food that endures (v. 27), and he reminded them that their request is itself the "work of God" (v. 29). That invitation in turn inspired the crowd to ask for a sign as reason and motive for their belief (v. 30). It may be helpful to remember that the entire first section of John's gospel has been called the Book of Signs (1:29-12:50). The changing of water into wine was explicitly noted as the first sign (2:11). The cleansing of the temple was acknowledged by bystanders as a sign (2:18-23), and Nicodemus admitted that no one could do such signs unless God was with him (3:2). The cure of the royal official's son was a second sign (4:54). At the beginning of the story of the multiplication of the loaves, the crowds had followed Jesus because of his signs of healing (6:2). His entire ministry was a series of events that illustrated and demonstrated God at work. Only someone who already has an idea of what God does can express that faith in words and point to certain actions as specific examples of God's work in our world.

God's Story Made Present

God speaks the "language of bread." Marcus kept looking for signs of what he should do with his life. He looked for "the billboard" that would tell him what to do, for the television program that would make it obvious, for the unexpected and startling event that would turn his life in a specific direction. Such signs never materialized, only the interests and natural give and take of life did so, yet Marcus seemed to keep missing those. He never recognized how God had been feeding his journey all along.

Manna

The people of Israel had once been sustained in the desert by the mysterious substance that they called manna (v. 31; literally, "what is it?"; see Exod 16:4). In typical Johannine fashion the speech moves with dizzying speed from the multiplication of the loaves (6:1-14) to "bread from heaven" (v. 32) to "bread giving life to the world" (v. 33) to Jesus identifying himself as "the Bread of life" (v. 35). Throughout all of history our God continues to feed, nourish, and strengthen his people in many ways: nutrition from the fruit of the fields, meaning and motivation from mission and purpose, direction and destiny from gift and grace. John's Jesus is himself the source of nourishment, strength, and vitality for his disciples who are forever fed by believing in him and his mission. Though people in the assembly at Mass may

never think of the "what is it" behind the word "manna," its very use by John could elicit a question that seeks to clarify the type of nourishment implied in each use of bread or food in these pericopes.

God's Story Made Present

God hand-feeds us. While God does feed us, too often we never come to realize how that has been going on all along.

The waiting area in the airport terminal seemed to become a nest of unsettled energy, everyone moving about with no more purpose than waiting ever seems to have. Alongside the ceiling-to-floor windows a young father was about the task of focusing his two-year-old son's restless wandering—holding him close, letting him pull away, reeling him back, giving him reign, all a kind of play amid the sights and sounds and feelings splashing over his two-year-old.

After a while the father pulled out a large purple plum, and with his arms around his son the two sat down on the carpeted floor along the windows. Back and forth the plum was handed between father and son, the father peeling the skin with his teeth then handing the meaty plum back to his son, the two-year-old gnawing away at it as his eyes took in the cache of busyness happening about him then handing it back to his father for more of it to be peeled, without ever taking his eyes off his world bubbling with life. And so it went until the time for boarding the plane was announced.

We are like two-year-olds being hand-fed by our God, without ever realizing the wonder of it all.

> **Tuesday of the Third Week of Easter**

---

1. Marietta Jaeger Lane, "From Fury to Forgiveness," in *Criminal Justice: Retribution vs. Restoration,* ed. Eleanor Hannon Judah and Michael Bryant (Binghamton, NY: Haworth, 2004), 164.

2. Kathleen Norris, *Amazing Grace* (New York: Riverhead, 1998), 69.

Wednesday of the Third Week of Easter

God's Story Proclaimed

ACTS 8:1B-8
They went about preaching the word.

Scattered for Harvest

Stephen became a catalyst for persecution because his witness and his ideas were strongly opposed by those with whom he had debated. After his death, the early disciples were scattered widely (vv. 1, 4). Even King Herod eventually got into the act by killing James and arresting Peter (12:2). As a result of such repeated instances of persecution, many members of the Christian community (except for the Twelve) left Jerusalem. Among them was Philip (v. 5) who went north to Samaria to proclaim Christ in that community. From the beginning the blood of martyrs has been the seed of faith. Their witness became a strong inspiration to others. By God's grace, painful experiences such as the death of Stephen can become blessings in retrospect. Those who fled for self-protection against the authorities in Jerusalem became the seeds of new communities of faith in neighboring towns and villages. Like dandelion seeds blown in the heat of summer, new growth can take place in unanticipated locations.

God is the catalyst for reorganizing faith. Being forced to pick up our lives and move on may come from various impetuses. It may be that one stage of life ends and another begins such as with graduation or empty nest or retirement. Yet it may also come because life collapses in one way or another. New venues always have the potential for new life but also for new and deeper faith. They may call us to a new trust; they may simplify our lives; they may free us from unhealthy attachments; they may demand that we surrender. The occasion may be difficult, but the results are wonderful.

Philip the Evangelist

Earlier in Acts we had learned that Philip was one of the Seven set aside to take care of the needs of Greek widows (6:5) in Jerusalem. Rather quickly, it would seem, some of these same individuals were inspired to become evangelists, as well as administrators of local food pantries. Stephen debated with members of the Synagogue of Freedmen (6:9), and Philip first went north to Samaria (8:5) then south to Gaza (v. 26). Acts describes the physical and spiritual healings performed by Philip (v. 7) and the great joy that filled the city of Samaria as a result (v. 8; see also the story of Jesus and the Samaritan woman at the well in John 4:4-42, where she is remembered by John's gospel as the primary evangelist to that community). Almost invariably, service to the poor and needy inevitably finds expression in verbal witness to the full Gospel of Jesus. In this passage Philip is proclaimed as an example of those whose faith became wonderfully fruitful in spite of, or even perhaps because of, the persecution they endured. How far Philip continued to travel is not known, but a fifth-century Martyrium has been found to his honor in the city of Heiropolis (Turkey), some hundred miles east of Ephesus.

God's Story Made Present

God collapses life and rebuilds life. In her book *Widow*, Lynn Caine wrote of her world after the death of her husband, Martin. She writes of a world that ended but also of the new world Martin's death ushered in for her.

Today I carry the scars of my bitter grief . . . marks of my fight to attain an identity of my own. I owe the person I am today to Martin's death. If he had not died, I am sure I would have lived happily ever after as a twentieth century child wife never knowing what I was missing.

But today I am someone else. I am stronger, more independent. I have more understanding, more sympathy. A different perspective. I have a quiet love for Martin. I have passionate, poignant memories of him. He will always be part of me.

But Martin is dead. And I am a different woman. And the next time I love, if ever I do, it will be a different man, a different love.

Frightening.

But so is life. And wonderful.[1]

For Lynn Caine the collapse of one world initiated the creation of another. That, too, is how God brings about a new creation.

ANTIPHON—PSALM 66:1
Let all the earth cry out to God with joy. (or: Alleluia)

Psalm 66:1-3a, 4-5, 6-7a

Psalm 66 is a hymn of praise that has been liturgically divided to serve as the responsorial song for two successive days this week. The initial verses used in today's liturgy are primarily expressions of praise with only generic references to God's deeds. Those verses reserved for tomorrow's Eucharist are taken from a litany of more personal reasons for that acclaim. The entire world and all its nations are invited to join in praise for the Lord's tremendous deeds among the children of Adam (v. 5). He changed the sea into dry land (v. 6) at the time of the exodus and rules forever. The liturgy suggests that perhaps these words of praise could be placed on the lips of the people of Samaria at the time of Philip's visit. They are now offered to those who gather for the parish morning Eucharist today.

The Refrain

As a result of the geographic spread of early Christian witnesses on the occasion of the martyrdom of Stephen, there is an implicit universal expression of Christian praise from the beginning. This refrain acknowledges that the entire world takes part in the joyful hymn (v. 1), each people in its own tongue and cultural rhythms. Perhaps the different ethnic backgrounds of the parishioners at weekday

Mass are a contemporary example of the same universalism described in the reading from Acts and celebrated in the psalm. Many are one.

GOSPEL ACCLAMATION—JOHN 6:40
Once again this song lifts up the final verse of today's gospel reading and prepares the assembly for appreciating its ultimate importance as the climax of the pericope.

JOHN 6:35-40
This is the will of my Father, that all who see the Son may have eternal life.

Wednesday of the Third Week of Easter

Bread of Life

The Lectionary has chosen to repeat the last verse of yesterday's gospel with its reference to the "bread of life" (v. 35) and to use it as the opening statement for today's passage as well. This indicates its importance for the development of John's thought this week. In contemporary American slang, the word "bread" can signify both food and the money used to purchase it. In a different but equally comprehensive sense *lehem*, the Semitic word for bread, signifies all the basic forms of human nourishment—including meat. Moreover, from another perspective, the ancient Semitic mentality presumed that those things that move are somehow alive—such as water, wind, clouds, sun, and other heavenly luminaries, while stationary plants are not. "Bread of life" or "living bread," therefore, is somehow "bread on the move," either in terms of the motion that it enables in the lives of pilgrim people or the way this bread moves through the world with life-giving energy and vitality. These are phrases rich in meaning, and John loves to play with them. The gospel passage concludes with the reminder that the life given by this bread is already the life of the next (eternal) age (v. 40).

God is the bread that feeds our lives. It has been said that we always become the kind of people we want to become. It seems to be true. If one seeks riches, that person will become if not wealthy at least someone focused upon the accumulation of wealth. If it is popularity, then one becomes focused upon the aspects of social life. The same can be said of aspects of faith. Seek patience, and life will take you there. Seek kindness, and it will come. Seek wisdom, and you will find it. There does seem to be something in us that nurtures and feeds our hungers. Is it simply human nature—or is it the very living bread of God that feeds us?

Wednesday of the Third Week of Easter

Belief as a Gift from God

Jesus noted that the crowd had seen him but still not believed (v. 36). Obviously, at least in this case, the popular saying about "seeing is believing" is not necessarily true! Apparently, therefore, true belief requires more than mere physical experience. It is a gift from God that enables a person to "come to Jesus" and results in never hungering or thirsting again (v. 35). Also woven throughout this chapter is the assumption of the need for God's life-giving grace. Although the word is not used, the text repeatedly suggests that belief is a gift from God, a grace that always respects human freedom. Faith does not forfeit freedom. Those whom the Father has given to Jesus (v. 37) come forward because of the transforming grace granted to them. The capacity to love God and neighbor is the fundamental grace of Christian existence and the source for all the obligations that follow from it. Jesus does not have further requirements or extra expectations, and for that reason he accepts disciples warmly and willingly, pending their free acceptance of that gift of divine love.

God's Story Made Present

God brings us to that point of readiness for faith-filled seeing. Anthony de Mello told of a similar coming to a point of readiness for seeing. "Before I was twenty I never worried about what other people thought of me. But after I was twenty I worried endlessly—about all the impressions I made and how people were evaluating me. Only sometime after turning fifty, did I realize that they hardly ever thought about me at all."[2] How does one see oneself clearly? How does one see God clearly? It is all by grace.

The Will of the One Who Sent Me

As we know, the prayer taught by Jesus includes the petition, "Thy will be done" (Matt 6:10) and specifies that those who obey include all creatures both in both heaven and earth. Curiously, Luke's wording of that prayer apparently assumes that the coming of the kingdom includes this same acceptance because the equivalent petition is absent from his simpler version (Luke 11:2-4). Even Jesus is not exempted from that invitation, but out of love, not obligation. John's gospel makes loving obedience a central element in the relationship between Jesus and his heavenly Father, and refers to their union often. This is also found in the loving accommodation of human spouses to each other's preference by choice, not obedience. Some early groups slipped into the heresy of "subordinationism"—that is, believing that Jesus is lower in divine dignity than the Father because of this obedience. They concluded, therefore, that the Son was less than the Father. Authentic Christian faith, however, does not see the loving obedience of Son to Father as implying subordination in any fashion. Early ecumenical councils had to struggle for decades to find the right phrases for this profound mystery. Love, even when between fully equal partners, inspires an eager spirit of cooperation and compliance; divine love between Father and Son creates a profound unity in mind and will. In John's gospel we are reminded early on that God sent his Son to save the world, not condemn it (John 3:17). Jesus embraced that mission wholeheartedly because he loved the world and everyone in it. He came to do his Father's will in its fullness (v. 38).

God wills to save us. Some more so and some less, most people are savers of one sort or another. Martha had a penchant for saving Hummel figurines. One was attractive and nice, but fifty in one cabinet made them all seem no more than trinkets. Others choose to save endless pieces of string, drawers upon drawers of plastic grocery bags, stacks of *National Geographic* magazines going back fifty years, rubber bands by the doorknob-full, and mounds of scrap lumber—just because you'd never know when the right length might be needed. To say nothing of empty toilet paper rolls, used Christmas wrapping paper, empty coffee cans, and old grocery receipts. What is it about us human beings that seems to betray an instinct for saving—some of us more so than others, but all of us to some degree? Yet it would seem, based upon this day's gospel, that the inclination to save is a very Godly instinct that is manifest again and again—the child who brings the parent to faith, the illness that brings us to our knees, and conflict that teaches us to forgive.

**Wednesday
of the
Third Week
of Easter**

1. Lynn Caine, *Widow* (New York: William Morrow, 1974).

2. Anthony de Mello, *One Minute Wisdom* (New York: Doubleday, 1986), 91.

Thursday of the Third Week of Easter

God's Story Proclaimed

ACTS 8:26-40
Look, there is water. What is to prevent my being baptized?

On the Way

Philip was on the way southwestward to the city of Gaza (v. 26), and the Ethiopian was on the way back home to Ethiopia in eastern Africa (v. 28). One was an evangelizer eager to speak about the Lord's death and resurrection; the other was struggling to understand the prophet Isaiah's teachings. They were both following God's will as best they could. Each was "on the way" to somewhere not as yet achieved. Their respective paths suddenly crossed and they shared their faith. The "way" was one of the earliest titles for the new Christian faith (9:2). It was the path of obedience to God's will, the practical journey one should make through life in this world to arrive in the fullness of the kingdom in the next. Jesus himself said that he was "the way, the truth and the life" (John 14:6). Some twenty centuries later, we are all still "on the way." Our lives intersect with others through shared occupations, mutual care, common service to the needy, and any number of shared projects for the betterment of our communities. We are, each and all of us, people on the way.

God's Story Made Present

God's Spirit brings people into our lives and lifts people out of our lives, at times for a moment and other times for longer. Our journey of faith is seldom a solo flight. Each is a gift for as long as they—spouse, children, friends—are with us. The wisdom of some can nurture us. The conflicts with others may strengthen us. Some individuals may open doors to growth; others will sustain us. "God's Way" is a path of others' comings and goings in the life we live.

Awhile back there was a group of high school students sitting around talking about whatever it is that sixteen- and seventeen-year-olds talk about. For whatever reason someone in the group, a Philip sort of person, spiked their conversation with the question, "What's a value you hold that nobody else does, or seems to?" Like a winter wind, it cut the conversation to a chill and a groan. "No really," he insisted. "Don't you have any?"

"Well sure," someone finally admitted, "but why are you asking?" "Just wanted to know, that's all. So what is it?" One by one most of them there gave voice to their value. For one it was being honest, no matter the cost. Another said that she respected her body—no drugs or smoking or alcohol. A number of them named their family, even above their friends. One said it was her faith. She was a bit older, and you could tell she felt a risk in saying it aloud to the group. Then just as quickly as that topic had begun, it splintered into why's and when's and on to other subjects. It is how the Spirit brings people into our lives and lifts them out again.

From Isaiah to Jesus

The ancient world always read aloud (v. 28). Early Judaism even insisted that one obtain the permission of the neighbors before establishing a school because the noise of a classroom of students reading could be so disturbing to adjacent families! Philip heard the Ethiopian and ran up to see if he could offer any help in understanding Isaiah's mysterious Fourth Servant Song (v. 32, citing one version of 53:7 from the larger unit of 52:13–53:12). This text was a favorite of the early church because it spoke so clearly of the servant's sufferings as a sin offering for others, and it contrasted the servant's abject humiliation with final glory. The ancient words of Isaiah offered a perfect description of the death and exaltation of Jesus, which we call the paschal mystery. The words of the prophet, therefore, also seemed to describe the shocking and painful death of Jesus, as well as his stunning resurrection. This text from Isaiah also explains why the first Christians gave the title of "servant" to Jesus in their prayers (Acts 4:27, 30). The same words from Isaiah give insight into the sufferings of countless contemporary Christians who share their Lord's paschal mystery through baptism and thus participate in the ongoing redemption of the world.

God's Story Made Present

Spiritual mentors or directors help us put the pieces of our life together. William Deresiewicz is a retired professor of English at Yale University who recently wrote a book entitled *Excellent Sheep.* As one reviewer states:

> He presents a devastating critique of the idea that college education is simply about learning marketable skills. . . . Whether the students are actually satisfied to be sheep is another matter. Deresiewicz writes movingly of their anguish. No reader of his book can doubt that elite colleges are full of fearful, driven kids whose miseries include "eating disorders, cutting, substance abuse, addiction, depression." Here are some voices from the meritocracy in training: "I only get two hours sleep per night. . . . I really, really fear failure. . . . I am just a machine with no life at this place. . . . I am a robot just going page by page, doing the work." It is like the mental Olympics, one student observes, but the contest never ends. Sometimes "the drug of praise" can temporarily numb the fear of failure. And sometimes it takes other drugs: "If I didn't take Zoloft," one former student told him, "I would hate myself."[1]

College students are not the only ones who feel they have no control over their lives. Many at all stages of life feel overwhelmed and unable to negotiate the winds of life. It is in such times that we value companions on the journey in order to see ourselves more clearly and honestly. With spiritual mentors we come to understand the rhythms of life more readily. We are opened to new directions and new paths. Like Philip to the Ethiopian, such individuals become guides on the way, sometimes short-term and other times long-term.

Antiphon—Psalm 66:1

Let all the earth cry out to the Lord with joy. (or: Alleluia)

Psalm 66:8-9, 16-17, 20

As noted yesterday, the editors of the Lectionary chose to continue using some of the verses from Psalm 66 for two days. Yesterday's selection from the initial portion of the Psalm focused on universal praise and songs of rejoicing. Today's section also invites praise but adds new motives for that jubilation—namely, the gift of life to individual souls and protection for feet that slip dangerously (v. 9) together with an invitation to hear what God has done for this individual (v. 16). The reference to safety for feet echoes the tale of the journeys of both Philip and the eunuch. God is praised for his faithful kindness (literally, covenantal *hesed*) and for not having ignored a desperate prayer (v. 20), perhaps like the urgent request of the eunuch for assistance. There is a sense in which these words from the psalm echo the sentiments of Isaiah's Servant Song. Yesterday's allusion to the exodus of the entire nation (v. 6) is now replaced by individual salvation from whatever burdens or troubles faced at the moment. Anyone from the day's Mass congregation can easily make the verses her own.

> **Thursday of the Third Week of Easter**

The Refrain

Every act of individual salvation becomes a motive for the rejoicing of the entire world. The biblical perspective presumes a profound and constant social connection between all people. The ancient world would find the radical individualism of our Western culture strange and unbiblical. The entire world is once more invited to rejoice (v. 1) over any protection given by God to his Servant *par excellence* or to any one of his servants, no matter what the time or place. The very same refrain is repeated in each of these two days, perhaps to signal the relationship between Israel's ancient salvation from the Egyptians and any individual action of God for the protection of people today.

GOSPEL ACCLAMATION—
JOHN 6:51

The Lectionary has selected the final verse of today's gospel reading as an introductory summary to the proclamation. This decision highlights from the beginning the identity of Jesus, as well as the inner relationship between this heavenly bread and the gift of eternal life.

Thursday of the Third Week of Easter

JOHN 6:44-51
I am the living bread that came down from heaven.

Unless the Father Draw One

With some of the best of Johannine subtlety and thematic interweaving, this sixth chapter moves from Word as faith-nourishing revelation to Word as life-giving Eucharist. In this morning's gospel passage we see more clearly the signs of the chapter's movement from bread as nourishment for faith that leads to eternal life (vv. 35-50), on the one hand, and bread that is truly the flesh and blood of Jesus (vv. 51-58), on the other. Thus, during the initial section of this chapter, Bread of Life refers to revelation in Jesus, but after v. 50 Bread of Life takes on eucharistic tones and implications. That midpoint of thematic departure is found in today's teaching regarding the necessity of grace for the believer. No one can come without the Father attracting him (v. 44). Theologians tell us that such an attracting occurs by the way in which God's grace works in our human minds and wills. Although we remain free and able to refuse or reject God's invitation, the transforming grace of God enables us to lay down our lives without the solid evidence normally required for such fundamental life decisions. The citation "from the prophets" (Second Isaiah as a contemporary of the returnees) originally promised that those who choose to return from exile and live in Jerusalem again will be "taught by the Lord" (54:13). Just as Jesus proclaimed himself as the "Bread of Life" in terms of revelation (v. 35), he now describes himself as the "living bread that came down from heaven" (v. 51) and adds a reference to his flesh (*sarx*), which will be given for the life of the world (*kosmos*). Jesus is both revelation and Eucharist. God's mind-altering grace is needed to recognize him as either.

God's Story Made Present

God brings each of us to faith, not we ourselves. Sometimes we do stumble upon the seeing when we search for God, just because often enough it does feel more like a stumbling upon than a looking and finding. At other times it does seem that God finds us, that we do come to see without ever looking or even knowing we should look, as if we were blind and didn't know we were blind.

In the novel *The Color Purple* it is Shug who has come to that wisdom in her own life. "Here's the thing, say Shug. The thing I believe. God is inside you and inside everybody else. You come into the world with God. But only them that search for it inside find it. And sometimes it just manifest itself even if you not looking, or don't know what you're looking for. Trouble do it for most folks, I think. Sorrows, lord."[2]

Listens, Learns, and Comes

In the midst of today's passage from the teaching of Jesus on living bread comes this gem: "Everyone who listens to my Father and learns from him comes to me" (v. 45). These few words describe the entire process that the other gospels might label "discipleship." We don't learn unless we are paying attention. Whenever we learn anything, we are changed. We can never be the same. Moreover, once we realize that we have been transformed by what we have heard, we tend to listen even more carefully and to pay even greater attention to what we hear. Learning like listening is a process of transformation. In some way we become like the person we listen to, and we share a bond that unites and changes us. When it is God to whom we listen (v. 45), we begin in some small way to become like God! Whoever believes already possesses eternal life (v. 47)—that is, the life of the next age. Because the Father and the Son have all things in common except their distinctive Fatherhood and Sonship, becoming like God automatically means becoming like Jesus. Listening and learning brings us to Jesus because we share the gift of human flesh and blood with him, and because we also share his life-giving Spirit. In these same few words we can hear intimations of the profound mystery of the Trinity, which distinguishes us as Christians from other religious traditions of our world. To pause over this single sentence can leave us wide-eyed in wonderment.

God instills the wisdom of holy common sense. All parents worthy of the name seek paths of common sense for their children. Without it life is so much more difficult. For those who seem to find it, in time that common sense seems to become more nuanced, both broader and deeper. We tend to call it wisdom among those who have grown to the far side of life. There does seem to be some common truths by which life is lived. Call it a natural law of human life, if you will. Those who seem to possess such wisdom seem to have been fed by the very wisdom of God. For them it has become their bread of wisdom, the bread of life.

Coming to Jesus

Sometimes the phrase "come to Jesus" is used as playful shorthand for a disciplinary meeting in which the hard facts of irresponsibility or disobedience are explained by a teacher or parent, and punishment is duly meted out. In today's gospel context, however, the phrase (v. 44) is a reference to the personal act of faith in Jesus the Living Bread. Faith is a new way of accepting the way God works in our world, not so compelled by evidence, however, as to lose one's individual freedom in the process. Rather we come as a whole person and not merely a will or intellect, even though the motivation for such a gift of self may not be completely clear.

God invites and welcomes us into the new life of faith. There are times when a couple may fall in love and fully commit themselves to each other even when friends and colleagues are left scratching their head and wondering "what she sees in him!" Such a couple has moved from self-centered infatuation to genuine love that cares about the other person freely and completely. Similarly, the gift of faith can move a believer to freely place oneself at the service of God's will without any level of irrefutable or demanding evidence as may be found in science or mathematics. Someone may see signs of God at work in our world and freely respond with the generous gift of oneself. At such times the grace of God's invitation is at work, waiting at times for the right moment, and then leads us into a new relationship. Often we mistakenly think that it is we who come, but in fact it is God who makes himself known to us in new and unsettling ways! It is then by God's transforming grace that we come to Jesus as disciples and partners and not as errant children.

**Thursday
of the
Third Week
of Easter**

---

1. Jackson Lears, "A Place & Time Apart," *Commonweal* 142, no. 8 (May 1, 2015): 16.
2. Alice Walker, *The Color Purple* (New York: Washington Square, 1982), 177.

Friday of the Third Week of Easter

God's Story Proclaimed

ACTS 9:1-20
This man is a chosen instrument of mine to carry my name before the Gentiles.

The Conversion of Saul

In the course of the account of the early church's growth as presented by Acts, the history of Saul's conversion is recounted three times (chaps. 9, 22, 26). Although insignificant individual details vary between the stories depending on the precise point to be made in each case, the very fact that the same basic tale is told thrice signals its importance for the book and for early Christianity as a whole. Saul's intense conviction about the truth of Judaism and his dedication to that religious tradition is a key piece of information for the story (v. 1), as well as the fact of a heavenly interruption into his life from somewhere beyond human control (v. 3). The profound identity between the risen Jesus and the disciples whom Saul persecuted is also a crucial element in Saul's new appreciation (v. 5). Subsequently two God-given visions in Damascus bring together the startled, fearful Ananias (v. 10) and the still-confused Saul (v. 12). Much to his surprise Ananias ends up healing Saul, baptizing him, and welcoming him into the very community that Saul had despised (v. 18). In a complete reversal, the fiery persecutor (v. 1) becomes an ardent evangelist of Jesus as Son of God (v. 20). It all happens "on the way" as early Christianity was called by its adherents.

God's Spirit forms us in times of transition. The rhythms of life will often offer transitional times from one period of life to the next. A time of engagement before marriage, boot camp as an initiation into military service, even the time of pregnancy, all serve as periods of preparation and transition.

As it was for Saul during his three days of blindness and waiting, the movements into faith can be quite similar. Although not so dramatic, there is a fundamental process for many Christians that can lead from ignorance or even hostility to the profession of faith. The individual starting points may be different for each person, but the process from childish or adolescent faith to maturity is universal. The journey to faith is part of "the way" for disciples of every age.

Professed religious life will usually offer a period known as the novitiate in order to prepare a person for the commitment one is about to make. Seminary life is intended to prepare for ordination. Similarly those who seek to join the Catholic Church participate in the RCIA process before they formally join the church. In much the same way, though to a lesser degree, daily reflective prayer can also be a time of briefly escaping distractions in order to focus upon the day ahead and the faith responses we may be called to make during the day.

Surprising Chosen Instrument

To a stunned and very uncertain early Christian by the name of Ananias, the Lord announced that Saul the persecutor was to become God's "chosen instrument" to carry his name to Gentiles and their kings as well as to the children of Israel (v. 15). To a doubtful Ananias, the Lord simply said, "Just go!" Scripture is filled with examples of God choosing improbable figures: Moses who stuttered (Exod 4:10), David whom his family didn't even bother to bring forward to meet Samuel (1 Sam 16:11), Jeremiah who claimed to be too young (Jer 1:6), Mary from Nazareth, a city never even mentioned in the Old Testament (Luke 1:26), and the list goes on. Perhaps the ultimate reason is to make it clear that the praise goes to God rather than to any mere human instrument. Saul, ardent Jewish protagonist and ruthless persecutor of Christians, is called to address Jews and Gentiles (v. 15) about Jesus and become a divinely chosen instrument in bringing together the ones he had initially discounted. Like a skillful surgeon or experienced carpenter, God knows precisely which instrument will best do the job—and we humans are almost always left shaking our heads in surprise.

 God's choices too often surprise. In many ways life is a box of crayons, all with their pointed tips so perfectly cast and placed in rows of matched and tinted hues. Each color seems so eager to make its mark, brilliant or shy or somber or faint—like a touch of some wistful bygone season. There has always been something about a brand-new box of forty-eight crayons, something that makes one pause a bit in awe and reverence. Burnt sienna, magenta, turquoise blue, mahogany, apricot, salmon, periwinkle, lemon yellow—the names themselves make you want to pull them out of the box and put them onto paper. Like life, they are simply waiting to be put into use, each perfectly suited for the specific color needed.

Life can be a box of crayons. When God chooses individuals for specific tasks, often enough it seems that God chooses the wrong person, the wrong color. To us a different color would fit the picture much more pleasingly, a different person would seem much more suited to the task. Yet God knows precisely which instrument will best do the job. And of course the surprise choice becomes the perfect choice.

ANTIPHON—MARK 16:15
Go out to all the world and tell the Good News.
(or: Alleluia)

Psalm 117:1bc, 2

 With only a total of two verses in all, this is the shortest hymn of the entire Psalter. Scholars have suggested that it originally served as the introductory summons to a prayer service, initially addressed by the priest to an entire congregation. The motive for this outburst of joyful praise is God's steadfast covenantal kindness (v. 2, literally, *hesed*) and enduring fidelity (literally, *'emet*, "truth"). No examples

are given nor any specific motives for the praise. Perhaps each participant in the congregational worship is expected to supply his own personal reasons for the tribute of gratitude. The fact that the nations are invited to join this praise (v. 1) may be the logical result of the fact that the prior reading from Acts describes how Saul had been chosen by God as the instrument of the Gospel to the larger Gentile world in a new and unexpected fashion.

The Refrain

In an unusual turn of liturgical practice, the day's refrain is not selected from the psalm response itself but from the end of the Gospel of Mark (16:15). Perhaps the editors of the Lectionary decided that the psalm was too short to give up either of its two verses, or they may have wanted to link Paul's vocation to the concluding command of Mark's Jesus to bring the Gospel to all. The original Greek of that request as found in Mark was literally "to every creature," which suggests the sum total of material creation, not simply human beings. Mark's phrase also recalls Paul's conviction that every creature (not only human beings) was waiting in groaning anticipation for transformation into glory (Rom 8:19-23).

GOSPEL ACCLAMATION—JOHN 6:56
Once again the Lectionary selects a verse from the proclamation that highlights a main point of the passage and prepares the congregation for what above all else they should hear: eating the Lord's flesh (*sarx*) and blood actually leads to unity with him.

JOHN 6:52-59
My Flesh is true food, and my Blood is true drink.

Eating Flesh

At this point in the fluid speech of the discourse spread through the verses of chapter 6, it finally becomes very clear that the Bread of Life of which Jesus speaks (v. 35) is not only transforming revelation but truly the lifegiving bread that we call Eucharist (v. 53). Jesus does not back down, reinterpret, or sidestep the physical reality that caused members of his audience to take exception or walk away. In fact, in this gospel passage Jesus not only uses the Greek word *phagein* (to eat or consume as food), but he intensifies the point by using an even more graphic term four times within these six verses—namely, *trōgein* (to chew or gnaw, vv. 54, 56, 57, 58)! No wonder some of the listeners began today's text by arguing among themselves (v. 52), and ended the debate by walking away from such a hard saying (v. 60, as we will learn at the beginning of tomorrow's reading)! Catholic tradition has not backed away from this teaching either, but clarified it by insisting that the eating is sacramental, not physical. We eat the flesh (*sarkx*, another very physical Greek word) of the Son of Man (v. 53) under the appearance of bread and become a member of the body we consume. Christ's gift of self not only transforms the banqueters but gives them a share in the life of the next age (vv. 54 and 58)!

**Friday
of the
Third Week
of Easter**

Being fed by God makes us sons and daughters of God. Each year at the end of the Thanksgiving Day Eucharist there is a local priest who will playfully remind those present that as they gather around their Thanksgiving Day table and gaze in awe at the beauty of the turkey before them, "Remember, you are what you eat!" The same is frequently noted about sharing in daily fast-food fare. We do become what we eat, for good or for ill. To reiterate that folk wisdom about the Eucharist, a very real sharing in the presence of the Lord Jesus, conveys a real truth as well. We cannot help but take on the reality of what the Lord Jesus is if we regularly share in the reality of the Eucharist.

Announcing "Life because of Me"

Amid the theologically dense speech of Jesus in this final teaching on bread in all its aspects, we hear a powerful statement: "whoever eats (*trōgein*) chews me, that very one will live because of me" (v. 57). Jesus is the living Word of God sent into this sinful world (*kosmos*) to bring life in abundance (John 10:10); he is also the source of life for others. By birth we are human at one level, but to consume Jesus in the Eucharist is to come alive in a new and more complete way. No matter how much we may experience vitality in daily life or at high peaks of our human existence, that life is minimal and almost insignificant in contrast to the kind of life given us by sharing the Bread of Life that is Jesus the Christ himself. It is the causal connection "through Jesus" (literally, "because of me," v. 57), which this portion of John's gospel wishes to stress. Eucharistic connection with Jesus and all human neighbors gives universality to life and provides us with a motive for action beyond our limited individual persons—namely, the motive of God's love for the whole world. It is through our relationship with Jesus the Lord that we can share even now the reality of full and future life. We become inserted into the redemptive mission of Jesus. We live because of him—because he died and rose to new life, which he shares through baptism into his death, which he intensifies through the Eucharist.

Jesus proclaims and offers a level of life beyond anything we can ever imagine. On so many levels, nutritionally and spiritually, we become what we eat. Whenever we give ourselves away to the poor and hungry, offer dramatic protection to the innocent and vulnerable at great risk and personal cost, or stand up for the bullied and mistreated, we live the self-sacrificing life of Jesus himself. We make his vision real in our limited human world and in our time. Having pondered the gospel stories, we bring them to life again in our families and neighborhoods.

Saturday of the Third Week of Easter

God's Story Proclaimed

Lectionary note: The editors of the Lectionary chose to omit ten verses that describe the turmoil experienced by Saul both in Damascus and in Jerusalem when he tried to engage his former colleagues with testimony about Jesus as the Messiah. Lowered in a basket out of an opening in the Damascus city wall (v. 25) to avoid physical danger, Saul went to Jerusalem where Barnabas took care of him by introducing him to the apostles (v. 27). Unfortunately, the theological polemics began all over again, so they sent Saul back to Tarsus for his physical protection and for peace in Jerusalem. That's where the Lectionary takes up the story again.

Acts 9:31-42

The Church was being built up, and with the consolation of the Holy Spirit she grew in numbers.

An Attractive Church at Peace

With Saul off the scene, at least for the moment, the church assembly (*ekklesìa*) was at peace (v. 31). The Semitic notion of *shalom* (in Greek: *irene*; peace), however, always signaled more than tranquillity. The fact that the text refers to the larger geographic area of Judea, Galilee, and Samaria underscores the good relationship that existed between these various small Christian enclaves within some forty or fifty miles from Jerusalem. They were somehow bound together, initially through their relationship with the apostolic leadership in Jerusalem but also by reason of sharing the same faith in Jesus their common risen Lord. The community lived in an abiding reverential fear of God and enjoyed the many gifts of the Holy Spirit, which were summarized as "consolation" (v. 31)—that is, comforting encouragement. To be "at peace" is to have all the parts working smoothly together and, therefore, to be healthy as a community. None of these communities were closed in upon themselves, and as a result they grew in numbers. These are characteristics that Luke deliberately describes in order to provide yet another template for measuring the health of subsequent Christian communities as they were established throughout that known world: (1) openness to all the gifts of God's Spirit and (2) numerical growth because of the attractive witness provided by the community. The cure of Aeneas and his new enjoyment of health (vv. 33-35) is also a symbol and sign of the larger community's well-being within which he lived. He became a concrete example of the *shalom* that outsiders found so striking and eye-catching. Both the health of the community (v. 31) in the biblical sense and the health of Aeneas (v. 35) became reasons for new members.

God's gift of peace makes individuals as well as their communities powerful examples and invitations. As then, so now people are attracted to communities that welcome others and live in respectful relationship with all those they welcome. We are created as social beings called to community membership. A spiritually healthy community is changed and strengthened by every new member. Gospel peace is anything but stagnancy! Every parish today could well engage in an assessment of its spiritual health by thinking about the same criteria listed in this reading from Acts. Such a discussion would be a perfect occasional agenda item for the pastoral council. Sometimes one neighboring congregation seems more vital and more attractive than its Christian neighbor. How is God served by our witness?

Tabitha the Seamstress

The book of Acts is filled with touching tales of the lives of individuals like so many people we know. Earlier we were introduced to folks like Joseph called Barnabas, for example, who sold some of his personal property and gave the proceeds to the apostles for the poor (4:36). Now we meet a widow by the name of Tabitha—or Dorcas as she is called in Greek (both words mean "gazelle," v. 36)—who sewed clothing for the poor (v. 39). After her sudden death (v. 37) she was restored to life in the community of Joppa through the prayers of Peter (v. 40). The ancient church fostered the Order of Widows—groups of women bound together by prayer and works of charity. These ancient groups have recently received renewed pastoral attention with an eye toward their possible restoration today. Only a community that exercises care for the poor is truly Christian. This story, however, also serves to emphasize the continuity between the ministry of Jesus, who raised the widow's son at Nain (Luke 7:14), this action of Peter on behalf of the seamstress, and Paul, who later raised the young man at Troas (Acts 20:9-12). The Gospel continues to be life-giving on many levels and in successive generations. Generosity toward the needy is one of the principal characteristics of faith in action. This is yet another common value shared by Judaism and Christianity alike. Aeneas was freed from paralysis (v. 34). Dorcas is raised from the dead so that with her widow friends she might continue to care for the needy.

Saturday of the Third Week of Easter

Care for the sick, the needy, and the dying are signs of the kingdom of God at work in our world. Most people at heart want to be good and want to do good to others. They find themselves instinctively drawn to be part of communities where that is happening. A homily for this day might point to where such activities are taking place in your own community of faith. When people speak with pride of their parish, what is it they mention?

ANTIPHON—PSALM 116:12
How shall I make a return to the Lord for all the good he has done for me? (or: Alleluia)

Psalm 116:12-13, 14-15, 16-17

Psalm 116 has been described as a hymn of thanksgiving that begins with references to former distress and anguish (v. 3) from which God delivered the soul—specifically, the person from death, eyes from tears, and feet from stumbling (v. 8). The editors of the Lectionary have omitted references to prior suffering in order to focus on the second portion of the psalm—namely, liturgical thanksgiving for deliverance. The use of these verses in today's response suggests that they might well be the prayer of Tabitha after being raised from the dead. By providing a Christian context for the second part of this psalm in liturgy, moreover, the editors of the Lectionary have enabled a contemporary parish congregation to understand the "cup of salvation" (v. 13) and the "sacrifice of thanksgiving" (v. 17) as referring in an unexpected and fuller fashion to the Eucharist that gathers folks together each weekday.

The Refrain

It is utterly impossible to make any truly adequate response or repayment to God for all the blessings each of us has received throughout life. It would be arrogance on our part to think otherwise. Nevertheless, the question posed by this refrain (v. 12) must be raised by any truly grateful person. Gratitude might well be expressed, not so much back to the donor, but rather by using the gift wisely and well—or by showing similar kindness to others in need. "How" seems to be the operative word. A proper response could simply be further service to others in the larger community. Tabitha may well have shown her gratitude by redoubling her efforts to work with the other widows in providing clothing for the needy. The "how" asks a question whose answer may also come from the needs of others around us.

GOSPEL ACCLAMATION—JOHN 6:63, 68
This introduction highlights a combination of the words of Jesus that exhibit the Spirit and give life in one reference to Peter's con-

fession of faith. They present one important dynamic found in this passage.

JOHN 6:60-69
To whom shall we go? You have the words of eternal life.

The Question of Jesus

What sounded like rank cannibalism to anyone not aware of sacramental reality might rightfully make some of those in the audience step back in horror (v. 60). This was particularly true within Judaism, which had great respect for blood (Acts 15:29) since they believed life was contained therein. Jesus spoke very realistically, and they understood that his teaching was no mere symbolism, but they did not as yet understand that the eating was sacramental—that is, under appearances of bread and wine (as was evident from the institution narratives of the Synoptic Gospels, and from the very first gatherings of Christians). In John's gospel Jesus is always utterly transcendent, knowing all things and being in complete control of his destiny. He also knew full in advance those who would eventually become unbelievers and betrayers (v. 64). Today's section of the gospel, however, returns to the need for God's grace to fully appreciate this jolting teaching, for "no one can come to me unless it is granted him by my Father" (v. 65). At the same time Jesus respected the freedom of disciples throughout the ages. He asks the fundamental question, "Do you also want to leave?" (v. 67). Faith must be freely given. Only God's grace can facilitate a positive response to this teaching. God does not force any acceptance against the dictates of human reason. Therefore the sad searching question of Jesus to the folks around him at Capernaum was simply, "Do you also want to leave?" (v. 67). The same question is addressed to Christians of all ages when faced by hard sayings.

God's words are Spirit and life. Addictions may be many things, but whatever they are, in one way or another they offer something perceived as life giving. Gerald May has written a book entitled *Addiction and Grace,* in which he lists 106 slices of life to which people find themselves addicted, attractively so, and then another seventy-seven that people addictively avoid (phobias).[1] The obvious attractions find their way onto his list—alcohol and smoking and gambling and the like. But then he also includes many unexpected behaviors—addictions to the stock market, being right, power, happiness, revenge, potato chips, chocolate, nail-biting, music, and almost a hundred more. While we may find ourselves surrendering to one or another, the person of faith also recognizes that ultimately God's word offers the richest life. At some point we say "yes" to that word and seek ways to live it out as best we can.

Peter's Response

The figure of Peter as described in all the gospels is characterized by goodness and generosity, as well as a certain impulsiveness. Peter blurts out a response to the question of Jesus regarding the identity of the Son of Man (Mark 8:29), and he even insisted on his willingness to go to prison and die with Jesus (Luke 22:33) prior to the arrest in Gethsemane. He would have some rude lessons yet to learn about his own weakness as we know from his eventual triple denials on the occasion of the arrest and trial of his Master (John 18:25-27). In this case, however, Peter's fundamental goodness and loyalty shines forth as he offers his famous confession of faith in Jesus the Holy One of God, "To whom shall we go? You have the words of eternal life" (v. 68). These same words could well be the daily prayer for any contemporary Christian faced with hard choices and difficult decisions.

God serves up a richness and depth for living life. These are days when institutional realities of any sort are held suspect—government, houses of finance, political forces, and also the organizational dimension of the church. As a result many walk away. For many, however, the response of Peter is their response: "To whom shall we go?" In spite of frustrations and disappointments, the institutional aspect of the church has been the vehicle for passing on the richness of the tradition—both doctrine and spirituality.

Saturday of the Third Week of Easter

---

1. Gerald G. May, *Addiction and Grace: Love and Spirituality in the Healing of Addictions* (San Francisco: Harper & Row, 1988), 38–39.

Fourth Week
of Easter

Monday of the Fourth Week of Easter

God's Story Proclaimed

ACTS 11:1-18

God has then granted life-giving repentance to the Gentiles too.

What God Has Made Holy

The first story of creation concludes with a touching moment when God muses about it all and decides that the world of newly formed creatures was "very good indeed" (Gen 1:31). The origin of the Jewish distinction between acceptable foods and those forbidden as "unclean" is extremely obscure. Avoidance of pork is shared by modern Jews and Muslims alike. The book of Leviticus attempted to offer some practical guidance for ancient cooks and menu planners (11:1-47). It would seem that the ancient Jewish custom of dietary restrictions served to underscore their ethnic distinctiveness and their difference from the surrounding Gentile nations. Peter's prior fidelity to that way of life (10:14) validated him as a leader and spokesperson for the Jewish Christians in Jerusalem. The book of Acts makes a point of showing Peter as the first to set aside those distinctive marks of Jewish identity as part of the postresurrection mission and indeed to do so by divine command (10:28-49). In the biblical background for today's reading, it may be helpful to remember that the fundamental notion of "holiness" is associated with something set apart and viewed as separate from daily life and common use. In today's reading Peter explains his actions to the leaders back in Jerusalem and receives their approval (11:18). The fact that the vision was given three times (similar to the fact that Paul's conversion is also reported three times in Acts) indicates its importance for the theology and practice of Acts (11:10). Although Jewish converts may (and perhaps should) continue their kosher practices, the restrictions are not binding on Gentile converts. Indeed God does grant considerable freedom to those who enter the wider family of faith. Everything that exists is in some fashion already holy by that fact.

God's Story Made Present

God creates each and every thing holy. In his poem "As Kingfishers Catch Fire," the nineteenth-century poet and Jesuit priest Gerard Manley Hopkins says, "Each mortal thing does one thing. . . . Crying What I do is me: for that I came." With their brightly colored wings, kingfishers dive for fish and catch the glisten of the sun on their wings is if they were aflame. They cannot not do so, he says. And a stone dropped into a deep well, he goes on, echoes back its plunk, just as a bell rings out its tone to the countryside. All of creation does what God has intended it to do. In the final stanza of the poem Hopkins comes to make his point that "the just man justices," which is to say that the person in relationship with God cannot but help to show the face of God in all that she or he does. That, too, is of the nature of someone who is a person of faith—something bred in one's bone. Hopkins writes with the deep conviction of faith that indeed each and every thing has been created holy.[1]

Peter and the Six Brothers

A subtle detail that might escape the attention of contemporary readers is the number of believers who visited the home of Cornelius in Caesarea—namely, the fact that the delegation was comprised of seven people. Seven seems to have been the number required for authoritative leadership in the early church. Seven individuals of good repute were set aside to care for the hungry (6:3), and they became a council of leaders for the early Hellenistic Christian community (though not necessarily "deacons" in our modern ministerial sense). An addition to John's gospel made a point of noting that seven disciples (21:2) witnessed the miraculous catch of fishes (v. 11) and the formal commission of Peter as one designated to feed the flock (vv. 15-19). Countless other examples illustrate the popularity of the number—the traditional seven days of the week and the seven gifts of the Spirit, and so on. Perhaps the number simply reflected the human experience that seven cannot result in an even, tied vote. In any case, the decision of Peter and the fact that seven witnessed the gift of the Spirit to the household of Cornelius make this action one of authority with binding consequences for our subsequent religious history. The seven witnessed God's gift of the Spirit to the Gentiles. That fact alone was important.

God confers authority upon communities of faith to recognize the Spirit. In the celebration of confirmation the faith community formally declares that the presence of the Spirit has been recognized in an individual. That same affirmation is recognized in a faith couple committing themselves in marriage. Baptism affirms someone to be Spirit-filled. Even the tradition of papal infallibility is a declaration of the community's long-held faith now formally affirmed as true. The faith community does have both the ability and the authority to recognize the Spirit.

Life-Giving Repentance

This reading concludes with the enthusiastic approval of the Jerusalem leadership for Peter's decision to meet with Cornelius' Gentile household and to welcome them into baptism (v. 16). The new converts did not thereby also receive, however, the obligation of following kosher dietary laws. The early Christian community could exist as united even if its members were separated between those who did live according to the kosher diet and those who did not. Apostolic leaders were filled with amazement in their discovery that God had granted "life-giving repentance" even to Gentiles (v. 18)! A few

chapters earlier, at the end of Peter's famous Pentecost speech (2:28), he had stated that God required two actions from those who suddenly realized their complicity in the death of Jesus: repentance (*metanoia*) and baptism. We know that the repentance required of those bewildered listeners was not penance in our sense of the word, but a more profound change in thinking regarding how God operated in their world. Their acceptance of baptism welcomed them into God's new creation. Their unity was found in their common need for conversion and repentance rather than in dietary practices or restrictions. The promised result of that conversion would be forgiveness of sin and the gift of God's creating and unifying Spirit (v. 28). All of that is wonderfully summarized when the leadership in Jerusalem realized that "life-giving repentance" had been granted to Gentiles, too (11:18).

God's Story Made Present

The yearning for God comes from God. We humans are filled with hungers. Some time ago BMW had an advertisement that described "Twenty Things to Do in This Lifetime." It obviously wanted to suggest that owning a BMW should be one of them. But then the ad went on to list others:

- flying over the Grand Canyon in a helicopter
- standing on the Great Wall
- seeing an opera at La Scala in Milan
- taking a balloon ride over the Serengeti
- playing the Old Course at St. Andrews
- seeing the sun rise over the ruins at Machu Picchu.

The ad was attempting to tap into our hungers to experience the richness of life, that there is more to life than what we now have and we shouldn't miss it. Except that the list doesn't really do it. In the end they all fail to last. Yet all of them ultimately can lead us to the realization of their futility, and so then to discover God. That discovery then becomes repentance and conversion.

ANTIPHON—PSALM 42:3A

Athirst is my soul for the living God. (or: Alleluia)

Psalms 42:2-3; 43:3, 4

Scholars agree that these two psalms (each of which contributed some verses to today's responsorial psalm) originally formed a single hymn. This is evidenced by the triple repetition of the same refrain (42:6-12 and 43:5) as well as the absence of an introductory rubric for Psalm 43. The verses chosen for today's liturgy omit any reference to enemies or faithless oppressors as found in other sections of these same psalms. The liturgical response simply describes a person's longing for the living God, almost like thirst (42:3), and a plea for the gift of light and faithfulness, which will bring the individual to God's holy mountain (Zion, 43:3). These verses would be perfect prayers for the new Gentile converts (and for all of us). That same verse that rejoiced in the ability to ascend to God's altar (43:4) once formed part of the initial prayers at the foot of the altar in the Latin Mass of Pius V prior to the liturgical reforms of the Second Vatican Council.

The Refrain

Contemporary Western households with easy access to purified running water simply cannot appreciate the level of thirst experienced so often in the ancient world. The daily walk to the village well at sunrise and the possibility that even then only stagnant water (namely, not fresh running "living" water) might be found for daily use, was taken for granted. Even in towns and villages, people consistently lived with physical thirst. Only in the Middle Ages did urban neighborhoods begin to have access to fresh water fountains throughout a given city. The daily experience of physical thirst was easily elevated to describe the deep desire of a religious person for the presence of God in daily life. This refrain is also useful as a liturgical response to the story of the baptism of that early Gentile community in Caesarea (11:16).

GOSPEL ACCLAMATION—JOHN 10:14

In both years of the Lectionary's weekday cycle, though the verses of the gospel passage vary, the same acclamation proclaims Jesus as the Good Shepherd. Note that the Greek word for "good" in this verse is not *agathos*, which would stress someone who is "morally and ethically upright," but rather *kalos*, namely, "excellently skilled and competent."

Lectionary note: In *Year A* of the Lectionary, the gospel passage for the Fourth Sunday of Easter is John 10:1-10 in which Jesus only proclaims himself as "the Gate." Consequently, in order not to duplicate the same reading on successive days, the gospel chosen for Monday of the fourth week is John 10:11-18 about the Good Shepherd. In *Year B*, when the Sunday gospel is 10:11-18 about the Good Shepherd, and in *Year C*, when the Sunday reading is John 10:27-30 about Jesus who knows his flock, the following weekday's gospel reading is John 10:1-10, namely, about Jesus as the Gate.

| Monday |
| of the |
| Fourth Week |
| of Easter |

JOHN 10:11-18 [YEAR A]

A good shepherd lays down his life for the sheep.

A Good Shepherd

As noted above in reference to the gospel acclamation, there are two very distinctive Greek words that might be translated in English as "good." One is *agathos*, which describes someone who is morally or ethically good, as in a "good woman" or a "good child." The other is *kalos*, which refers to someone recognized as excellently capable of performing a task well, as in a "good cook," a "good carpenter," a "good seamstress," a "good teacher." It is the latter that Jesus applies to his shepherding abilities in this verse. In caring for his flock, Jesus knows what he is doing and does it superbly. In the earlier portion of the chapter (vv. 1-10), Jesus had spoken of his easy access to the fold, but only through the proper gate (v. 2). He also asserted his ability to call them by name and his duty to lead them out into good pastures (v. 3). This is what a capable and effective shepherd does for his flock. In this text, he goes further and insists (three times) that a true shepherd even lays down his life to protect his flock if necessary (vv. 11, 16).

God patterns life for us. All of creation has the power to lay down its life. It would seem to be bred in its bone by the one who is Creator. The yearly seasons lay down the bounty of their harvest, and daily our own lives pour forth their energy into tasks and labors, often for others—all a kind of "laying down." Indeed, most people want to be and are generous. Most people want to forgive, be patient, and sacrifice for the sake of love, all of which are a kind of giving back what is received. Most people want to give of themselves for the happiness of others.

Monday
of the
Fourth Week
of Easter

Just as readily all of creation has the power to take up life again. Springtime returns; weakened bodies heal. We seek relationships of love; we desire to enflesh that love with children. We work hard; we long to be creative; we strive to be good people. That dual rhythm—of laying down and taking up—is but the echo of the Lord Jesus and how he chose to shepherd us. It was his Father's command to him, bred in his bone and in his spirit. It is a command that continues to show itself in our lives.

Others Not of This Fold

John's community was characterized by the ideal of genuine love for each other. Repeatedly Jesus referred to this as his Great Commandment (13:34; 15:12-17). The phrase is clearly a variant form of the ancient Jewish commandment of love of God and neighbor (Deut 6:4; Lev 19:18; Mark 12:30). Commentators wonder at times if there is an implied contrast between the Synoptics who insist on "love all your neigh-

bors," and John's "at least love one another!" Sometimes it is in fact more difficult to love those closest to us because we experience their foibles so frequently. On at least two occasions John's gospel makes a point, perhaps to broaden the picture, of adding a comment regarding Christ's care for those beyond his immediate flock (10:16; 17:20). This concern for the larger world is an essential element in the mind of Jesus. It is also one of the important bases for the ecumenical movement of our age. All followers of Christ are expected to follow his example of concern for outsiders as well as insiders, whoever they may be in any given age.

God's family is always larger than we think. Something is there that moves us to care for the lost among us. It does so often enough instinctively, and at times even contrary to our own best interests. It can be a bit like Tom, who is allergic to cats. His eyes turn red, and he starts to wheeze so that he has to excuse himself and leave. Oddly enough, Tom befriended a neighborhood stray at his back door. He doesn't touch it, and he won't allow it into his house, but he feeds it regularly and even misses it when it doesn't show up on his stoop.

In much the same way, believers find themselves enlarging their world to care for lost souls. We seek ways to help immigrants and offer to be foster parents. We stock food pantries and become members of St. Vincent de Paul Societies. We serve as Big Brothers and Big Sisters, visit prisons, and mentor students. Love enlarges our world.

JOHN 10:1-10 [YEARS B & C]
I am the gate for the sheep.

A Gate for the Sheep

Flocks of sheep, both ancient and modern, were given shelter at night either in caves, rough huts, or areas hedged high by thistles and brambles with the single access of a "gate." Shepherds were always concerned to protect their flocks from human or animal predators. In applying the image of "sheep gate" to himself (vv. 7, 9), Jesus emphasized his duty to protect his charges but also the need to offer legitimate access to those who shared his responsibility for the "flock" of God's people. Ability to enter was obviously not limited to the physical dimensions of the gate. It was the spiritual qualities, like those of Jesus, that dictated one's right to enter: shoulders broad enough to carry burdens, a heart big enough to contain compassion for everyone, and hands flexible enough to help in many different ways as needed. Only those who share his attitudes are welcome to have access to the sheep because they would be truly concerned for the flock's welfare. Jesus provides the spiritual measurements and sets the conditions for anyone desiring to serve in the pastoral work of the church. Some six centuries before Christ, the prophet Ezekiel had some very harsh things to say about priests, prophets, and kings who simply took advantage of God's people for personal pleasure or profit (Ezek 34:1-10). Those false shepherds were denounced and rejected by God because they only pastured themselves. Today's gospel passage goes further to call them thieves and robbers (vv. 1, 8), falsely presuming to take what did not belong to them. In preaching and praying today, special care and attention should be paid to avoid any "supersessionist" suggestion that all first-century Jewish leaders were rejected as such. At the time of Jesus those who made ingratiating compliance with Roman authorities for their own advancement or benefit more important than genuine care for the welfare of sheep were the ones targeted by this phrase and rejected by Jesus. In this passage Jesus proclaims himself as a model of authentic care for his sheep (v. 7), providing real protection, safety, care, and nourishment. He also promises to care for all the members of his flock, healthy or ailing alike. Whatever our weakness, needs, or limitations, Jesus makes sure that we are protected from danger and provided with shepherds who will

represent him and make his care tangible and effective. Jesus, both Gate and Shepherd, cares for his flock.

The wisdom and care of Jesus unlocks the doors to life. Every once in a while you and I get lost in our search for whatever it is that we sense is missing in our days. We say we need to put some life back into our lives. Maybe it's when someone tells us to "get a life." Or maybe it's when we end up feeling sorry for ourselves and so we pull down the window shades not only on our living room but also on our deepest insides, and we sit in a darkness that is heavier and more fearful than any nighttime walk through a cemetery. What all that feels like is life without purpose or meaning or maybe even God. It's at that point that we desperately long for someone to show us how to find our way back to light. Enter Jesus the shepherd. Whenever you and I live the way of that shepherd, then our lives seem richer. When we care for others more than for ourselves, when we forgive (even though it may be grudgingly) or are generous or peaceable or faithful. And whenever you and I do not live in such a way, well then that's when life is lifeless. So we say Jesus is the gate because we realize his wisdom is the measure of every other wisdom that seeks to settle into our lives. And we say Jesus is our shepherd because when we feel lost nothing else or no one else seems better able to show us how to be found.

> Monday
> of the
> Fourth Week
> of Easter

Life in Abundance

The gospel passage selected for the day concludes with a triumphant statement of the ultimate goal of all the service that Jesus offered his disciples and the larger world—namely, "life in abundance" (v. 10). In the largest sense of the word, Jesus is completely "pro-life." Far more than mere physical vitality and natural good health, Jesus repeatedly offers a share of life in the next age, life of a vastly different quality, life that surpasses anything we can know or experience in this present world of ours. This type of life "of the coming age" is often translated as "eternal," but the phrase in fact should suggest something more than merely "endless." Those who believe and are baptized already have a share in that utterly transcendent gift, even here and now. As the saints remind us, the utter joy of living completely for others even in this world brings blessings and satisfaction beyond measure.

God's Story Made Present

God serves up a taste of the banquet. Perhaps it is when we say "it doesn't get any better than this" that we are already experiencing just a taste of the banquet to come. A typical pastor's week at this time of year might include such common events: looking out the backyard window only to see a tiny field mouse skitter along the edge of a melting snow dune; seeing birds that had been cowering against the cold and wind for most all of winter ventured out to the bird feeder swaying in the sun; a parishioner who comes to talk leaves with her coat draped over her arm because the warmth is beginning to make a comeback and "it was too good to miss"; a teenager stopping to tell of the "awesome beauty" of a gurgling creek he has come upon while cross-country skiing through the woods; third-graders spending twenty minutes looking at projected photos that parishioners have taken on a recent trip to Haiti, and so the students want to know what they can do to help the people of Haiti in a lasting way; a recently engaged couple who come in to make arrangements for their marriage, and the bride-to-be is so excited that she can barely stay seated in her chair. There is a yearning in each of us, from the tiny field mouse to those who fall in love, a yearning that life can be more than what it has been. And indeed we sense that maybe we are on the verge of falling into it.

Monday of the Fourth Week of Easter

---

1. Peter Milward, "As Kingfishers Catch Fire," *A Commentary on the Sonnets of G. M. Hopkins* (Chicago: Loyola University Press, 1969), 114.

Tuesday of the Fourth Week of Easter

God's Story Proclaimed

ACTS 11:19-26
They began speaking to the Greeks as well, proclaiming the Good News of Jesus Christ.

A Decisive Moment of Grace

Perhaps the early Christians from the island of Cyprus (south of present-day Turkey) and from Cyrene (a country on the North African coast, south of Greece) were more accustomed to conversation with strangers, especially given the extended commercial enterprises of their homelands. It was precisely those folks who first began speaking about their faith with non-Jewish Greeks in the great city of Antioch in southeastern Turkey (v. 20). That action, however it may be explained, marked a major turning point in the history of early Christianity, much to the benefit of all consequent Gentile Christians throughout history. What had been an exclusively Jewish movement suddenly became open to the larger world. The shift was not an easy one, however, and Barnabas was sent from Jerusalem to review the situation and judge its fidelity to the teachings of the risen Jesus (v. 22). At a critical moment, he blessed the decision for all time. It was a pivotal moment in the history of religion. This "moment" became an enduring eternal reality for the rest of human history. It belongs to us, too, because we are still called to be open to the larger world that may be different from ourselves.

Each day God casts life and then breaks the mold. We all have expectations of what life should be, and, when it turns out different, we can grow angry and confused. We have expectations for our nation, but then immigration changes the dynamics, the economy tanks, or political winds change. We have expectations for the church, but popes come and go and change the ways of being church, liturgical prayers change, and questions of what we should be about as church arise. We have expectations of family, but children do not always meet those expectations, nor do spouses. The journey of transition made by the Hebrew community in adapting to Gentiles is no different than the journeys we make today. Changes, though sometimes painful, can be wonderful new beginnings.

Barnabas the Great

Joseph, nicknamed Barnabas (son of encouragement) by the apostles, had first been introduced as a generous member of the community who sold his property for the needs of the poor (5:36). He quickly became a prominent and much respected leader of the early Christian community in Jerusalem, "filled with the Holy Spirit and faith" (v. 24). As a result he was the one chosen and sent by the apostles as a representative and judge of the situation in Antioch (v. 22). Wise discernment is part of effective leadership. Apparently Joseph a.k.a. Barnabas was delighted with developments and fully endorsed their initiative to the Gentiles. Sensing the need for better catechetical training in Antioch, Barnabas sent for Saul a.k.a. Paul of Tarsus (13:9), a very well-educated Pharisee, to take over the position of Director of Religious Education in Antioch. Although Paul usually gets all the credit for the missionary efforts described in Acts, it was Barnabas who approved the initiative of outreach to the Gentiles, sought the best personnel, and developed the recipe for success. Maybe he needed a better press agent. His historical role was crucial. In contemporary popular literature Paul often gets the credit, but Barnabas did much of the initial work.

God raises up the right person for leadership in every age. John XXIII opened the windows and unsettled the status quo of the church. Paul VI negotiated a path through Vatican II. John Paul II centralized authority, to the delight of some and to the chagrin of others; in his travels he also reached out to embrace the whole world. Francis has come, emphasizing compassion, something that may not have taken place so effectively had we not had a highly centralized church.

Antiphon—Psalm 117:1a

All you nations, praise the Lord. (or: Alleluia)

Psalm 87:1b-3, 4-5, 6-7

This psalm has been described by scholars as hopelessly disjointed, and so the verses have often been rearranged to provide a logic not found in the text. Perhaps the original was intended to reflect the jubilant mood of a pilgrim upon first experiencing the Holy City. In any case, the Lectionary has achieved a literary integrity by simply breaking up the verses as written and using an antiphon borrowed from Psalm 117 to provide discreet units. Thus, even as the text stands, it is logically separated into three sections—namely, an initial recognition of the physical temple and its gates (vv. 1-3); a list of nations from the farthest southern and northern regions who come on pilgrimage to Zion (v. 4); and a final festive song by those who claim ancestral roots, at least by faith, in the Holy City (vv. 5-7). This acknowledgment of religious heritage easily reflects the reading's account of the initial Christian missionary efforts as far as Phoenicia and Cyprus.

Tuesday of the Fourth Week of Easter

The Refrain

From the beginning, the Christian experience has been marked by a new universalism. Even at the time of Abraham, however, Israel was called to be a blessing to the nations (Gen 12:1-3) and was only summoned to be separated from them for the purpose of offering such a blessing in turn to that larger world. In today's renewed interreligious climate, there is a sense in which Christian peoples are invited to use Israel as a model for our own obedience to God's will. We are asked to make that same complete dedication to God, but with all the cultural elements that make each Gentile nation unique. Every culture and nation is commanded to enter the chorus of international praise, each in its own language and with its own customs and character. This psalm's universalism anticipates the "catholicism" of the missionary outreach of Acts.

Gospel Acclamation—John 10:27

Jesus insists that the members of his flock hear his voice and follow his lead. With a certain directness that reflects the harsher tenor of his debates as described in John's gospel (whose final revision reflected the growing religious divisions of the 90s AD), Jesus declared that his interrogators were simply not of his flock. Those who gather for daily Eucharist at the parish may find themselves humbly grateful for the graces of discipleship that they have received as faithful members of the Lord's flock.

John 10:22-30

The Father and I are one.

The Liberating Works of God

In 164 BC the Maccabean family arose in religious revolt against their pagan oppressors. The flashpoint for the rebellion was a cultural uniformity suddenly and rigorously enforced by Hellenistic rulers who made sacred Jewish practices (kosher diet, circumcision of infants, and respect for the Torah) punishable by death. As a result of military success, however, the Jewish people regained their independence and proceeded to rebuild and solemnly reconsecrate their temple in 164 BC. The great December feast of Hanukkah celebrates that new religious freedom each year. It was that same feast that formed the background for today's reading (v. 22). At the time of Jesus some two hundred years later the Jewish people again felt restless under greedy and sometimes harsh Roman domination. They were seeking the type of leadership that might once again restore political and religious freedom to their nation. Against that historical background it was logical that devout Jewish worshipers should press the question of Jesus as a possible "anointed" leader chosen by God for the political restoration of his people. Tell us plainly, they begged (v. 24). When Jesus attempted to correct and depoliticize their expectations, they accused him of speaking obscurely in riddles. His response was to point to his works (v. 25), and to insist that his works were the works of God who cares for the sheep in spite of venal human leaders. His Father's sheep hear the voice of Jesus and follow him because he knows their deepest needs (v. 27). His works will make sure that they never perish (v. 28) and that no one will ever remove them from the Father's loving hand (v. 29). His works operate on a level distinctive from mere political leadership. The works bring freedom of a new and different type. His proposed leadership was beyond anything they could imagine.

God rearranges life and expectations. Often enough we find ourselves shifting our expectations and understandings from how we think what life should be and begin to realize how God makes himself known in how life really is. At such times we find ourselves rethinking life and our role in it, or we continue on in the struggle to try to fit life into our predetermined molds. Poet Robert Frost echoes that shift in his own perceptions in his poem "A Minor Bird." He muses about his irritation over a noisy bird outside his home but then concludes that the fault lies in himself, as he cannot recognize the beauty in creation as it is.

Unity of Father and Son

John's gospel is often described as providing what is called "high christology." Written toward the end of the first century, John's teachings about the Christ had already benefited from the deepening faith of the earliest Christian communities. His gospel illustrated the developments already achieved by their effort to understand the mysterious workings of God, and therefore to resist the initial heresies of that age. In contrast to the traditional devotion of Judaism to the singular Oneness of the Lord their God, and in keeping with that shared conviction, Christians tried to find some way of ascribing divinity to Jesus without blurring the individual personalities of Jesus and his Father. John's gospel declared the unity of Father and Son (v. 30) without compromise or confusion. It would require another two centuries and more, however, to find the correct terminology to express this mystery. That finally occurred, although with considerable initial acrimony, at Nicea (AD 325). Our Scriptures proclaim the mystery; our theologians struggle to find the words to make that mystery both reasonable and illuminating; and we struggle to live the reality in our daily lives. Nevertheless, there remains a sense in which this final statement is and perhaps should be shocking to all who continue to venerate the utter majesty of God. Jesus does his work in the name of his Father (v. 25). Moreover, God the Father so unites himself to the mission and work of Jesus that the works of Jesus are the works of the Father! The heavenly Father does everything that Jesus does.

Tuesday of the Fourth Week of Easter

God's Story Made Present

All that we are about and all we do is the unfolding of God's presence.
An often misquoted phrase of Henry David Thoreau observes that "it is not enough to be industrious; so are the ants. What are you industrious about?"[1] Life and its many demands upon our time tend to muddle our industriousness. Keeping priorities clear and assuring that our values give life is never easy. What grounds us as disciples of the Lord Jesus is God's word. We listen to the voice of the shepherd, which keeps us from scattering too far from God's presence. It is why we gather in prayer on a weekday, why we consider the wisdom we find here, and why we open our lives to the Way that is Jesus.

Christ's Sheep Never Perish

The Scriptures regularly take images and experiences common to the life of the people of their day in order to expand and transform them. Any good shepherd worthy of the name, for example, is constantly concerned with the safety and welfare of his or her flock. Referring to the responsibilities of a shepherd, Jesus speaks of knowing and calling the sheep (v. 28). In turn, their trusting confidence preserves and protects them from physical harm and danger. Although earthly flocks eventually provide food and clothing for their owners, the flock of Jesus the Good Shepherd receives a share in "eternal life" (literally, the life of the next age) and will never perish because no one can snatch or steal these sheep from God's hands (v. 29). With typical Johannine skill, the gospel moves from the natural safety of the well-tended flock in this age to the life of the next age, which members of this flock receive from their loving Shepherd God.

Tuesday of the Fourth Week of Easter

God's Story Made Present

The shepherd leads us to newness of life. In a *Luann* comic strip Quill asks his friend, Gunther, why he seems down in the mouth and whether it's because Gunther's girlfriend has chosen to live thousands of miles away. Gunther responds, "No, I've let go. I know we always had different paths. . . . I'm just . . . full of *questions*. Like, who *am* I? Am I still who I was? Am I a *new* me trudging the path of the *old* me? And where does that path go? Where should it go?? Should I *stay* on the path? Where am I going? Why am I going there??" Quill replies, "I can see why you're down. You're under four tons of question marks."[2]

People of faith sooner or later look at their lives through the lens of faith and tend to recognize some greater wisdom shaping their lives, some nurturing presence intertwined with their own efforts at life. They begin to recognize different strands. It's then that Jesus' words make sense: "I give them eternal life, and they shall never perish. No one can take them out of my hand."

1. Henry David Thoreau, letter to Harrison Gray Otis Blake (November 16, 1857), in *Great Short Works of Henry David Thoreau*, ed. Wendell Glick, Perennial Library 598 (New York: Harper & Row, 1982), 100.

2. Greg Evans, *Luann* (Kansas City, MO: Universal Uclick, April 28, 2015).

Wednesday of the Fourth Week of Easter

God's Story Proclaimed

Acts 12:24–13:5a
Set apart for me Barnabas and Saul.

The New Missionary Vocation

In the reign of the Roman emperor Claudius (10 BC–AD 54) severe famine broke out throughout the ancient Near East. As a result Saul and Barnabas were promptly sent from Antioch to the religious community in Judea with relief supplies (11:28-30). The report of that mission, as well as the account of the arrest, imprisonment, and miraculous release of Peter (12:3-19), was omitted by the Lectionary. Unmentioned, therefore, is the ancient link between material generosity to the needy and evangelization. Caring for the physical needs of the hungry led to the Spirit-inspired impetus to care for spiritual hungers as well. Then, in what seems like a whirlwind of apostolic activity, we read in the fuller text about Barnabas and Saul returning from Jerusalem back to Antioch where they were quickly chosen by the Spirit for a new missionary venture (13:2). Like all genuine vocations, that mission came from the Holy Spirit, but only with the approval of the community. Moreover, it was conveyed sacramentally by the laying on of hands in the context of common prayer. Off they went, first to the port city of Seleucia in the northeastern corner of the Mediterranean Sea some twenty-eight miles from Antioch, then to the city of Salamis on the island of Cyprus where they preached in the synagogues (v. 4). These two apostolic activities—namely, relief to the poor and proclamation of their faith—demonstrated that believers in Antioch had reached a new level of mature faith. Perhaps that development was the fruit of Saul's first catechetical work there. In both instances Saul and Barnabas, by now good friends, were officially sent as representatives of their home community, accompanied by the prayer and best wishes of the church. They were sent to herald the Lord's death and resurrection and to explain its implications for the history of the world.

The Spirit sends each of us out as heralds of faith and charity. In so many parish communities, groups of parishioners are sent out to serve the needs of the larger community: youth and college students heading out on mission trips, others supporting meal programs at local food sites, parishioners visiting sister parishes, and teams sent to areas of natural disasters where tornados and hurricanes have caused devastation. The fact is that every single person since the first Pentecost has been set apart for some specific task, depending on talents, circumstances, and need. All become partners with God in the work of the Gospel. Saul and Barnabas are specific models and concrete examples for every baptized person throughout subsequent history.

Prophets and Teachers

The earliest Christian communities continually struggled to find the most helpful and accurate titles for their leaders, as well as for the different functions fulfilled by the various men and women who were active members. To speak in priestly terms was initially impossible because of inevitable confusion with the roles served by functionaries at the temple in Jerusalem. In Paul's First Letter to the Corinthians, for example, he spoke of "apostles, prophets, teachers, performers of mighty deeds, healers, helpers and administrators" (1 Cor 12:28). Elsewhere he listed "prophets, evangelists, pastors and teachers" (Eph 4:11). By God's gift, different individual believers each have gifts to offer that should be identified, welcomed, developed, and respectfully utilized. Here Luke simply mentions the leadership of prophets who spoke in God's name and teachers who helped the community's members understand the biblical and religious roots of their new faith in Jesus (13:1). Five individuals of different backgrounds are listed among the religious leaders at Antioch. From among them, Barnabas and Saul were further designated by God's Spirit for special ministry to the larger world (v. 2).

God raises up prophets and teachers in every Christian community if they are to hear the word of God in the specific circumstances of their daily life. Consider those who have spoken prophetically in our own day:

- Susan B. Anthony (USA)
- Cesar Chavez (USA)
- Mahatma Gandhi (India)
- Martin Luther King Jr. (USA)
- Nelson Mandela (South Africa)
- Archbishop Oscar Romero (El Salvador)
- St. Theresa of Calcutta (India)
- Archbishop Desmond Tutu (South Africa)
- Lech Walesa (Poland)
- Madala Yousafzai (Pakistan)
- the youth who stood before the tank in China's Tiananmen Square.

Wednesday of the Fourth Week of Easter

ANTIPHON—PSALM 67:4
O God, let all the nations praise you! (or: Alleluia)

Psalm 67:2-3, 5, 6, 8

In the light of the sentiments of verse 7, which refers to the harvest yielded by the earth, it would seem that Psalm 67 is a brief prayer of jubilant gratitude for a bounteous and fruitful harvest at the end of the annual growing season. Moreover, verse 2 echoes the famous priestly blessing of Aaron and his sons (Num 6:24-26, a text most familiar to con-

temporary Catholics as the "Blessing of St. Francis"). Although neighboring farmers at the time of the psalms may have been of different ancient Near Eastern faiths, all were invited to praise God. This psalm has a universal sense about it. All peoples and nations to the ends of the earth (vv. 3, 4, 5, 6, 8) are addressed and invited to join the harvest prayers of gratitude. The organizers of the Lectionary also found in these verses the perfect response of communal joy to the initial mission of evangelization to which Saul and Barnabas had been commissioned.

The Refrain

Curiously, the antiphon actually selected for this response is not among the verses offered in the Lectionary for the day's song. Perhaps the editors were determined to underscore universality without repeating specific wording. There is an interesting subtle contrast by the fact that Saul and Barnabas went to the specific synagogues (v. 5) in the cities first visited, but it is the larger world of Gentile nations who are invited by this refrain to join in praise of God (v. 4). All who benefit from the harvest of the fields and all who will be blessed by the renewal of Jewish faithfulness (Gen 12:1-3) through the preaching of Saul and Barnabas are encouraged to join the chorus.

GOSPEL ACCLAMATION—JOHN 8:12
The Lectionary borrows a verse from an earlier chapter of the gospel in which Jesus identified and proclaimed himself as the "light of the world" (*phōs tou kosmou*) who illumines his followers. This citation thus immediately introduces the theme of light and serves to prepare this morning's congregation for a consideration of the illuminating ways Jesus entered our *kosmos* as light (12:46).

JOHN 12:44-50
I came into the world as light.

Lectionary note: This passage begins at a new and different juncture in John's gospel. Yesterday's passage concluded with selections from the tenth chapter's treatment of sheep and shepherd. In moving toward today's gospel, the Lectionary omitted the lengthy story of the raising of Lazarus (11:1-44), the session of the Sanhedrin that decreed the death of Jesus (vv. 45-54), the anointing at Bethany (12:1-11), and the triumphant entry of Jesus into Jerusalem (vv. 12-19). All of these had been recently proclaimed and pondered as the Lenten season came to its annual solemn celebration of the Lord's death and resurrection. To repeat the sections after Easter would seem liturgically out of place. Hence they are omitted, and the Lectionary begins anew with a summary teaching on belief that in fact provides an echo from yesterday's reading (10:26).

Sent and Sender

In John's gospel Jesus will be presented as the "way" to the Father (14:6). Today's reading begins to prepare for that revelation by insisting that whoever believes in Jesus by that very fact also believes in the one who sent him (v. 44). Then Jesus quickly adds that whoever sees him also sees the one who sent him (v. 45). He proclaims a profound transparency into the mystery of God through his very physical being. Such a relationship is not foreign to daily human experience because the physical features and mannerisms of children often remind others of their parents. Even to see the former can quickly remind family friends and colleagues of the latter. In the case of Jesus, however, the similarity resides, not in physical likeness, but in values, attitudes, and priorities. Jesus speaks what his Father has told him to say (v. 50) and nothing else.

Jesus only says what he has been sent to declare (v. 49), and when we in turn see him we see the Father (v. 45). In some similar and profound fashion, people should be able to see something of God in our own human lives because of our baptism into Christ!

God shines in goodness done. In the Middle Ages, when science seemed to be stepsister to the arts and not the reverse as in so many ways it is today, the people thought that phlogiston was an element inside objects that made them flammable. The more phlogiston in something, the more readily flammable it was—that was how they understood the inner workings of physics. This phlogiston theory explained why rocks did not burn and why straw readily did. Though phlogiston has long been shelved, its theory is not so far removed from how the Spirit of God burns in our lives. If some effort of ours glows with light and heat, others will recognize something of God's presence taking place—not unlike phlogiston.

Jesus as Light

During Israel's forty-year journey out of Egypt, God was their guiding "cloud by day and fire by night" (Exod 13:21; 40:38). The mysterious Servant was a "light to the nations" (Isa 42:6; 49:6) as a God-given instrument of true and effective salvation from harm and destruction. The accounts of the transfiguration insist that even his clothing was radiant (Mark 9:3). In John's gospel Jesus has repeatedly been described as a light that has come into this world (1:6-9; 3:19; 8:12; 9:5; 12:35). As such, he reveals in a definitive fashion how God works in our world, and he indicates what forces are ultimately forms of darkness opposed to the God of Israel. He invites us to become "children of light" (12:36). Like noontime brightness, Jesus eliminates all shadows and makes all things clear. Also note that the Easter candle, which is so prominent in the liturgy of the Easter season, serves as a daily reminder of Christ's luminous presence in the midst of his redeemed people. In every generation Christ remains the Lord of Light, luminously revealing the ways of God at work in our world.

God's wisdom eases our journey. It has been said that we never become believers before the age of thirty-five. Whether or not thirty-five is the magic number, it does seem to suggest that it takes some life experience to recognize both the hand of God and the wisdom of God. Before that we do tend to stumble our way through our choices. Through it all God keeps trying to show us how to make it—Jesus being the brightest star.

**Wednesday
of the
Fourth Week
of Easter**

Thursday of the Fourth Week of Easter

God's Story Proclaimed

Acts 13:13-25

From this man's descendants God, according to his promise, has brought to Israel a savior, Jesus.

Lectionary note: The choice of liturgical readings results in passing over an interesting editorial comment—namely, that Saul was "also called Paul" (13:9). Prior to that verse, the only name used in Acts was "Saul," and afterward, only "Paul." Curiously, "Paul" is a Latin word meaning little; perhaps it served as a playfully fond nickname like "Shorty," somewhat like Simon was called Peter, or "Rocky," by Jesus (Matt 16:18). Similarly, Barnabas was also a familiar name for Joseph (Acts 4:36), and even Mary was called *Kecharitomene* ("deeply graced") by the archangel Gabriel (Luke 1:28). At some point Jesus nicknamed John and Andrew *Boanerges* ("sons of thunder," Mark 3:17), perhaps in reference to their short fuses in times of opposition. Jesus was quickly given the title of *Christos* ("anointed") as if it were a proper name rather than an exalted title. The many close bonds of friendship and cooperation in the early Christian community fostered names of affection. Perhaps even today each of us has our own secret name known only to God.

Children of Israel and God-Fearers

 Luke seems to be the only evangelist to use the phrase "God-fearer" (v. 16) as a technical term. First applied in Acts to the Roman centurion Cornelius (10:2), the designation is now used as a description for a distinctive group in attendance at the synagogue service in Pisidian Antioch. God-fearers were Gentiles who found the monotheism and moral code of Judaism very attractive. Although not accepting the full kosher dietary regulations of Judaism or the rite of circumcision, they shared a common vision of God with their Jewish neighbors. As such they were often welcomed at synagogue services. In Paul's address, which rehearses the early history of Israel, he immediately noted their presence within the congregation and acknowledged them out of courtesy (v. 16). This group was frequently sought out by early Christian missionaries as a fertile field for converts to "the Way." Note that the same greeting is repeated again halfway through Paul's exhortation (v. 26) and will serve as the introduction to tomorrow's Lectionary segment from this same speech. Paul's introduction can provide a practical template for modern sermons in the fact that it recognizes the diversity of faith groups present at every worship service and addresses each in its unique situation. He rehearses salvation history for all who were present, Jews and Gentiles. Paul as a wise pastor, albeit a visiting guest, senses the diversity and speaks directly to its religious needs and hopes.

God's people are a patchwork quilt sewn from various cloths of faith. Even presuming that all who gather at the table are Catholic, what each believes tends to be an amalgam of various understandings and lifestyles. Each assembly draws in cafeteria Catholics as well as robotic Catholics, those who look upon God as a fatherly male in a white beard as well as those who will explain God as the Force, those for whom Jesus is the Son of God and those for whom he is simply the wisest and best of all humans, those who pray to the Father or to Jesus or to the Spirit or do not pray at all. Yet somehow they have all been drawn in, each coming for his or her own reason. And to each the word of God is then preached.

A Word of Exhortation

Modern visitors to Pisidian Antioch in central Turkey can stand amid recent excavations of an ancient synagogue, allegedly the very same first-century building where Paul (as he is now named in Acts after 13:9) preached the Good News of Jesus to the children of Israel and their God-fearing neighbors (Acts 13:16). Invited by the authorities of that synagogue to offer a word of encouragement (*paraklēsis*, v. 15), he readily accepted the opportunity and launched into a brief history of salvation. The focus of this speech was a succinct summary of Israel's experience in a masterful fashion. Subtly included was an implicit invitation to the congregation to see their respective place in the historical sequence of divine work in the world. Not every homily should be a recitation of history, but an awareness of the way God continues to work in the unfolding of our contemporary world can provide both fresh understanding as well as added motivation for a positive response in faith.

Thursday of the Fourth Week of Easter

God writes history with broad swaths of the pen. Each New Year's Eve some friends sit down and try to remember an event from each of the past years, beginning with the most recent and working their way backward as far as they can. After the first couple of years, they always find themselves reduced to remembering only vacations or deaths or life transitions of one sort or another—only the biggies. All of the other issues over which they have spilled much angst have somehow receded into oblivion and insignificance. While we dither over many small issues of life, God is interacting with our present history, making of it the lives we live.

ANTIPHON—PSALM 89:2
For ever I will sing the goodness of the Lord. (or: Alleluia)

Psalm 89:2-3, 21-22, 25, 27

The editors of the Lectionary were very careful in the portions that they selected as the response to this reading. The entire original Psalm 89 for example is divided into three sections: a hymn of praise for God's faithfulness (vv. 2-19), a

litany of specific examples in which that faithfulness was evident, especially in the story of David (vv. 20-38), and finally a lament over the bitter experiences of the Babylonian destruction of Jerusalem and the seeming absence of God (vv. 39-53). In this liturgical response, the latter portion is ignored in order to focus on God's faithfulness throughout the history as described by Paul in his address to the synagogue at Pisidia.

The Refrain

The hymn of praise placed on the lips of the congregation this morning contains a series of technical words for aspects of God's relationship with his people. Although the English translation of the refrain uses the word "goodness" (v. 2), the Hebrew is *hesed*—that is, mutual covenantal responsibility. The refrain thus clearly suggests that Israel (and the contemporary Catholic assembly) is invited to sing forever of that wondrous divine gift and grace throughout history. God's faithfulness (*'amunah*) is extolled in the same verse (v. 2). The following verse of the psalm reverted to the original *hesed* (v. 3), even though the liturgical text uses the English "kindness," which does not communicate anything covenantal. Note that the final portion of the response concludes with a repetition of the key words *'amunah* and *hesed*, this time translated as "mercy" (v. 25). Our English can hide as well as reveal the deeper meaning of God's word.

GOSPEL ACCLAMATION—REVELATION 1:5
The book of Revelation begins with a greeting from John the visionary and from Jesus described as witness, firstborn, and loving liberator from sin. The original third-person description is now used as an acclamation and liturgically changed into an expression of personal praise from the day's parish community for the risen Lord. This in turn prepares for the gospel's account of the washing of their feet and virtually places these words of praise on the lips of the disciples who humbly accepted the Lord's washing of their feet.

JOHN 13:16-20
Whoever receives the one I send receives me.

Lectionary note: This week's liturgy offers sections from three different literary contexts of John's gospel—namely, chapter 10 (Wednesday), chapter 12 (Thursday), and Chapter 13 (Friday). It may be helpful, therefore, for anyone who preaches or prays out of these respective passages to recall the theological framework of each section in order to properly root the homily or reflection in its proper context.

The Disposition for Service

The editors of the Lectionary have thoughtfully inserted a reference to the prior washing of the disciples' feet by Jesus (v. 16a). Although these actual words are not in the original inspired text of this passage, the reference to that moving event enables the congregation to recall the initial context of this discourse and its point of origin. The gesture of washing the feet of guests was customarily performed by slaves who were expected to be available as needed. The allusion to that action of Jesus at the Last Supper serves to explain the opening reference to slaves and masters (v. 16), and it underscores the mission of Jesus as sent to function as a servant (*doulos*). The verse's reference to one who is "sent" also creates a literary linkage with Wednesday's passage about the "sender and sent" (12:44). Remember that the Gospel of John does not contain the description of the eucharistic institution narrative as found in the other three Synoptic Gospels. John apparently chose to emphasize the effects of the Eucharist—namely, a ritual empowerment and a motivational encouragement for loving service. This passage emphasizes the fundamental willingness required of every disciple to serve others in every way. The church's inclusion of this portion in the Easter season liturgy signals the need to remember the perennial danger of betraying Christ's love (v. 18) by self-centered lives. Selfishness can perdure, even after Easter.

If we choose to limit our charity or to exclude any particular group, we neither represent Christ nor serve his true mission.

God's Story Made Present

God sews an instinct of service into the human spirit. Sometimes we serve out of obligation, sometimes out of love, and sometimes simply because a task needs to be done. At times it is a conscious choice and at other times it may be done without reflection. The believer recognizes it as an echo of the command of Jesus, however it occurs.

Robert Hayden recounts his father's sense of service to the family in his poem "Those Winter Sundays." He tells how his father got up early on Sunday mornings to build a fire to warm the house before everyone else arose and even polished Robert's shoes. Much later in life the poet rues, "No one ever thanked him." But then service is not done for the thanks but rather for the love. It can be a lonely journey as the poet finally realizes, "What did I know, what did I know / of love's austere and lonely offices?"[1]

I AM

In response to the inquiry of Moses at the burning bush, the God of Israel had revealed his name as the mysterious "I will be what I will be" (Exod 3:14). Jesus refers to that name on several occasions in this gospel (e.g., 8:28). One might also recall from the passion according to John that was read at the church's Good Friday liturgy that Jesus twice responded "I am" (*ego eimi*) to the crowd seeking to arrest him in the garden (John 18:5-8). Scholars insist that the answer not only signaled his personal identification with the object of their quest on a human level but also reaffirmed his divine identity. If one remembers that this small passage that forms today's gospel was originally placed on the lips of Jesus at the Last Supper, his reminder to the

Twelve of his mysterious identity, and his request for their faith (v. 19), no matter what may happen in the events to come, constitute a powerful teaching moment. The other gospels, written earlier in the first century, are not as explicit as John in this affirmation of the divinity of Jesus.

God sprouts faith amid the rockiness of our lives. Sometimes the fragility and tensions that seem to rip life apart are the very means amid which we recognize God's presence. In an interview by Bill Moyers, the poet Jane Hirschfield comments on a poem by Izumi Schikibu.

> If your house is walled too tightly, if your psyche is so defended that it won't let in the cold winds— won't let in suffering or anger, won't let in grief—neither will it allow entrance to the desirable, beautiful moonlight. If you don't allow yourself to experience the full spectrum of human life, you won't wall out only the hard parts, you'll close yourself off from the luminous as well.[2]

Thursday of the Fourth Week of Easter

The Missionary Imperative

The ease with which this gospel passage moves from the washing of feet (v. 16) to the notion of being "sent"

(v. 20) is a very helpful reminder of the close connection between Eucharist, service, and missionary witness. Jesus was sent by his Father to save the world, not to condemn it (3:17). His death achieved the redemptive restoration of the universe after human sin. That divine gift of self is celebrated, renewed, and extended to every parish eucharistic community throughout all ages. Those who are sent (initially through baptism, renewed in confirmation, and repeatedly thereafter through every celebration of the Eucharist), must truly represent their divine Sender. It is not that the church has a mission, but (as contemporary experts in missiology remind us) that the mission has a church.

God has a mission for each of us, yet for most of us it is quite different than that experienced by those who went out into the towns of Israel. We are not a people on the road. We have commitments to honor, families to support, children to raise, employers and employees to honor. Perhaps it is attitude that makes the difference for us—whether we see ourselves as merely trying to "make it for ourselves" in life, or whether we see ourselves as "one who is here to do what needs to be done for you."

1. Robert Hayden, "Those Winter Sundays," in *Collected Poems of Robert Hayden,* edited by Frederick Glaysher (New York: Liveright, 2013), 41.

2. Bill Moyers, *Fooling with Words: A Celebration of Poets and Their Craft* (New York: Perennial, 1999), 107.

Friday of the Fourth Week of Easter

God's Story Proclaimed

Acts 13:26-33

God has fulfilled his promise by raising Jesus from the dead.

Word of Salvation

This second portion of Paul's "word of encouragement" began conveniently with the same repeated initial address to the mixed congregation of Jews and Gentiles (v. 26) in the community of Pisidian Antioch. To their synagogue assembly, immediately after the readings from the law and the prophets (v. 15), Paul spoke of the entire history of God's activity in Israel as a "word of salvation." Biblically "word" (*dabar*) means a message in action, a communication that is expressed in events. The prophets regularly demanded that people "hear the word of the Lord" then proceeded to describe what God was doing by way of either comfort or judgment. The actions of history around us are the words of God. That is how God chooses to speak to each and all of us. It is the responsibility of the community that we call "church" to help us interpret those events and to do so with the help of similar events from the past. There is a consistency in God's way of dealing with his human partners.

God speaks to us in the events of our lives. Too often the ordinary does not seem very salvific. Yet it is in all that seems so ordinary, in all that surrounds us every day, that God does speak. Sadly so often we seem to miss it.

Jay Williams's classic children's book, *Everyone Knows What a Dragon Looks Like*, tells the story of how a mandarin once asked the Great Cloud Dragon for help so that the city in which the people lived might be saved from a terrible invading force. What the city received was a short, fat, bald man announcing that he was the answer to the mandarin's prayer. The ruler was quite sure this couldn't be a dragon for dragons were proud conquerors that had great powers. But when the invading force arrived, the short, fat, bald man puffed himself up into a fiery weapon who overcame the invaders. That was when the mandarin realized that a short, fat, bald man could, in fact, be a dragon![1]

Fulfilling the Prophecies

In Paul's speech at Antioch, he insists that the condemnation of Jesus and his death fulfilled the very prophecies that had been regularly proclaimed on the Sabbath in synagogues over the years (v. 27). One of the tasks of early church teachers was to trace out the threads of truth from the Scriptures and to help the early followers of Jesus to see continuity and development in the events associated with the life and ministry of their newly risen Lord. Paul understood that his preaching was a vital element in unpacking the prophetic teachings and fulfilling God's will for the world.

God's comprehensive vision and plan spans all ages. In the Arthurian legends Merlin was a kind of mentor for Arthur, especially in his younger days. While you and I grow older day by day, and so Arthur as well, Merlin grew younger. Thus he had a wisdom beyond Arthur's, a wisdom of the future in reverse. He lived with the larger picture that placed the events of any day in perspective. For us who profess to be believers, the Scriptures are a sort of Merlinesque wisdom—a faith perspective that offers God's vision for life.

Asking Pilate for a Death Sentence

Jewish authorities in Jerusalem did not have any authority to put a person to death; only the local Roman representative of Caesar had such power (John 18:31). Their concern was to signal as clearly as possible (1) their distance from any social unrest and (2) that any public disturbance was not their doing. The

Jerusalem authorities may even have wanted to protect their friends and neighbors (and themselves) from any sudden brutal exercise of Roman control. The fact that Jesus had constantly spent time with tax collectors, prostitutes, and other social outcasts, often giving them a new dignity associated with their conversion, made the leadership worry about losing their control, and they responded accordingly.

God's Story Made Present

The God-life at the heart of creation overcomes death. Each year the old man's garage had been sagging more and more until the entire garage was out of line. The doors would no longer close completely, the corners were beginning to pull apart, and the roof was askew. He decided to put in a new foundation, and so he jacked up the entire garage and laid cinder block under it. Along one side, where there was a bed of lilies of the valley blooming, he poured gravel over the plants for a solid footing and then sand over the gravel—and on top of it all he placed the cinder blocks. Then he lowered the garage on top of the new foundation. The next spring the lilies of valley sprouted and blossomed as abundantly as before.

In spite of human efforts to squelch new beginnings and new dreams, life that was meant to come forth seems to find a way. The hunger for democracy sooner or later blossoms into freedom. The human desire for justice and equal opportunities refuses to be suffocated by racial prejudice. Truth that lies hidden in time is made known.

Friday of the Fourth Week of Easter

ANTIPHON—PSALM 2:7BC

You are my Son; this day I have begotten you. (or: Alleluia)

Psalm 2

Psalm 2 was chosen as today's response because it was quoted in the final portion of Paul's address in the synagogue at Antioch. In this liturgical context the verses readily become the song of the entire church. Psalm 2 was in fact an important item in the preaching arsenal of the first Christian missionaries because of its mention of royal sonship (v. 7). Most of these same verses were also selected as a psalm response earlier in Eastertide—namely, on Monday of the Second Week (to which the reader is referred). Today's portion of the psalm omits any reference to the raging of the nations (vv. 1-3), however, since the initial response of the people at Antioch was positive. The psalm's reference to God as the King in Zion (v. 6) reflects the annual celebration of YHWH as royal leader in Jerusalem—and everywhere believers gather in praise and petition.

The Antiphon

Kings in the ancient Near East were often understood as sons of the god under whose patronage the nation had been placed. An oracle of adoption (v. 7), uttered by a representative of the priests or prophets attached to the court would always be proclaimed on the day of coronation and subsequent anniversaries. As a "son," the human king was a representative and co-regent of the god. He was regularly so declared during temple services and rituals. Christians often use the same verse in order to acclaim Jesus as a divine Son in a transcendent sense, especially at Christmas and during the Easter season. John's gospel did not hesitate to proclaim Jesus as King, especially in the context of Pilate's private interrogation of Jesus (18:33-37) after the arrest and in the inscription affixed to the cross (19:19-22).

GOSPEL ACCLAMATION—JOHN 14:6

In selecting the final verse from today's gospel passage as the acclamation, the Lectionary prepares the congregation for the proclamation of Jesus as the unique "Way, Truth and Life." In a subtle way therefore today's liturgy highlights that teaching from the very first syllables of the solemn reading of the gospel. The expression gives an initial reason why the hearts of the disciples should not be troubled (v. 1).

JOHN 14:1-6
I am the way and the truth and the life.

Troubled Hearts

This passage from the very beginning of a new chapter of the last discourse of Jesus to his disciples strikes a different note. Jesus encourages his little flock to remain confident and not to allow their hearts to be troubled (v. 1). Biblical anatomy presumed that the heart (Hebrew: *leb*; Greek: *kardia*) was the place where human plans were laid and decisions made. As they gathered in the Upper Room that evening prior to the arrest, the disciples became more aware of the ominous political clouds gathering in Jerusalem's corridors of power. That may have been apparent especially because it seemed to have happened so quickly after the triumphant entrance of Jesus into Jerusalem just a few days earlier. When burdened by disappointment over immaterialized plans, opposition from neighbors, or unexpected obstacles we also know something about our own experience of troubled hearts—and the difficulty of making firm plans. The most effective remedy is a confident renewal of our faith, both in God and in Jesus (v. 1). When we remember that God is most certainly in charge of the universe, even the most virulent of human opposition is ultimately rendered inane and powerless, and we feel more confident about planning.

God's Story Made Present

God gives the gift of courageous and confident faith. In a book entitled *Unconditional Love*, John Powell tells of a twenty-four-year-old student of his dying of cancer. Tommy seeks out Powell and allows him into some of the corners of his heart. He thinks a greater sadness could befall someone, sadder than dying at the age of twenty-four.

"What's it like to be only twenty-four and dying?"

"Well, it could be worse."

"Like what?"

"Well, like being fifty and having no values or ideals, like being fifty and thinking that booze, seducing women, and making money are the real 'biggies' in life. . . . The essential sadness is to go through life without loving."[2]

It is amazing how at the age of twenty-four Tommy is able to see to the heart of life in ways that some never do and so journey into death seemingly without fear.

Having Faith in God

Jesus acknowledges that his disciples in the Upper Room are persons of faith in God, weak and wavering as they will soon prove to be, but asks that they extend that same faith to him as well (v. 1). Serious studies in Johannine theology over the past half century have demonstrated that this faith (*pistis*) is much more than simply accepting a series of statements or propositions such as are found in our creeds. Biblical faith is to enter into a personal relationship with the One who is holy and divine.

Friday
of the
Fourth Week
of Easter

The place God prepares is rooted in the human heart. Those we generally regard as saints (whether they have been canonized by the official church or by our own spirituality—and particularly those who speak to our own spirituality) are most often the ones whose lives somehow have reflected the gifts of God's presence—patience, generosity, forgiveness, inner peace, trust, surrender, and many other such qualities. They have not been lived doctrinal truths that have drawn us to them, but rather the enfleshed realities lived by Jesus. Their lives and activities are clear, concrete signs of a fruitful living faith in God.

God's Many Dwelling Places

American residential neighborhoods are among the most creative in the world. Our cultural individualism finds ready expression as family homes, often side-by-side, reflect a wide diversity of styles reminiscent of Tudor, Cape Cod, California mission, or Spanish hacienda. Ancient Near Eastern builders—and probably city planners in most other parts of today's world as well—would be astonished by the diversity in American home design. Throughout most of human history homes were virtually always the same. In first-century Palestine, for example, the basic architecture of a house was a U-shaped building with work and storage rooms gathered around an inner courtyard with olive trees and an oven. The open area was walled off from the street for protection and privacy. In the summer people usually slept on the roof. When Jesus assures his disciples of "many dwelling places" (v. 2; older translations used the more pretentious word "mansions"), he is assuring them of God's determination to provide ample and uncrowded space for everyone. Diversity of architecture to fit individual tastes was not his point. Like a roadside motel for travelers, God's sign advertising "vacancies" was lit for everyone.

Friday of the Fourth Week of Easter

God's eternal dwelling includes rooms for everyone. New construction will often seek to find ways of including ideas and plans and adaptations from many contributors. In the end there seems to be a room for each of them. The places in which we live are always more than physical buildings. We live in our personal worlds of God-inspired values, hopes, and dreams. Since we are God's partners in the transformation of the world, God is even willing to incorporate our "dwellings" into his designs for the final perfection of the world. Our ideas of democracy and economics and culture, our ways of education and healing and nurturing, our various spiritual journeys—they all find their ways into who we are and thus into eternal life as well. We are co-architects, at work every day of our lives.

Knowing the Way

Ancient Near Eastern roads were never marked with direction pointers or estimates of mileage. One simply followed the main commercial routes and asked the locals as uncertain turns or puzzling crossroads appeared en route. The off-handed comment of Jesus regarding "knowing the way to his destination" (v. 4) inevitably provoked a question from a slightly exasperated Thomas, whom we know from later resurrection stories was perpetually dubious and often stubbornly required further clarification. The issue is not really geographical, however, and the destination not a matter of cross-country travel. One attains to the heavenly home of Jesus by embodying his attitudes and being transformed by the paschal mystery. Jesus announced to Thomas, "I am the way" (v. 6). Imitation of his daily actions was the only trustworthy travel route for arriving at the homes of heaven. Jesus himself alone is the GPS guide for life. The apostles needed to understand that basic reality.

God's Story Made Present

God maps our hearts to find the way. The journey into deepening faith is often marked by confusion and uncertainty and doubts. At times the only answer is to be faithful to the journey, trusting that God is doing the leading along the way. Thomas Merton's prayer of abandonment expresses that well:

My Lord God, I have no idea where I am going. I do not see the road ahead of me. I cannot know for certain where it will end. Nor do I know myself, and the fact that I think I am following your will does not mean that I am actually doing so. But I believe that the desire to please you does in fact please you. And I hope that I have that desire in all that I am doing. I hope that I will never do anything apart from that desire. And I know that if I do this you will lead me by the right road, though I may know nothing about it. Therefore I will trust you always though I may seem to be lost and in the shadow of death. I will not fear, for you are ever with me, and you will never leave me to face my perils alone.[3]

**Friday
of the
Fourth Week
of Easter**

1. Jay Williams, *Everyone Knows What a Dragon Looks Like* (New York: Four Winds, 1976); see also Belden C. Lane, *The Solace of Fierce Landscapes: Exploring Desert and Mountain Spirituality* (New York: Oxford University Press, 1998), 93.

2. John Powell, *Unconditional Love: Love without Limits* (Niles, IL: Argus, 1978).

3. Thomas Merton, *Thoughts in Solitude* (New York: Doubleday, 1968), 81.

Saturday of the Fourth Week of Easter

God's Story Proclaimed

ACTS 13:44-52
We now turn to the Gentiles.

Opposition and Local Rejection

One must be careful to note that Paul, Barnabas, and those who became jealous over the initial success of the Christian preaching (v. 45) were all Jewish. To suggest any hint of a Christians-versus-Jews story is not only dangerous—as the horror of last century's holocaust amply demonstrates—but false. The fact is that some local women of prominence and leading Jewish men of the city began to resent the success of the apostles and took issue with their teaching (v. 50). Paul and Barnabas responded with boldness (*parresia*, v. 46) and decided to turn their attention and witness to the Gentiles in Antioch who frequented the synagogue. For Paul, that decision was not an easy one because he felt so strongly about Jesus as the God-given Messiah of Israel. Only in his letter to the Romans did he finally work out his thought about the Jewish people—namely, that their covenant remained forever irrevocable (11:29) and that God would grant mercy to Jews and Gentiles alike in their full and future reconciliation at the end of the world. The initial rejection on the part of some Jewish leaders in Antioch (v. 46) was neither universal nor final. The complete history of salvation for the world would eventually have its own times and seasons. In the meanwhile, as the quotation from Isaiah suggested, the light of Israel's faith was a source of salvation to the world (v. 47, citing Isa 49:6).

them" the Canadian singer and songwriter Leonard Cohen articulates it this way: "Forget your perfect offering. There is a crack, a crack in everything. That's how the light gets in."

Rejoicing in Suffering

To be expelled from Antioch in Pisidia by the very people they had come to love and serve was not easy for Paul or Barnabas. Scholars tell us that it was customary among the more pious Jews of that time to shake the dust of foreign pagan lands from their feet upon returning to their ancient land of promise in Judea. For Paul and Barnabas to enact the same gesture upon leaving this town in modern central Turkey, even if out of the pique of the moment (v. 51; see also Matt 10:14, where that action is prescribed against those who refused to listen), indicated that at least for the time being they considered Pisidian Antioch as pagan, and temporarily off-limits. The passage concludes on a very positive note, however, by stating that Paul and Barnabas were filled with much joy over the initial success of their preaching to the Gentiles of that city. The experience of misunderstanding and mistreatment only made them more like their Lord. Success and failure was in God's hands, and even the suffering entailed in a temporary rejection could be used for good. Later at the end of their first mission journey, Paul and Barnabas returned once more to Antioch (14:21) to strengthen their first converts and to encourage perseverance. Obviously, neither the resistance nor the departure was final. The immediate moment was not the end of the story.

God's Story Made Present

Because of darkness, God shines as light. As has been noted previously, so often it is the darkness that enables the light to shine. It was the rejection of Jesus by some that brought the Light of the World into Gentile communities. In his song "An-

God's Story Made Present

God spurs a path between the pricklies of life. At the local beach I watched a father and his four-year-old son walk barefoot along the shore of the lake. It was a warm summer day, and because the sand on the beach was

too hot they were walking in the dry stubby grass paralleling the beach. As they made their way hand in hand, I overheard their conversation.

Son: Dad, I need to ride on your shoulders because the pricklies hurt my feet.

Dad: Step between the pricklies and they won't hurt your feet.

Son: Dad, do the pricklies hurt your feet?

Dad: Sure they do, that's why I step between the pricklies.

Son: Dad, it looks like your feet are bleeding.

Dad: It's just the wet sand.

Son: I know, but it just looks like your feet are bleeding.

And so the two of them simply kept on walking side by side.

There's a difference between riding high above life's pricklies and negotiating life's pricklies. For the believer the way we negotiate conflict and suffering—which is really to say the way we negotiate life—is not through escape but by faith.

ANTIPHON—PSALM 98:3CD

All the ends of the earth have seen the saving power of God. (or: Alleluia)

Psalm 98

 Psalm 98, remarkably similar in tone and sentiment to Psalm 96, would seem to be associated with Israel's annual ancient divine enthronement festival. Although God is not called King, nor is royalty as such ascribed to him in this hymn, God's universal power is proclaimed and celebrated. Though unspecified, some new deeds of deliverance by God apparently deserved a new song (v. 1), since the older familiar hymns suddenly seemed inadequate. In spite of the negative events recently experienced and described in the liturgy's first reading from Acts, the psalm recalls God's faithfulness to the house of Israel (v. 3). The responsorial psalm therefore suggests that this turn of Paul and Barnabas to the Gentiles now holds a new promise of salvation to the nations (v. 2) without, however, in any way

suggesting final rejection of the Jews. In God's designs all will be eventually reunited and welcomed.

The Refrain

The positive response of the Gentile God-fearers in the synagogue at Antioch surprised and delighted Paul. They were invited not to join Israel but to accept the implications of Christ's resurrection for their lives as Gentiles and for the eventual salvation of the larger world. Even the ends of the earth sang for joy upon seeing how far God's gift of salvation could eventually reach (v. 3). The Gentiles became God's people in a new way. The ancient blessing of Abraham and his family (Gen 12:1-3) found new fulfillment in Paul's ministry just as Isaiah had once promised light and salvation to the nations through God's mysterious Servant (Isa 42:1-6). The contemporary parish community at prayer might for a moment consider itself at that edge, rejoicing to be included by God's goodness!

Saturday of the Fourth Week of Easter

GOSPEL ACCLAMATION—JOHN 8:31B-32

This acclamation encourages the folks in the Upper Room to remain rooted in Christ's word so that they (and all successive generations of believers) might truly be the disciples of Jesus and know his truth. This in turn also prepares the modern parish congregation for the theme of truly knowing Jesus and his heavenly Father. "Word" and "knowing" are the initial thematic links between these readings.

JOHN 14:7-14

Whoever has seen me has seen the Father.

Seeing the Father

In yesterday's gospel it was Thomas who did a bit of whining out of his frustration—almost like an adolescent utterly lost in the maze of his parents' adult reasoning. If he didn't know *where* Jesus was going, he lamented, how could he ever know the way (14:5)? As any traveler understands, he concluded, one's destination determines the route. Today, however, it is Philip who echoes virtually the same type of complaint. Jesus has just stated that those who know him also know the Father and have seen him (v. 7). The puzzle was apparently too much for Philip who blurted out in exasperation, "Master, just show us the Father!" (v. 8). Jesus responds by offering some of the early church's first steps toward understanding the mystery of the Triune God—namely, "I am in the Father and the Father is in me" (v. 10). As noted earlier this week, it would in fact take centuries for the early Christian church to unpack the deepest meaning of that statement and to find the best philosophical language for that truth of faith: Three Divine Persons in One God. It was the Council of Nicea in AD 325 that finally found a way to express the heart of the faith that we now recite in our creed each Sunday at Mass. Jesus said it more simply: "whoever has seen me has seen the Father" (v. 9). Because the eternal Word of God became flesh and dwelt among us (John 1:14), we believe that seeing the face of Jesus and watching his human actions can actually give us a profound insight into the infinitely mysterious nature of our God. The insistence of today's gospel passage—that is, seeing something of God in the words and actions of Jesus—is admittedly an echo from this past Wednesday's Lectionary selection but serves to highlight yet again an important truth throughout the Easter season. In the risen Jesus we see hints of God's majesty, and in the lives of his baptized disciples we see traces of the Christ of glory. This reality, as John's gospel repeatedly seems to insist, is a fundamental truth of Christianity that merits repetition and our prolonged reflection.

Saturday of the Fourth Week of Easter

God absorbs us into his presence. It is not uncommon for us to recognize the mannerisms and conversation of our parents in our own lives. It can seem as if we have absorbed who they are. Similarly we tend to think that we take on or absorb the values and lifestyle of the Lord Jesus and so reflect him and God whom he called Father. On the other hand, perhaps it is God who absorbs us into his presence, so that slowly and over the course of a lifetime and without our realizing it there are those aspects of God that shine in us. All of that takes place as we regularly spend time in prayer, are available to the needs of others, and build bridges among the divisions of life.

The Works of the Father

Perhaps Jesus experienced his own share of frustration as he attempted to explain the profound truth of his relationship to the Father. Throughout his human life Jesus struggled to find human words for this profound reality of his relationship to his Father. Even today we humans all struggle to find the right (if faltering) words for our deepest loves and hopes. In response to Philip, therefore, Jesus said, "At least believe because of the works" (v. 11)! Over the years of the public ministry of Jesus, the disciples had seen for themselves how "the blind regain their sight, the lame walk, lepers are cleansed, the deaf hear, the dead are raised and the poor have the good news proclaimed to them" (Matt 11:5). The same testimony that Jesus had once given to the disciples of John the Baptist could be given to Philip (and to us). These are all examples of the blessings of the sovereign action of God (a.k.a. the kingdom) at work in our world. In a similar fashion Isaiah's Fifth Servant Song had insisted that the mysterious Servant of God had been anointed "to bring good news to the afflicted, to bind up the broken hearted, to proclaim liberty to captives and release to prisoners" (Isa 60:1). In Luke's gospel—which was the first volume of this magnificent testimony to the history of human salvation by God—Jesus had quoted the same words to his former neighbors in Nazareth (Luke 4:16-21). These are the things he was sent to do, just as his words are those he was sent to speak. They represent, therefore, the words and works of God, not merely his own human expressions (v. 10). The gospel even promises that those who believe in Jesus will do even greater works (v. 12). Our works are intended, therefore, to give glory to God alone, not to enhance our human selves in the eyes of our neighbors.

God's Story Made Present

The Philip part of us takes time for God to dawn faith in us. We who were born into Christianity as children were taught as we were raised that Jesus is the Son of God. The Twelve and those who lived and walked with him learned it another way, through his works—inside out, one might say, or through the back door. Or perhaps it is we who have come to know him backwards. The point is that they who lived with him came to conclude over time that this man Jesus with whom they interacted was indeed the Son of God. There is a sense in which we, too, come to adult faith through observing the works of God going on in others.

Terry Anderson was a news reporter who was abducted by Islamic terrorists in March 1985 in Beirut, Lebanon. In December 1991 he was released. When asked how he felt toward those who held him hostage, his response was, "I forgive them. I have to. I'm a Christian. I'm a Catholic. I have to forgive them." There are many works of God such as this. Individuals choose to donate a kidney to a total stranger. Great generosity is offered in times of natural disasters. All forms of sacrificial love take place that are indeed the works of God in us and through us. A believer sees these and comes to ever deeper faith recognizing them as God's activity in human life. Despite our catechism learning, it does take time for us, too, to catch on as to what it means that Jesus is Lord.

Fifth Week
of Easter

Monday of the Fifth Week of Easter

God's Story Proclaimed

ACTS 14:5-18

We proclaim to you Good News that you should turn from these idols to the living God.

Geographical note: The account of these first missionary journeys and the stops in central Turkey can be confusing, especially when broken into shorter daily readings and referring to ancient place-names. Paul and Barnabas traveled to *Antioch in Pisidia* (Central Turkey) where Paul gave his extended speech in the synagogue (13:13-33; Thursday and Friday of the Fourth Week of Easter) from whence they were expelled after turning to the Gentiles in that city (Saturday of the Fourth Week). Unwelcome at *Iconium*, they traveled on to *Lystra* where they healed the man lame from birth and fended off those who wanted to sacrifice to them as pagan gods (Monday of the Fifth Week). When that became difficult because of the city's sudden negative shift in mood and an attempted stoning, they traveled through *Derbe* before returning back through Lystra and Iconium to *Pisidian Antioch* where they encouraged the new disciples and then returned to their home base at *Antioch in Syria* to conclude their mission (Tuesday of the Fifth Week). The geography can be confusing because there were several Hellenistic kings named Antiochus, each having a tendency to name cities for themselves.

Proclaiming the Good News

Jewish and Gentile leaders in Iconium (today known as Konya) joined forces to attack Paul and Barnabas (v. 5). Pagan Gentiles protected the economy of their temples, and some Jews feared that their traditional beliefs were being eroded. Apparently stoning seemed to be the weapon of choice; so the team of Paul and Barnabas was forced to move away through the cities of Lystra and Derbe. As if oblivious to the repeated negative reactions, however, they continued to proclaim the Good News (v. 7) of Jesus risen from the dead for the salvation of the world. Rejection and even stoning did not deter them from their mission. The core of their message included the announcement of life after death and God's promise of ultimate victory over all opposition, hardship, and persecution. Jesus had suffered it all in his own flesh, and therefore they even felt encouraged if they were privileged to endure their own taste of such rejection and physical abuse. They continued to proclaim the Good News of the risen Jesus and the need to turn away from idols (v. 15).

God's Story Made Present

God is known in the nature of our commitments. One knows who one is by one's commitments. Just as each nation must sort that out, so must each individual, or one is doomed to wander nameless in the desert of life. Like Barnabas and Paul, those committed to God's word and to trusting in that word will be known by the struggles of their lives. People of faith are not without struggles. They are people who strive to remain faithful to their commitments—to continue to grow in marriage, to raise responsible children, to bring justice to their dealings with others and in their work, and to be faithful in prayer, lifestyle, and calling.

> If we lived in a state where virtue was profitable, common sense would make us good, and greed would make us saintly. And we'd live like animals or angels in the happy land that needs no heroes. But since in fact we see that avarice, anger, envy, pride, sloth, lust, and stupidity commonly profit far beyond humility, chastity, fortitude, justice, and thought, and have to choose, to be human at all . . . why then perhaps we must stand fast a little—even at the risk of being heroes.[1]

Lame from Birth

Walking has been a longstanding biblical metaphor for the moral life. The psalms celebrate those who walk in the Lord's paths and refuse to walk according to the advice of the wicked (Ps 1:1). The moral teachings of Jesus provided abundant travel plans for all his disciples as they journeyed through life. Healing of the lame was a sign of restoring people to the fullness of their moral life before God and neighbor. By way of biblical continuity, Jesus healed the lame (Matt 15:31) as did Peter and John in the temple (Acts 3:2-10), and now Paul and Barnabas perform the same action. Perhaps because they were early missionaries, often traveling on foot, their healings of the lame and crippled were chosen to be highlighted in these accounts. The beggar had been lame from birth, but suddenly he walked and jumped (v. 10). Although the crowds initially misdirected their praise to Paul and Barnabas as if they were themselves gods, the citizens recognized the miraculous nature of the wonder when they saw it. Everyone who gathers for Mass could well begin with the implicit recognition that they also have been "lame from birth" as they seek forgiveness, healing, and a fresh start in life's journey.

**Monday
of the
Fifth Week
of Easter**

God's Story Made Present

The power of Jesus touches our own sinful limping. One of the marvels of Christian spirituality is that those who continually seek to live in the image of Jesus do grow in faith and goodness, all despite their own continual sinfulness. While human sin may get in the way of maturing holiness, it does not prevent it in those who genuinely seek to be faithful. M. Scott Peck has well noted that it is not necessarily an easy journey, yet a necessary one.

> When my patients lose sight of their significance and are disheartened by the effort of the work we are doing, I sometimes tell them that the human race is in the midst of making an evolutionary leap. "Whether or not we succeed in that leap," I say to them, "is your personal responsibility." And mine. The universe, this stepping-stone, has been

laid down to prepare a way for us. But we ourselves must step across it, one by one. Through grace we are helped not to stumble and through grace we know that we are being welcomed. What more can we ask![2]

The Witness of Fruitful Seasons

In Paul's quick if exasperated speech to the citizens of Lystra who were trying to offer sacrifice, he tried to introduce his proclamation of Jesus by reminding his audience of God's perennial natural goodness. He pointed out that the very rains from heaven and the seasons of the year served as witnesses to God's kind and caring purposes (v. 17). All of creation's orderly natural sequence was briefly invoked as evidence of God's providential care for Gentiles everywhere. Paul and Barnabas were convinced of the eternity of the seasons because of an ancient divine promise after the flood to keep a world safe and orderly (Gen 8:22). This was the apostles' first argument against foolish idols (v. 15). We are reminded of the final admonition in John's first epistle: "Children, be on your guard against idols" (5:21).

The wonders of God's creation bring us to awe and wonder. Amid the talk of climate change and its dangers we find ourselves treasuring the gifts of creation all the more. The smell of fresh mown grass, the awesome display of thunder, the delight of morning dew, the majesty of plains and mountains, the power of the ocean. The believer begins to realize anew that without these gifts one avenue to knowing God would become muted.

ANTIPHON—PSALM 115:1AB
Not to us, O Lord, but to your name give the glory. (or: Alleluia)

Psalm 115

This psalm was probably chosen as the perfect song of response because of its very first verse, which echoes Paul's plea to the people of Lystra and forms the hymn's refrain. Psalm 115 was also perfect for communal worship as evidenced by the various specific groups invited to reject idols and to praise God: Israel, house of Aaron, and God-fearers (vv. 9-11). Contemporary idolatry may be more subtle than its ancient forms, but no less real. The verses that specify those groups are not selected for today's liturgy because the psalm's intended focus is praise of God alone who blesses his people and makes the heavens and earth (v. 15).

The Refrain

 The refrain is perfect for the narrative just proclaimed. As Paul fought off the devotion of the citizens and resisted mightily the attempts of the local pagan clergy, he could well have pleaded in the very words of the refrain. He insisted that praise for everything—natural wonders of providence and miraculous healings alike—belongs to God alone. The words are offered for contemporary congregations as well. Using the word "name" preserved the ancient custom of respectful reverence for the sacred unspoken title of the God of Israel. This is a refrain that might be cited whenever praise is offered for any human accomplishment, for all glory does indeed belong to God alone who makes all things possible.

GOSPEL ACCLAMATION—JOHN 14:26
The acclamation uses the final verse of the gospel to highlight the promise of the Holy Spirit to teach us and remind us of everything Jesus taught. These words remind the congregation of their need to pay attention to the role of the Holy Spirit as they listen to the gospel.

JOHN 14:21-26
The Advocate whom the Father will send will teach you everything.

Law and Love

 Carefully observing the commandments, wishes, and preferences of God is itself a sign of one's love for Jesus (v. 21). Because we love, we try to please, and our love itself increases as we please those we love. The word "love" occurs seven times within the first verses of this reading. The term obviously encompasses a wide range of human emotions and sentiments as we know from experience. Nevertheless, the notion of "love" emphasizes the fundamental decision from which all our offers of assistance or expressions of affection originate. Infatuation becomes authentic love when we decide to make it a deep part of our unselfish relationship to the larger world in which we live. The gospel recognizes that we all try to please those we love. In this sense love always precedes law. Because of love, we try to obey—rather than obeying to become worthy of love.

God's Story Made Present

Love, from God and for God, colors all we do. One of the more oft quoted observations of Fr. Pedro Arrupe, the former superior general of the Society of Jesus, is that "Nothing is more practical than finding God, that is, than falling in love in a quite absolute final way. What you are in love with, what seizes your imagination, will affect everything. It will decide what gets you out of bed in the morning, what you do with your evenings, how you spend your weekends, what you read, who you know, what breaks your heart, and what amazes you with joy and gratitude. Fall in love, stay in love, and it will decide everything."[3]

> **Monday of the Fifth Week of Easter**

Revealing Oneself

 Jesus himself suddenly introduced the notion of self-revelation (v. 21). Because Jesus states that he reveals himself to those whom he loves, Judas (not the Iscariot as the gospel pointedly notes in v. 22) simply can't resist a question. Since Jesus had referred at times to his love for the entire world (3:16), why, wonders Judas, would he devote his time and energy to so few people rather than reveal himself more universally to everyone? To us moderns, it seems like a very good question. The subtle response of Jesus makes the point that loving someone somehow results in living within them (v. 23). Perhaps that beloved person then becomes the instrument for sharing God's love with others—and others—and others—until the entire world is encompassed. True love is personal and individual. God uses us to love and reveal himself to others. We have no secrets from those we love, and we in turn can't resist speaking to others about those we love. Perhaps love and self-revelation are two sides of the same coin.

God unfolds faith in relationships. Can someone come to faith if they have not in some way been loved or cared for? While nothing is impossible for God, it does seem unlikely that in the course of daily living faith will occur without a caring person to reveal that faith. Yet such revelations are not the result of mere catechetical teaching or of the insistence or even demand that someone practice religion. Faith is "caught" amid the daily exchanges of life. Think of the persons who have enabled you to trust God because they have trusted you. As one's own words rely on trust, so too the power of God's word relies on trust, i.e., on faith.

The Advocate

Among the four gospels John is the most explicit witness to the existence of the Holy Spirit. Today's liturgical passage ends with the promise that the Father will send the *Parakletos* (v. 26). Note

Monday of the Fifth Week of Easter

that the same word occurs four times in the farewell discourses. It had been used earlier in v. 16 (which the Lectionary has chosen to omit from the Easter weekday readings) to teach and remind the disciples of everything that Jesus had said over the years. The same word will be used again in 15:26 (Monday of the Sixth Week in Ordinary Time) as a testifying witness to Jesus, and finally in 16:7 (likewise omitted in the Lectionary) to judge the world. Literally, the Greek word *parakletos* refers to "someone called to one's side." Because, as our own human experience reminds us, we can call for help in very different situations, the word *parakletos* has received diverse but legitimate translations in the New Testament. If, for example, we call on someone to help us make a case for receiving something we need (like the keys to the family car, or the use of a neighbor's tool), we call that individual at our side an "advocate." If, however, we simply need help in sorting out a perplexing personal problem, our call might be for a "counselor." The same word is translated differently, therefore, according to the need at hand. Jesus reveals the future gift of God in the form of someone truly divine at our side to assist us in all things, forever explaining, teaching, helping, and even transforming us into members of the Body of Christ at the time of our baptism.

The Spirit's task of teaching is lifelong. Parenting can be frustrating as children grow and mature in wisdom slowly. For some the simple reality of common sense trips them up. Avoiding irreversible tragedies becomes a task for guiding teenagers. Adulthood is marked by the need for discerning life choices. It seems we never outgrow our need for the Spirit's presence.

1. Robert Bolt, *A Man for All Seasons* (New York: Vintage, 1990).

2. M. Scott Peck, *The Road Less Traveled: A New Psychology of Love, Traditional Values, and Spiritual Growth* (New York: Simon & Schuster, 1985), 167.

3. Pedro Arrupe, in spontaneous remarks to a group of religious sisters, qtd. in Kevin Burke, "Love Will Decide Everything," *America* (November 12, 2007), 21.

Tuesday of the Fifth Week of Easter

God's Story Proclaimed

ACTS 14:19-28
They called the Church together and reported what God had done with them.

Recovery Surrounded by Disciples

The reading opens with a rather remarkable summary, perhaps so cursory as to be easily overlooked. The popular mood at Lystra had changed suddenly and dramatically from the crowd's earlier acclaim and their desire to offer sacrifice to Paul over the miraculous cure of the man lame from birth (v. 18) to their complete rejection of Paul as a result of the mysterious negative words of folks from Pisidian Antioch. We learn that Paul was stoned and dragged out of the city where he was left for dead (v. 19)! The text simply reports that when his disciples gathered about his body, he got up and went back into town (v. 20) and then traveled onward the next day! Talk about a sudden recovery! Two astonishing truths immediately come to mind. First of all, when surrounded by the faith and love of fellow believers, Paul came back to health again. We simply cannot even begin to measure the positive healing effects of charity in our lives. Being stoned apparently to death is no slight event; yet Paul's phenomenal resiliency, rooted in his faith and combined with the care of his friends brought the gift of remarkably restored health. Secondly, he simply got up and went back to the same town again. Talk about stubborn apostolic conviction! Like the bulldog that he was, Paul refused to give up. He would not relinquish his vocation and mission, no matter how severe the obstacles.

God's Story Made Present

The Holy Spirit gives courage and fidelity to those who love the Lord.
The story is told of a Chicago pastor who personally knew St. Frances Cabrini when she was working among the Italian poor of Chicago. Apparently she was a very determined woman with stubborn apostolic conviction, so much so that when that pastor heard that she was to be canonized a saint, he commented that it was easier for him to believe in the eucharistic presence than it was to believe that she was a saint of the church. Not unlike St. Paul who could be irksome in his own way, apparently the gifts that we are given for a noble purpose can also carry the barbs that can make life with others difficult. The Spirit's gifts at times do not seem hesitant to make life difficult for others.

Entering the Kingdom through Hardship

Paul and Barnabas began their return trip home, retracing their steps back from Derbe through Lystra (the place of the stoning) and Iconium to Pisidian Antioch (v. 21) in central Turkey and then eventually back to home base in the sea port of Syrian Antioch (v. 26) from which they had first been sent (13:3). Acts tells us that the group lingered briefly at Pisidian Antioch for a bit of community formation in that place where Paul and Barnabas had first turned to the Gentiles. It was there that Paul coined the classic phrase of Christian spirituality: "it is necessary to undergo many hardships (*thlipsis*) to enter the Kingdom of God" (v. 22). The Greek word signifies pressure, oppression, affliction, or hardship. Though a fundamental joy may pervade everything, life for a true believer will not always be easy. One sometimes pays a social price for one's convictions. Reaching out to others in need may cost something in time, resources, and even reputation. Entering the kingdom, namely, allowing God's will to rule one's choices and daily existence, means saying "no" to one's own desires at times. There is no other door into the kingdom! "Did you not know that the Christ had to suffer so as to enter his glory?" (Luke 24:26). The same theme runs through Luke's gospel and his Acts of the Apostles.

God's enables us to accept his will and even endure the resistance of others, especially if that decision leaves a few bruises and scars. President Abraham Lincoln was initially condemned for his dogged opposition to slavery. The lives of the saints recount numerous instances in which they endured oppression and hardship for the sake of the Gospel. Saint Thomas Aquinas was vilified and his literature burned before he was ever recognized for his intellectual acumen and eventually declared a Doctor of the Church. Saint Theresa of Ávila and St. John of the Cross both encountered rejection as they sought to nurture and foster holiness in their communities. During the 1950s some very eminent Catholic theologians were painfully silenced by church authorities until they were vindicated by the new perspectives of the Second Vatican Council. One has never needed to be a martyr to suffer for the Gospel. Even daily life can have its share of heartaches.

Tuesday of the Fifth Week of Easter

Homecoming and Accountability at Antioch

This passage ends with the apostolic team back at the home port of Syrian Antioch (not Pisidian) from which they had initially been sent (13:4). Now that the work to which they had been first commended had been completed, the apostles called the church together (remember that *ecclesia* means the assembled community) to give an account of their ministry. The pattern is set forever. There can be no lone rangers in service to the Gospel. Those who preach must be called and sent (see Rom 10:14). They returned, mission accomplished, to render an account of their labors to the same community that had first delegated them for the work of the Gospel. All true ministry is exercised with ultimate accountability to God, certainly, but also to the church. Such reporting is a joy, not a burden, since the work is done in God's name and by God's grace. The fact that Paul and Barnabas spent "no little time" back home serves to validate the idea and practice of apostolic "R & R."

From God comes the work and to God be the glory! Most of us do not like being held accountable. We tell ourselves that we are our own persons. Yet there is a wisdom in the community that can often be a corrective, whether that be the system of checks and balances in our national and state governments or the need for communication between family members. Communities spark both needs and wisdom. Somewhere in that stew of life is the movement of the Spirit.

ANTIPHON—PSALM 145:12
Your friends make known, O Lord, the glorious splendor of your kingdom. (or: Alleluia)

Psalm 145

Psalm 145 is an alphabetical acrostic; that is, each verse begins with a different successive letter of the Hebrew alphabet. This imposed structure makes the flow of ideas somewhat generic and repetitive. The Lectionary has chosen, however, only the central section of the hymn, thus concentrating on the works of God that sing praise (v. 10) and his faithful (*hasidim*) who are invited to speak of God's kingdom (v. 11). The fact that the word "kingdom" occurs three times in this brief portion of the psalm serves to highlight Paul's teaching about the hardships required for entrance into the kingdom. Moreover, the invitation to make known God's might (v. 12) echoes the final report given by the team to the church community back at Antioch.

The Refrain

Apparently some liturgical adaptation has taken place in this verse, perhaps to include the parish's contemporary congregation in the action. The original Hebrew text says, "[they speak] making known to the sons of men your mighty acts, / the majestic glory of your rule" (v. 12; NABRE). The Greek Septuagint is virtually the same as the Hebrew. This Lectionary version turns the object into the subject and gives them (like the apostles returning to Antioch) a role as "friends" of God, in speaking about the mighty deeds of God. Thus the editors of the Lectionary took some liberty in crafting this liturgical refrain. A weekday community at Mass should not miss the compliment of being called "friends of God."

GOSPEL ACCLAMATION—LUKE 24:46, 26
The Lectionary uses a citation from the teaching of Jesus on the way to Emmaus to introduce the sufferings of Jesus as a necessary and inevitable element in his mission of salvation.

JOHN 14:27-31A
My peace I give to you.

Christ's Peace

Today's gospel text presents another opportunity to review the basic meaning of the Semitic word "peace" (*shalom*) (v. 27). In contrast with contemporary English usage that often combines "peace and quiet" to signify tranquillity and absence of noise, the biblical notion of peace provides a focus on reintegration and placing the pieces back together again after some disruption or fracture. To that end, the Hebrew word often also includes restored unity and renewed prosperity. When used as a greeting, it signifies both an initial "hello" and a final "good-bye." Thus the casual daily greeting among Jewish people suggests the blessing of coming together and then the subsequent joy of departing in renewed friendship and unity. In this gospel pericope, the peace (*shalom*) that is left and given by Jesus (v. 27) suggests both an inheritance resulting from the saving death of Jesus and a special gift. The text contrasts the way in which the peace of Jesus is given with the way peace is given by the world (*kosmos*). One way of describing that contrast is to recall that *kosmos* in John signifies an attractive reality that is

fundamentally opposed to the Gospel. Such a merely human sense of that world operates out of power and bases any peace on self-interest. By contrast, Christ's peace is given generously and freely out of total self-sacrificing concern for the well-being of the recipient. Christ's peace transforms and ennobles the person who accepts the gift as well as the society within which that person lives. Christ's peace always also encompasses the entire community, not only its individual members. The exchange of the sign of peace at the daily Eucharist is both a recognition of the gift given by Christ and a wish for its ever greater effect in our lives.

God's Story Made Present

Christ's peace changes the person, changes the world. The 2012 PBS documentary *Freedom Riders* tells the story of the brave Americans who risked their lives in 1961 to travel together on buses and trains through the segregated Deep South. It tells of Jim Zwerg, one of a handful of white Christians who joined the nonviolent movement. At the bus terminal in Montgomery, AL, a racist mob knocked his teeth out and were about to kill him when a black man stepped in and ultimately saved his life.

In an interview in *USA Today*, Mr. Zwerg described what went through his head and heart as he was being beaten unconscious: "In that instant, I had the most incredible religious experience of my life. I felt a presence with me. A peace. Calmness. It was just like I was surrounded by kindness, love. I knew in that instance that whether I lived or died, I would be O.K."[1]

> **Tuesday of the Fifth Week of Easter**

What the World Must Know

Today's pericope concludes with a reference to the fundamental message of Jesus: his love for the Father and his total compliance with the Father's commands (v. 31). To a self-centered world (*kosmos*) that stands in fundamental opposition to the Gospel, Jesus proclaims his love of God and his subordination, both of which are often equally difficult for the world to understand and accept. These two spheres stand in stark opposition to each other. The witness of Jesus is given, not to condemn the world, but to save it (3:17). His witness is offered in order to demonstrate the inherently destructive results of self-centered existence. He speaks by the witness of his life, not by any power achieved through physical force.

God's Story Made Present

God provides our witness with a positive and saving effect on those around us. In his book *Civility: Manners, Morals, and the Etiquette of Democracy*, Stephen Carter calls us back to our need to be civil with one another, a virtue that seems to have been set aside in our culture. In many ways they are the very ways of love that Jesus proclaimed. All of them foster a kind of peace that echoes today's gospel:

> Our duty to be civil toward others does not depend on whether we like them or not.
>
> Civility requires that we sacrifice for strangers, not just for people we happen to know.
>
> Civility has two parts: generosity, even when it is costly, and trust, even when there is risk.
>
> Civility creates not merely a negative duty not to do harm, but an affirmative duty to do good.[2]

Tuesday of the Fifth Week of Easter

---

1. Tony Gonzalez, "Accidental advocate risked life to fight segregation," *USA Today*, May 26, 2013. See also Matt Malone, "Of Many Things," *America* 211, no. 1 (July 7–14, 2014): 1.

2. Stephen Carter, *Civility: Manners, Morals, and the Etiquette of Democracy* (New York: HarperCollins, 1998).

Wednesday of the Fifth Week of Easter

God's Story Proclaimed

Acts 15:1-6

They decided to go up to Jerusalem to the Apostles and presbyters about this question.

Back to the Center for Direction

Today's reading refers to some Jewish Christians who came down to Antioch (v. 1) with suggested corrections for proper Christian life, and others who went "up" to Jerusalem (v. 2) to seek counsel. The real issue was going to the heart of things. Spiritually Jerusalem was always the center and high point of Jewish life. For that reason the folks from Antioch went back "up" to Jerusalem to seek apostolic direction and certitude regarding what was truly important in their new faith. They consulted their apostolic leadership because the Twelve were the primary witnesses to the Lord's resurrection and the authentic teachers of "the Way" as early Christianity was first called. It was in Jerusalem that the experience of Pentecost had occurred, and to Jerusalem that they turned for the first major controversy that needed resolution.

God summons us back to the heart of the community to restore our balance and keep our bearing at moments of challenge and change. At key moments throughout history, Catholics have resolved issues by reclaiming their deepest identity in faith and charity. The baptism of infants, not only mature adults, was judged acceptable, for example, when the early church authorities affirmed the importance of baptism and recognized the importance of family life in passing on the faith. Later in another pastoral situation, the ancient practice of only receiving the sacrament of reconciliation once in a lifetime was put aside during the third century out of mercy for those who had denied their faith during terrible persecution but then realized their error and sought readmittance to full active membership in the faith community. Amid much controversy, the church made a decision in favor of mercy. God calls us back to the heart of the community for clarity, especially in difficult questions, regarding who we really are and what we should be about. Some years ago the US Bishops' Committee for Pastoral Life and Practice developed a statement entitled *Always Our Children* by way of guidance for Catholic parents confronted by the reality of their homosexual children. Even contemporary pastoral councils develop practical goals and strategies for being truly Catholic and Christian in challenging moments of controversy.

The Fundamental Requirement

Some obligations are more important than others, and therefore some laws more significant. In response to one of the scribes Jesus had said that love of God is the first commandment, and love of neighbor the second with none greater (Mark 12:30), yet the first command we hear when he came on the scene after his baptism was "repent and believe the Gospel" (1:15). Centuries earlier, Jeremiah had insisted in the name of his God, "I didn't ask you to offer sacrifice, I said, 'Listen to my voice!'" (Jer 7:22). When Paul and Barnabas had begun evangelizing non-Jews, they apparently did not require circumcision. Some Jewish Christian leaders came to Pisidian Antioch from Jerusalem to insist on circumcision (v. 1), and the same thing was demanded by others when Paul and Barnabas went to Jerusalem (v. 5). This was the great argument of the first century that necessitated resolution: Must one become Jewish in order to become Christian? Answering that question required a solemn assembly and the deciding voice of the Holy Spirit as we shall learn later this week from the same chapter of Acts. For Paul and Barnabas belief in Jesus and baptism stood out as central to early

Christian discipleship. They could never have guessed that twenty centuries later the question of circumcision would hardly be remembered. Each age has its own major debate regarding some issue of belief or practice. Each disagreement requires respectful listening to all parties concerned, but most of all to God who helps us sort out the key issues and brings us to the unity that God desires of his church.

The gift of the Spirit respects diversity but also sustains unity. Conflict and disagreement seem to be part of human existence. None of this, however, should necessarily be considered destructive, because no one view has a corner on wisdom. Disagreement can even be a gift, eventually bringing clarity and better understanding about how God works with us and what God wants from us. The Spirit cannot be contained. So perhaps a litmus test for those times of disagreement might be whether we can name the wisdom in the position contrary to our own. Until we can, it would seem, we are not on solid footing to adopt any one position—politically, ecclesially, or societally.

Wednesday of the Fifth Week of Easter

ANTIPHON—PSALM 122:1
Let us go rejoicing to the house of the Lord. (or: Alleluia)

Psalm 122

In its present arrangement, the combined 150 hymns of the Psalter contain several smaller, more ancient collections. One of the subsets extending from Psalm 120 through Psalm 134 is distinguished by the repeated title "A pilgrim song" (literally, a "song of ascents") at the beginning of each hymn. There were several times each year when ancient Israel was encouraged to make pilgrimages to Jerusalem: the feast of Unleavened Bread (to which Passover was added, Exod 23:15), the feast of Weeks at the first harvest, and

then the feast of the Final Harvest or Tabernacles in autumn (Exod 23:16). It would seem that Psalm 122 was regularly sung at the time of the pilgrims' departure for home at the conclusion of their stay in Jerusalem. Their feet had already stood within the holy gates (v. 2), and they had witnessed the city's compact neighborhoods (v. 3) and the crowds arriving from different tribes of Israel (v. 4), each obeying the command to give thanks (v. 5). Surprisingly, the latter portion of the psalm is not used in this day's responsorial, even though the pilgrims were encouraged to pray for the peace (*shalom*) of the city (v. 6), to acknowledge that such peace dwelt within its walls (v. 7), and to conclude the visit with a greeting of peace upon relatives and neighbors (v. 8)! This could have been a striking echo of the prior day's gospel greeting of Jesus (14:27), as well as an expression of the purpose for the apostolic trip up to Jerusalem amid the circumcision controversy described in the first reading. They went to Jerusalem in an attempt to restore unity (*shalom*) to the early church community.

The Refrain

A pilgrimage was always a time of great excitement and rejoicing, especially for those who lived a distance from the Holy City and visited the temple rarely. It was a time of singing and social interaction among families and friends en route. For Israel it was also a time for the resolution of arguments and reconciliation within families. This same refrain could well serve as a personal prayer whenever a modern parishioner leaves home for daily Mass or for any parish activity.

GOSPEL ACCLAMATION—JOHN 15:4-5
The congregation is immediately introduced to the need for a permanent personal relationship to Jesus in order to be well rooted throughout life and to bear much fruit for the larger world. "Remaining in him" must be the starting point for our entire life of faith and charity.

JOHN 15:1-8

Whoever remains in me and I in him will bear much fruit.

The True Vine

In its present context in John's gospel, this discourse on the vine and the branches seems abruptly introduced and arbitrarily forced into the logical flow of the text. The prior verse as a matter of fact concluded the speech of Jesus and even ended with the command, "Get up, let us go" (14:31). Now suddenly Jesus begins to speak of an entirely new theme. Ever since Isaiah, the image of a grapevine had been used to represent the people of Israel, transplanted from Egypt to the fertile soil of the Promised Land, carefully cultivated by God but then (with much divine regret) abandoned and punished for infidelity (Isa 5:1-7; 27:2-5). In this passage, Jesus begins by referring to God as the vine grower (v. 1) but then quickly takes to himself the image of being the vine itself and teaches that his own life is the source of true vitality, shared with his disciples. Remaining personally connected to him alone (and to his body of believers, including in some way all the baptized in any Christian church) is a crucial requirement for authentic Christian life. If we ever wish to know what a living and flourishing vine is really and truly all about, Jesus suggests that we think of him and his disciples. Jesus insists that those who do not remain in him "will be thrown out like a branch and wither" (v. 6), lifeless and only fit for use as firewood.

God's Story Made Present

The fruitfulness of life is the product of God's élan at work in us. A fruit tree grew in the backyard of my grandfather's home. As I grew up it seemed to me to be an apple tree, though I'm not really sure only because it also bore pears— both on the same tree. When the tree was a sapling, my grandfather once explained, he decided that as an experiment he would graft a pear branch onto the trunk of the apple tree (or maybe it was the other way around). At any rate, the graft took, and as the tree matured it bore two fruits, apples and pears. I remember friends coming to visit and scratching their heads in disbelief, wondering how one tree could bear two such different fruits. To an outsider it seemed as if the tree was unable to decide what it really was, and so it chose to be both.

In some ways, I suppose, the tree is not unlike many of us. We humans always seem to want to be something other than what we are. I know a car mechanic who would rather be a poet, and a nurse who wishes she could landscape and work outdoors, and a priest who loves to refinish furniture. The point of the parable is that the life force, whether it be in the tree or in us, is what produces the fruit. The fruit always seems to be a by-product of that life force, of the God whose power is at work in us.

Pruned for Bearing Much Fruit

In the parable of the sower and the seed, Jesus taught about the possibility of an extraordinary harvest in spite of the obstacles of birds, hard-trodden paths, stones, or thorns (Mark 4:3-9). Even though the same parable was later allegorized and each element explained for its potential symbolic meaning (vv. 14-20), the original point of that parable of Jesus seems to have been the inevitability of an enormously fruitful crop—by the power of God and despite all the difficulties a person might face in life. The Gospel of John points out the value and even the necessity at times of pruning even the choicest of vines (v. 2). Over the centuries expert vinedressers have learned the art and the necessity of removing a plant's suckers which too often drain off important vitality and limit the vine's ability to produce abundant fruit. John's Jesus alerts us to the fact that God prunes away whatever is not life-giving or mission-serving. The prospect of a thirty- or sixtyfold return

(Mark 4:8) might stretch the imagination of the original audience of Jesus, but a hundredfold was beyond the wildest dreams of any farmer in the crowd (v. 8)!

Like chosen vines of carefully selected stock, we are always pruned by our God. Life's experiences have a way of reshaping our personalities. Some refer to it as sanding off our rough edges. Others will say that we need to be social- ized out of our selfishness. The gospel alerts us to the fact that God prunes away what is not life-giving. Whatever one calls it, such activity does happen. Parents do it to their children as they grow up. Spouses do it to one another as they look to grow a marriage. Parishioners do it to their priests as they seek to build a faith community. In reality, however, it is not we who do the pruning but our God who does it to us and for us.

Wednesday of the Fifth Week of Easter

Thursday of the Fifth Week of Easter

God's Story Proclaimed

Acts 15:7-21

It is my judgment, therefore, that we ought to stop troubling the Gentiles who turn to God.

Confirmation by the Gift of the Spirit

Yesterday's reading ended with the arrival of Paul and Barnabas in Jerusalem where they were welcomed by the apostles and elders (v. 4) but encountered the same debate as at Antioch in Syria (v. 5). A bit of history may be helpful. Their first action both earlier in Antioch and again here in Jerusalem was to offer an account of what God had done with and through them (v. 4; see also 13:4–14:28). A key element in their report was the way God had opened the door of faith to the Gentiles (14:27). This report of Paul and Barnabas now occurred in the presence of all the apostles. Today's reading begins with words from Peter (v. 7), who took the occasion to recall by the briefest of allusions the way in which his own experience with the Roman centurion Cornelius at Caesarea (Acts 10:24-33) had concluded with the gift of the Holy Spirit upon the entire Gentile household of Cornelius (vv. 34-43), whereupon Peter had ordered the baptism of the household of Cornelius (vv. 44-49). In that earlier event they all glorified God who had granted "life-giving repentance to the Gentiles too" (11:18). Now this same experience of Peter is again briefly summarized and concluded with the reminder that "God . . . bore witness by granting them the Holy Spirit just as he did us" (v. 8), making no distinction between Jews and Gentiles (v. 9). Then James, who at some point had begun taking the role of head of the Jewish Christian community in Jerusalem (at least as Acts describes things), rose to add his opinion on the matter, quoting the prophets (Amos 9:11). James proposed that they should "stop troubling the Gentiles who turn to God" (v. 19) with extra burdens, but there will be more about that in tomorrow's

reading. Apparently, the clinching argument for James here was the gift of the Spirit at Caesarea, just as the disciples had received in the Upper Room in Jerusalem at the time of Pentecost.

The Holy Spirit is the criterion of whether someone is a true disciple.
Any organization of its nature seeks to fine-tune itself, to improve and make itself better, always balancing the qualities or "marks" of faithfulness with openness. There can be something good about that. Peter, Paul, and Barnabas all told stories of how the presence of the Spirit surprised them. The danger is that as a church we can become rigid, perhaps purist in seeking its ideals. We may even find ourselves seeking more from one another than was ever originally expected or intended. Pope Francis has raised similar concerns. It seems such was the instinct of some in the early faith community, who expected everyone to become Jewish, even if that was not necessarily God's plan. Similarly we also may ask more of each other in the Catholic community today than God would require, or we can impose the cultural expectations of one ethnic group on the rest of the world. Peter was not only reluctant but insistent that those who were disciples of the Lord Jesus not fall into such a trap. It would be a worthwhile discussion in today's church as to how much significance we should place upon two such marks—*orthodoxy* and *spirituality*.

First Peter with All His Weakness

This question of "Petrine primacy" in all his rare combination of frail moral limitation plus remarkable courage remains implicit in the structure of the Acts of the Apostles. The same contrasting combination in fact runs throughout all of Luke's testimony regarding him. It is presumed in this passage, for example, by the fact that Peter rises first to speak when Paul and Barnabas come for consultation. The author of Acts was concerned to demonstrate that Peter had some priority in the early church's momentous decision to welcome Gentiles into "the Way" without requiring that they come through the door of Judaism. After all, earlier in the Gospel of Luke it had been Peter who, in response to the Lord's question, "Who do you say that I am?" (Luke 9:20), made the pivotal confession of Jesus as the Christ. It was also impetuous Peter who was predicted as a source of strength for others after his own post-denial recovery (Luke 22:32). The triple cowardly denial of Peter is noted in all three Synoptic Gospels, including Luke (22:54-62). In Acts, however, fortified by the gift of the Holy Spirit, Peter was the one who spoke on Pentecost morning (2:14), cured the sick in continuity with the signs performed by Jesus (3:5), became the first face and courageous voice of the community before the Sanhedrin (4:8), and now welcomed Gentiles like Cornelius to baptism (10:47). In Luke's mind, Peter had to go first to demonstrate continuity with Jesus and to prepare for Paul's eventual journey to Rome (28:16). He demonstrated in his own life the power of the paschal mystery's weakness and victory. In Matthew (16:18), as in Luke, Simon Peter was the rock upon which the church of Jesus would be built even though he had to be rebuked and corrected by Jesus (16:22). With all his limitations and weaknesses, Peter became by God's transforming grace "the Rock" so that the real strength was most clearly that of God alone. After Peter's witness (v. 12) the whole assembly fell silent and then turned to listen to the testimony of Paul and Barnabas regarding "the signs and wonders which God had worked among the Gentiles through them." Peter's testimony set the scene for the rest of the story.

Thursday of the Fifth Week of Easter

God surfaces strength when human weakness abounds. How often the naïve questions of children can galvanize a community into action for greater justice or charity. In Israel's history it was the nonmilitary figures of Judith and Esther, not the generals, who saved their people in times of crisis. In times of national revolution women often become the heroines, and Joan of Arc was the voice that brought victory in her day. In our own time it has been the peoples' movements that have sparked freedom in eastern Europe, in the Middle East, and in northern Africa. Again and again in our own nation such racial minorities have stimulated change in the relationships between law enforcement and citizens. Around the world and throughout history, human weakness testifies to a deeper power—the presence of God.

ANTIPHON—PSALM 96:3
Proclaim God's marvelous deeds to all the nations. (or: Alleluia)

Psalm 96

Scholars seem agreed that ancient Israel celebrated several important events in the autumn each year: the feast of Tabernacles on the occasion of the great harvest together with the annual covenant renewal, the solemn enthronement of the Lord, and the inauguration of a new year. Psalm 96 was a favorite hymn for that annual celebration. Festive song and music filled the temple (v. 1), to which representatives of all lands and people had come (v. 3). As in any ritual for covenant-making or renewal, the recitation of benevolent actions on the part of the covenant grantor was an important element (v. 3), and the supreme kingship of YHWH was acclaimed once more (v. 10). Including the element of universality was especially appropriate for a response to the first reading in which the welcome of Gentiles was described and approved. Every parish community also celebrates its ethnic diversity (and evangelical openness) each time it gathers for the Eucharist.

The Refrain

The God of Israel is a God who continues to act amid the currents of human history. In worship, therefore, it is always the deeds of God that are announced and celebrated. Just as the call of Abraham had been recounted in ancient covenant renewal ceremonies at the time of harvest (Deut 26:5-10), the actions of the Lord of history were themes of special pride whenever Israel gathered for worship. The kingship of God was never merely theoretical or generic; the litany of precise historical deeds was always the motive for Israel's praise and thanks. The thanksgiving of any contemporary parish Eucharist should also include the specifics for which the weekday congregation is especially grateful that day. Each person has her own list of "marvelous deeds" (v. 3). Even the book of Lamentations, which gave voice to Israel's grief after the destruction of Jerusalem in 587 BC, included the conviction that "the Lord's acts of mercy (*hesed*) are not exhausted . . . they are renewed each morning; great is your faithfulness" (3:22). In sorrow and in joy, God's marvelous deeds are proclaimed to the nations.

GOSPEL ACCLAMATION—JOHN 10:27
Today's gospel teaching about Christ's enduring love for his disciples is introduced by an image from the Good Shepherd discourse about the sheep who listen, know, and follow their faithful guardian.

JOHN 15:9-11
Remain in my love, that your joy may be complete.

As the Father Loves Me

The first verse of this morning's brief gospel passage contains an implicit invitation to take count of the concrete signs of God's love and to trace the specific pattern of the Father's love for Jesus so that we can understand the enduring love of Jesus for each of us in turn. He learned how to love from his Father, not as a fickle sentiment limited to any period of time, but as a permanent life-long commitment. Almost like the petals of a he-loves-me-he-loves-me-not game,

the larger Gospel of John provides multiple indications of how God's love continues to work in our world. Moreover, the key-words are "as" (v. 9) and "remain" (vv. 9, 10) because they establish the Father's perduring love as the measure for Christ's love for each and all of us. By the very fact that he lifts up the Father's eternal love for himself as a concrete measuring stick for his own love for all his disciples (v. 9), therefore, today's disciples at Mass are encouraged to pause and make our own list of how we are loved! A moment of reflection suggests at least six signs of the Father's eternal love for Jesus: (1) the gift of a body with all its senses including the capacity to know, love, and grow in wisdom (Luke 2:52); (2) the gift of existence during a specific era or period of history; (3) the gift of a unique and precise task for that time; (4) the gift of companions and colleagues to share the job whatever it may be (there are no lone rangers in God's plans!); (5) the gift of a seemingly insurmountable obstacle sometimes called the cross; and (6) finally, eternal victory by God's grace. Those are the ways (supplied by the entire rest of John's gospel) by which the Father continued to show his love for Jesus. Because Jesus is "the Way" (John 14:6), each and every disciple can therefore expect to receive similar gifts specifically tailored for her years in the history of the salvation of the world. God's love is the basic pattern for us and ours. "All things work for good for those who love the Lord" (Rom 8:28).

> *Jesus loves us the same enduring way he was loved by his Father.* He learned his lessons well. We have each received the gift of a specific physical body. We live at the beginning of the twenty-first century with all its specific blessings and heartaches. Each successive phase of our life is a *kairos*—a decisive opportunity demanding some action on our part and seeking a specific and generous

Thursday of the Fifth Week of Easter

response, often in service to the people we meet and with whom we work. Virtually every season of life brings its own cross and invites us to name the colleagues with whom God wants us to work. Thus the measure of God's infinite love for his Son, even in the very finite time and space of his earthly life, is also the measure of Christ's love for us. In this gospel passage we are implicitly encouraged to name our specific individual blessings, burdens, and opportunities. We may not have a circle of twelve apostles, but we do have family members, as well as neighbors and colleagues at work, who travel with us through life. Christ's love walks with us when we love and are loved by friends and family, when we carry our crosses of illness or opposition (often over many years), or struggle to make our corner of the world a better place. For people of faith, life itself is a gift, as are the friends who journey with us through the years. They are all signs of Christ's love for us, even the crosses that stubbornly stay with us, because they enable us to be his partners in the redemption of the world.

Thursday of the Fifth Week of Easter

Staying in Love

Today's gospel passage is very brief and compact but also exceptionally rich in content. Jesus requests that we in our time, together with those special friends of his in that ancient Upper Room, "remain" in his love (v. 9)—as if such a sentiment is entirely within our control. He suggests that one way of demonstrating our desire to remain in love is to keep his commandments (v. 10) day in and day out, and he even indicates that doing so is actually one way of assuring that we do remain in that love. Once again, obeying his commands is never a way of meriting his love, but rather a way of proving that we treasure his love so much that we are willing to shape our lives around his will and his

values. He loves us, no matter what, but respects our decisions even when they oppose God's plans for this fragile world of ours. He gives us the freedom to live, basking in that love or hiding in the shadows far distant from it. The love is there, but it is we who determine how we relate to it and how thoroughly it shapes our lives.

God gives both the gift of love and the gift of staying in love. We know from human experience that falling in love is relatively easy. We constantly encounter individuals whom we find attractive for countless reasons: physical appearance, intellectual stimulation, compatible interests, common backgrounds, and so on. God creates each of us with an inner proclivity to enjoy the companionship of others, sometimes at a profound level. We are made to be social, and that sociability is part of God's gift to each person. The perduring challenge, however, is "remaining in love" (v. 10), driven by an enduring desire for the good of those we love; hence the specific command to remain in love and, in the process, to go beyond the physical surface of things. True friendship and enduring companionship always cost something in terms of personal preferences and "druthers." In our relationships with other human beings, we gradually discover the frayed edges of their limitations (and ours), and the very things that once were delightful can become annoying by reason of repetition. Married people often admit that staying in love, especially after the first infatuation, often takes hard work and daily effort. Experts speak of a seven-year cycle of initially falling in and out and in love again. Saints all speak of the period of purifying dryness that comes into life as they work under God's grace to deepen their love for the God who created them and offered friendship. Only after this second period of more realistic appraisal can we find the deepest peace of appreciating the gift of love.

Friday of the Fifth Week of Easter

God's Story Proclaimed

Acts 15:22-31

It is the decision of the Holy Spirit and of us not to place on you any burden beyond these necessities.

A Decision Shared with the Spirit

Yesterday's text seemed to make a point of all the various voices involved in the first major decision of the early church—namely, the degree of ritual independence accorded to Gentiles in the fundamentally Jewish Christian community of the first century. The text summarized Peter's experience and concluded with the suggestion of James that a letter be written to the effect that only four ethical requirements would be asked of Gentile converts (v. 20). Curiously, there was no indication in Acts of further discussion or vote. Today's text begins with the list of those representatives selected to bear the message back to Antioch—namely, Paul and Barnabas, Judas Barsabbas and Silas (v. 22), together with the wording of the letter to be sent. The letter itself includes the powerful phrase, "It is the decision of the Holy Spirit and of us" (v. 28). Precisely how they determined that the Holy Spirit had concurred in their decision is not mentioned. They were all convinced, however, that God's will was being done in the matter. A decision was made by apostles and elders (presbyters) in agreement with the whole church (v. 22). Apparently each distinctive group had contributed its conviction and concurred with that conclusion. The process is assumed and the agreement recorded, with the explicit note of their concurrence with the Holy Spirit. The text affirms the fact without describing how they knew its truth. The final and decisive "vote" in this major matter was God's.

God's Spirit casts decisions out of wisdom. How does the community come to any major moral decision?

In debates that inevitably surface in determining Christian policy and practice regarding the application of the gospel in any age, how do we know we are on God's side? How do we discern God's will? Paul's letter to the Galatians offered a list of the fruits of the Spirit: "love, joy, peace, patience, kindness, generosity, faithfulness, gentleness and self control" (5:22). The ultimate presence of such sentiments would be among the primary indications of the conformity of our decisions with the will of God. Moreover, fundamental consistency with the great commandment of love for God and neighbor (Luke 10:25-28) together with the paschal mystery of the Lord's dying and rising (Luke 24:26) would offer other measuring sticks. When all our contemporary debates are said and done, we remain with the final questions: How do we know God's will? And how much weight do we give it? We often live with big questions and complicated challenges, the "hot-button" issues of our day. Life is seldom simple. Spending some time thinking and talking about what it would be like to live with each alternative may help in clarifying the final decision. Patiently and thoughtfully listing pros and cons for each side may be another. Giving voice to the principles as a basis for the alternatives could be another. Certainly praying humbly for God's wisdom is crucial. And, finally, if uncertainty persists and if time allows, perhaps the decision should simply be deferred.

The Four Fundamental Criteria for Authentic Moral Life

In yesterday's reading James had outlined the four fundamental requirements for Gentile converts as he saw them (v. 20). His words of advice had special weight as the leader and spokesperson for the Jewish Christian community that had gathered around the apostles in Jerusalem. Apparently his suggestion was accepted by all (although in a slightly different order) since the same four areas of moral behavior are now repeated in the formal letter sent back to Syrian Antioch (vv. 23-29). The actual history of resolving the controversy was in fact much more complicated and volatile than it would appear from Luke's version in Acts (Gal 2:11-14). The four moral requirements established by the apostles for Gentile Christians (v. 29) were: (1) abstention from meat that had been sacrificed to pagan idols; (2) avoidance of blood since they assumed that life was in the blood (that is, basic respect for life); (3) avoidance of strangulation (nonviolence); and (4) avoidance of marriages judged unlawful (that is, incestuous) because of familial connections. Note, first of all, that the requirements are primarily ethical rather than doctrinal (though doctrine may be implicit at times). Earliest Christianity was faithful to its Jewish roots and considered ortho-practice more important than orthodoxy. Of course, all were assumed to be believers in the Lord's world-transforming resurrection. Note secondarily that in another context Paul himself seems to have had a slightly different take on the sacrifices since virtually all meat came from the temples and pagan priests were involved in all the butchering procedures (1 Cor 10:18-33). In that other context Paul suggested that it doesn't really matter, unless the use of such meat became a stumbling stone for weaker members of the community. Apparently the context is also a consideration in determining the morality of an action.

Friday of the Fifth Week of Easter

God's Spirit shapes faith out of ordinary episodes of life. The fundamental command to believe in the risen Lord and the obligation to love God and neighbor take on specific form and shape as we live from day to day in any family or larger community. Precisely how to welcome new neighbors, for example, or how to encourage family members in doing the right thing or how to forgive without condoning are specific situations that sometimes require our response as disciples of Jesus. Prayerful humble openness to God's Spirit is the starting point for any decision or action. People are moved by the Spirit when they can finally forgive others who have hurt them deeply in the past or when they spend years in patient loving care for sick parents or children. Parents are moved by the Spirit to work long hours in menial jobs to help pay for the college education of their children.

Final Consensus and Peaceful Acceptance by Faith through Grace

Although there may in fact have been some grumbling among those whose opinions had not won the day back in Syrian Antioch, Luke simply says that the recipients of the letter were delighted (v. 31). The decision of the apostles in Jerusalem confirmed their convictions. Not all church debates end so smoothly as the angry debate between Peter and Paul in Galatia indicates (Gal 2:11-14). It may require a great deal of time before such peace is achieved. People argue over what they judge truly important. Wise leaders know, therefore, that the values of each party should somehow be respected and preserved. True evangelical peace and perhaps even joy comes from obedience to the gifts of the Spirit and will not be easily disturbed (John 15:11; 16:22-24). Such peace and joy is the fruit of the Spirit (Gal 5:22) and is found when people of faith conclude that they are doing the right thing, no matter what the price at the moment. It was Paul who reminded the Ephesians that "by grace they were saved through faith . . . not by good works alone" (2:8). The ability to accept the community's decision is not by our own intellectual prowess alone, but by God's grace. Acceptance of what we thought all along, however, is not really *obedience*. Only humble submission qualifies for that title.

God's gift of peace flows from embracing the Gospel. When a community can find the ultimate rationale for its decisions in the Gospel (not merely in a single verse), they also find some assurance of the fundamental rightness of their actions. Pope St. John XXIII's personal episcopal motto (inspired by Dante's *Divina Comedia*) was *obedientia et pax*. There may be an initial price to be paid in such obedience, but dying to our individual desires leads to the deeper joy of rising anew to a higher and better life. In resolving any difference of opinion regarding matters of faith or morality, the leadership in the community needs to tend first to the "losers" as the Rule of St. Benedict wisely counseled. Often quietly living with a decision enables prior opponents to determine its ultimate rightness or how some further adjustments in wording or nuance may render the decision more correct. Course changes keep a ship on target. Our own country's struggle with the immorality of human slavery and the scourge of persistent racism over the decades, for example, provides an insight into the extended time often needed for resolving such major perplexing human (and moral) questions. Painful contemporary arguments over issues of human sexuality or capital punishment are among the questions of our own day. Current ecumenical dialogues, when faced by serious differences in such matters, sometimes find clarity by studying more carefully how decisions are made in each respective church. Patient unpacking of the issues in the context of our Christian faith and in light of the fundamental truths of Catholic reasoning together with respectful treatment of opponents can assist the churches in their search for God's will in such matters.

ANTIPHON—PSALM 57:10A
I will give you thanks among the peoples, O Lord. (or: Alleluia)

Psalm 57

Psalm 57 is a classic two-part lament psalm. There is the initial description of distress and bitter opposition from sharp-toothed enemies (vv. 2-7), followed by expressions of joyful gratitude for God's protection (vv. 8-12). If the individual had not in fact already experienced the salvation, the psalm presumes its speedy arrival by the very fact of God having heard the complaint and promised a solution! There may even have been an oracle to that effect by one of the priestly attendants at the shrine; scholars suggest that the oracle followed the lament and preceded the word of gratitude. Our response today omits the first lament portion of the psalm in order to focus on the joyful heart of the petitioner who sings praise (v. 8) loudly enough to wake the dawn (v. 9), celebrating God's mercy (*hesed*, or covenantal faithfulness, v. 11) to the highest degree (v. 12)!

The Refrain

In today's liturgical context the thanks of Israel is here celebrated among the peoples (v. 10) and nations of the earth as if it were expressed because the Gentiles had been admitted and welcomed as members of God's people by the apostles without having to become Jewish first. The refrain expresses an echo of the joy of the folks in Syrian Antioch upon receiving the letter from the apostles. Gentile Christians today need to be very careful, however, lest they look down upon and disregard what is no longer required of us or consider traditional Jewish piety to be of minimum value before the Lord.

Friday of the Fifth Week of Easter

GOSPEL ACCLAMATION—JOHN 15:15
This liturgical statement immediately introduces the notion of friendship in announcing the specific type of love that Jesus has for his disciples. The notion stresses mutual respect and affection, not only functional cooperation. It's almost as if the new friendship established between Jews and Gentiles, as described in the first reading, now becomes an introduction to the words addressed by Jesus to his closest disciples in the Upper Room.

JOHN 15:12-17
This is my commandment: love one another.

Friendship

To be considered friends (*filoi*), as well as disciples and apprentices, of Jesus is a great honor and gift. Elsewhere in John's gospel, Pilate would be sharply reminded by those who wanted Jesus condemned that he had been granted the formal title of "friend of Caesar" (19:12) and was expected to act accordingly. Here Jesus grants that title of friendship to his disciples and makes it somehow related to fulfilling his wishes (v. 14). Jesus also makes a point of underscoring the manner in which he reveals to his true friends everything he has learned from his Father (v. 15). Lack of secrets, the willingness to lay down one's life, and the promise of pastoral fruitfulness (v. 16) are noted as three signs of the friendship that Jesus extends to his disciples. This entire pericope is gift-wrapped as it were, beginning and ending in the genuine love of Christ for his disciples (v. 12) and their love for one another (v. 17). Such loves as well as its expressions are never burdensome. At its core, this love is genuine self-sacrificing concern for those whom we care about deeply.

Friday of the Fifth Week of Easter

God's friendship chooses us for ever-deepening life. We like to think that we choose to love, but rather it is love that seems to choose us. Or maybe it is God who chooses us to love and live in the love we find. So much of life is beyond our choosing. We like to think that it is we who decide whom we will marry. Yet many will point out that they did not choose the marriage in which they find themselves. Somehow it seems quite different. We do not choose the children we have. We may not choose to be single. We do not choose our disabilities or our family situations or the jobs into which we might find ourselves settled. Always it is precisely in those situations that we grow into people who love, chosen so by our God to love one another.

Laying Down One's Life

John's gospel is often dated some fifty years after the Lord's death and resurrection. Over that extended period the early church had ample time to ponder the paschal mystery and to explore the relationship of Jesus to his disciples. They found helpful images for understanding its inner dynamic and meaning. Elsewhere in the gospel, for example, we are told that the true shepherd, in contrast to the mere hireling who runs away in danger, is willing to lay down his life for the sheep (10:11). Here it is true friendship that enables such a sacrifice of self (v. 13). In each of the Synoptic Gospels, Jesus predicts his betrayal, death, and resurrection three times. Implicit is a certain free acceptance of that eventuality on the part of Jesus. This triple repetition indicates its importance in the teaching of Jesus and in the events of the redemption of the world. Laying down one's life for others in large matters as well as in more trivial concerns is a key element in Christian spirituality and life.

True human love echoes divine sacrificial love. In an effort to motivate others to volunteer, some will do so by explaining how they themselves have always received more than they have given. The risk then is that someone may choose to quit serving if that person does not feel good about what they have received back. Service in the image of Jesus, however, is always sacrificial, which is to say that it is not based upon what we receive in return. The most powerful example is the Lord Jesus who was willing to lay down his life for us.

In other words we do not give with the desire to receive back, but rather because we have already received, we give back. The farmer knows that. He receives from the earth its fruit, its richness, and he gives back to that earth lest its store be depleted.

It is what his father knew, and his father before him, and the generations before them. We receive and so we give back.

The parent knows that. The child they receive is a gift. That child is theirs not to keep but to nurture and raise and then give back to life. And should they break that rhythm, should they cling to that child even into adulthood, then something in them and between them dies. We receive and we give back.

Love knows that as well. To be loved is indeed a gift, something we do not deserve. It is a fearful and awesome treasure, so fragile and yet so fierce. We receive and we give back.

Friday
of the
Fifth Week
of Easter

Saturday of the Fifth Week of Easter

God's Story Proclaimed

ACTS 16:1-10
Come over to Macedonia and help us.

Lectionary note: The Lectionary has chosen to omit the story of Paul's decision to begin a second missionary journey in order to revisit their first communities (15:36). His purposes were their ongoing apostolic supervision and "quality control." The Lectionary also omits any reference to the disagreement between Paul and Barnabas over whether John Mark should be part of the team. Apparently, the differing opinions were so strong that they went separate ways with Barnabas and Mark going to Cyprus (v. 39) and Paul and Silas returning to central Turkey (v. 40). Evidently Paul could be very determined at times, possibly even stubborn in his convictions. Every gift has its own price.

Adding Timothy to the Team

Paul's second missionary journey (15:36–18:22) lasted about three years. Back among old friends at Lystra, they met a young man by the name of Timothy (16:1) who had precisely the qualifications needed to fill out the team membership: (1) the ability to understand Jewish practices from his Jewish mother, (2) sympathy for Gentile perspectives from his Greek father, and (3) a reputed circumcision to make him acceptable to Jewish audiences. The pressing need of Paul and Silas was to deal respectfully with the two different sections of early Christianity without imposing the needs of either on all. The presence of Timothy helped to demonstrate their seriousness in this effort as they traveled. At the same time an apostolic pattern was being set for future generations in the church—namely, the need first to determine which priorities were faced by a missionary team and then the obligation to assess which individuals might best assist in accomplishing that goal.

Sometimes God even uses human disagreements to help us review a situation and initiate fresh starts. In any process of discernment, whether in a search for parish council members or the quest for a new pastor or bishop, the same questions endure: (1) What needs to be done at this time in history? and (2) Who can best help us accomplish the task? This is not unlike our civic process of voting—though often highly politicized—in which the goal is to choose the right person for the particular time in history.

A Summons to Macedonia

Even though Troas today is a small village of Turkish homes clustered about a fishing harbor, the town marks a moment and place of significance for the history of early Christianity. Near the ruins of ancient Troy, the village of Troas is surrounded today by the rubbled remains of ancient walls and gates amid olive orchards. More importantly for Luke, it marked the spot of Paul's first missionary vision (v. 9) in which a Macedonian fellow (northern Greece) begged for a change in Paul's apostolic travel plans so as to aim toward Greece in continental Europe rather than back to central Turkey. It was in fact a major step toward the eventual proclamation of the Gospel in Rome (Acts 28). Apparently Troas also marked the place where Luke joined the team as evidenced by the sudden inception of the "we" travel diary (v. 10). Who knows what sites of seemingly human insignificance turn out to be major turning points in the history of our individual lives or of the Gospel?

God's Story Made Present

God's Spirit can insist upon its own path of growth. The twists and turns of daily living all seem to fit into the Spirit's daily instincts. What works and what does not, what gets in the way of decisions and what opens new doors, both agreements and disagreements, whether there be detours or new paths—for Paul they were all acceptable. It is a good model for learning to trust in the events of life.

> Over the years the old man had planted many trees. Oaks and maples and chestnuts. Apple trees and pear. Some pine, as well as willows and birch. He would plant them and give them over to Lady Nature to raise, as he would describe it.
>
> Yet it was the two outside his window that he fussed over the most. Though planted straight and to the sun, one grew bent toward the east and the other to the west. He tried staking them for a summer or two but to no avail. In time one seemed to slowly redirect itself toward the sun, though in somewhat twisted fashion. The other simply grew leaning over as if it were meant to be so. Thus, he would eventually say, he simply had to learn to love them as they were. In his words, it seemed to be their calling—one to grow twisted and one bent over. The view from life's window is not always what we would expect it to be.

ANTIPHON—PSALM 100:2A
Let all the earth cry out to God with joy. (or: Alleluia)

Psalm 100

Psalm 100 is a short but jubilant song of praise, perhaps designed to serve as a call to worship to be sung at the entrance into the temple. Although the specific reference to "entering the gates with thanksgiving" (v. 4) has been omitted in this responsorial song as used in the liturgy, the remaining words of the poem serve to generalize the hymn and relocate the song from a temple building to the scene of the apostles' entrance into continental Europe. All lands—even Europe as inferred from Paul's decision in the first reading—are addressed (v. 2), and both creation and salvation history (v. 3) are invoked as motives for the praise of the congregation gathered for formal prayer. The verses selected for this hymn of praise include three divine attributes: God's goodness, his kindness (the covenantal mercy of

hesed), and his fidelity toward all generations (v. 5). The refrain (v. 2) includes in a remarkable fashion the three elements that summarize both the responsorial psalm and the world's response to Paul's decision to turn to the European mainland: (1) once again the inclusion of a multiplicity of nations beyond Israel alone, (2) the invitation to join joyous and jubilant praise, and (3) praise directed to the Lord as its primary object forever.

GOSPEL ACCLAMATION—COLOSSIANS 3:1
The Lectionary has chosen a verse from the second reading of Easter Sunday to introduce the idea of Christ choosing his disciples out of the world and raising them up to new life in Christ.

JOHN 15:18-21
You do not belong to the world, and I have chosen you out of the world.

Not Belonging to the World

Again and again in this final discourse of Jesus to his disciples on the eve of his Passion, Jesus refers to the world (*kosmos*) as a hostile force opposed to his message and his mission. He explicitly states that such a world hates and rejects them as it hated and rejected him (v. 18). Jesus offers a motive for that rejection of the disciples—namely, that the disciples no longer share the same viewpoint as their neighbors and therefore do not "belong" to the larger society opposed to God's world (v. 19). If we belong to a family, nationality, movement, or group of any kind, we presumably share its history, values, concerns, objectives, and dreams. The disciples of Jesus have nothing in common with their opponents except for standing on the same planet, breathing the same air, and sharing God's enduring love for that wayward world (3:16). By these words, Jesus rejects two specific stances as outlined in H. Richard Niebuhr's famous treatise on *Christ and*

Culture—that is, either complete identification so that the church and the world are precisely the same reality, on the one hand, or complete severance so that the church is completely separate from and out of the world, on the other. Jesus has chosen his disciples from the larger political, economic, and social society (v. 19) and reoriented them for the purpose of changing and transforming the very world from which they have been taken and in which they still live. In this sense his disciples remain in society so that they might change and transform those whom they serve. They are chosen from and sent to that perennial enemy of Jesus and his people as evangelizers, prophets, and potential colleagues. It is this critical yet loving attitude toward the world that defines a "Catholic."

God's Story Made Present

Saturday of the Fifth Week of Easter

God plants us in two worlds to have a foot in each world: God's new creation and the old world, which is passing away. The story of *Les Miserables* by Victor Hugo is in part the story of a failed student uprising in the Paris of 1830 as the students protest the reestablishment of the French monarchy. In recent times the novel has become a hugely successful musical.

In one of the scenes the students gather just before they go out to confront the forces of an oppressive establishment. They are driven by the dream of a democratic France, and they sing of a new day. Their hope is that the citizens of Paris will be moved to join them in giving birth to democracy. When they do not, the students stand alone, and in the end give their lives to the dream that has overtaken them.

Conflicting visions of life will always spark conflict—Democrats and Republicans, immigrants and citizens, town and gown, urban and rural. The vision of Jesus that believers bring to life instinctively asks people to take a stand.

Persecution

At first, Christianity was viewed as one of the many forms of Judaism existing in the religious world of the first century. It didn't take long, however, before Christians were seen as problematic for other Jews because they venerated Jesus as sharing in God's divinity. Moreover, Christian refusal to participate in the religious life of the Roman city also brought a charge of "atheism" from the Romans, so Jewish leaders tried to distance themselves from Christians for political and religious reasons. Although there were places where Christians attended the synagogue well into the fourth century, the antagonism and polemics of that time deepened the divide and increased mutual recrimination. John's gospel, which found its final formulation toward the end of the first century, speaks of the disciples of Jesus being expelled from the synagogue for claiming Jesus as the Christ (9:22). The authentic teachings of the Gospel of Christ are best respected when we remember the teaching of Paul that Judaism remains special to God forever because the "the gifts and call of God are irrevocable" (Rom 11:29). Unfortunately, the hostility between Jews and Gentile Christians was mutual over the centuries, with enough guilt to go around for everyone. The experience of persecution, however—even that pain that we somehow bring down on our own heads—can be associated with the Lord's paschal mystery and can help bring salvation to the world. The teachings of the Second Vatican Council, especially the statements of the Declaration on the Relation of the Church with Non-Christian Religions (*Nostra Aetate*), suggest a new spring in the relationships between Judaism and Christianity. This fresh start needs careful nurturing and attention in today's world. Careful preaching about each other is a first step toward the reconciliation desired by God and the church.

God journeys with us through good times and bad times. Some years back the "Footprints in the Sand" story became very popular. It clearly articulated for many people a deep hunger—that in life's journey they needed to know that they were not making that journey alone but that God was with them and even carrying them, particularly when times became difficult and filled with conflict.

**Saturday
of the
Fifth Week
of Easter**

Sixth Week
of Easter

Monday of the Sixth Week of Easter

God's Story Proclaimed

ACTS 16:11-15
The Lord opened her heart to pay attention to what Paul taught.

On to the Crossroads of Philippi

The ruins of Philippi lie some fourteen kilometers inland from the modern Greek seaside town of Kavala (ancient Neapolis). Once an important stop along the famous Roman *Via Egnatia*, it made sense that Paul, Silas, and Luke should seek out the city of Philippi (v. 1) as a place of political prominence. The location also offered a popular site of convergence for merchants and military personnel who were traveling along the main route from the Adriatic to the Aegean Seas. For initial missionary contact and a suitable place of evangelization, Paul often chose urban locations and points of commercial activity. Jesus himself demonstrated a similar strategy in selecting Capernaum at the beginning of his public ministry (Mark 1:21) since that city marked a major commercial crossroads for travels from Damascus to Egypt. Where better to herald the kingdom than at resting places for people on the move? Ideas sown in a private conversation over tea could be disseminated quickly across the Middle East. Sometimes "location, location, location" makes all the difference in the world.

There are times when the Spirit sprouts by accident. God is especially active where people's lives cross paths. The word of God is then sown like a seed (Mark 4:3-9). The casual graces of charity, justice, forgiveness, hospitality, generosity, and kindness are exercised in chance conversations. A certain openness of mind and heart often marks weary travelers. In much the same way the Spirit happens in the context of truck stop ministries, as well as religious reading rooms at busy shopping malls but also between fishing friends sitting in a boat on a quiet lake or between neighbors over coffee at a kitchen table. Placing a booth for cookie sales or parish dinner tickets in the church vestibule where people go in and out of Sunday Mass can make the project successful.

Lydia the Fabric Dealer

Jewish places for prayer, especially in the diaspora, often sought sites where fresh water was available for ritual purification. Today's passage begins with the observation that "we" (remember that this book had suddenly become a first-person travelogue since Acts 16:10) went outside the city to a river for prayer on the sabbath (v. 13). That someone like Lydia should also have chosen such a location would have been almost predictable. Paul and Timothy (see 16:3) therefore found like-minded individuals of faith beside that little river. Today a modern little crossroads village named Lydia marks the spot, together with a fresh-flowing mountain stream and a new Greek Orthodox chapel dedicated to Saint Lydìa. Paul sat down to speak with the women who had gathered there by the river. Driven by his zeal for his risen Lord, Paul's conversation would not have been mere idle chatter, at least not for long. Moreover, he would quickly have realized the social and intellectual prominence of the woman named Lydia (v. 14), a leader in the group. She in turn with all her business acumen would have been equally adept at taking the measure of this foreign speaker and assessing his worth. We are told that she was a "worshiper of God"— that is, someone who accepted Jewish monotheism and took the ethical norms of Judaism seriously, without necessarily adopting all the dietary norms of full practice. Apparently commercially successful (since she was a dealer in fine purple in the major commercial center of Thyatira in Asia Minor) and religiously devout, Lydia was also a decisive God-seeker who paid careful attention to Paul's witness and was promptly baptized (v. 15). There is a bit of a wry smile behind the final words of the reading—namely, that she was also so persistent and persuasive in offering hospitality that "she prevailed" (v. 15), even over Paul who was no pushover or slouch at debate! She even cleverly places her own credibility on the line as part of the motive for accepting her invitation: "if you consider me a believer. . . ."

God's Story Made Present

Faith is a surrender to the life God unfolds. God works within and among people. Naturally gifted young college students or office workers sometimes hit it off remarkably well to form highly successful enterprises like Google, Apple, or Microsoft. Is it quirky happenstance or providential? Similarly, Ignatius of Loyola found like-minded friends at the University of Paris and together they evangelized their world. The history of the church is filled with such examples of men and women mysteriously brought together for the Gospel mission. It is seldom that any of us commit our lives so suddenly but also as decisively as Lydia seems to have done. Yet when we do so, impulsively or with great consideration, there is a surrender that the commitment involves. S. P. Somtow's novel *Jasmine Nights* is set in 1960s Bangkok, and it tells the tale of young Samlee who finds herself frightened by the culture in which she lives. So she decides to visit a shaman to seek advice for her life.

Monday of the Sixth Week of Easter

"Daughter," says the shaman, "you must walk your chosen path to its end. For twenty-five satang, you can take the tram, which is confined to its tracks, and can never deviate from its predestined course. For two saluengs, you can catch the white bus to Phrakanong, which has no tracks and could duck down some unknown [back alley] to avoid an accident in the road. But trams and buses are not *life*. . . . *Life*, you see, is like a taxi. You must bargain with the driver for the fare, you must pick your own destination, and once you have set out, you're on your own, not

knowing whether the driver is a madman, a kidnapper, or a saint who will take you to the appointed place without giving you a heart attack along the route."[1]

Antiphon—Psalm 149:4a
The Lord takes delight in his people. (or: Alleluia)

Psalm 149

Psalm 149 is an exuberant and joyful invitation to festive celebration and worship. As the second to final psalm in the collection, the words of this hymn begin to move toward the Psalter's concluding crescendo of praise in music, dance, and song (v. 3). God deserved their very best efforts of praise. Though many scholars place the psalm's initial popularity at the time of the rededication of the temple (December 14, 164 BC) during the time of the Maccabean revolt, the words themselves could well have been more ancient and familiar to worshipers of all periods. Note that the Hebrew word consistently translated as "the faithful" (vv. 1, 5, 9) is in fact *hasidim*—that is, those who take pride in being covenanted with God and in living lives marked by God's covenantal kindness (*hesed*). The Hasideans, people known for their loyalty and strict observance of the Torah, were sometimes viewed as predecessors of the Pharisees. In every age and nation, God is the great king around whom the children of Zion continue to rejoice (v. 2).

The Refrain

Although most of the verses cited in the psalm response deal with the people's joyful praise for the God who gives victory to his people (v. 4), the refrain prefers to see it all from God's point of view. The refrain (v. 4) translates the divine action as "delighting" in his people, but the liturgical translation of the psalm text itself says that the Lord "loves" his people. The original Hebrew present participle *rotze'* ("be pleased") tends to stress God's good will toward them, perhaps akin to the opening phrase of the liturgical hymn of the Gloria where (in spite of persistent popular misunderstanding) peace is wished not to people who possess good will but for those who are the objects of *God's* good will (*bonae voluntatis*).

GOSPEL ACCLAMATION—JOHN 15:26B-27A
The introductory acclamation immediately provides a focus on the reality of witness, both the witness provided by the Spirit of truth to Jesus and the subsequent witness found in the words and lives of his disciples.

JOHN 15:26-16:4A
The Spirit of truth will testify to me.

Literary note: In the extended reflection that scholars often entitle the farewell discourse of Jesus at the Last Supper (John 13–17), the phrase "Spirit of truth" occurs three times. The Lectionary first presented the term last Monday (14:17) in connection with the word *parakletos* (advocate, v. 16), and then it uses the phrase again at the beginning of today's passage. The Lectionary will do so again this Wednesday (16:13). Last Monday we explored the meaning of *parakletos*.

The Spirit of Truth

The Hebrew word for "truth" is *'emet*, often translated by the Greek *aletheia*. Those familiar with the scholastic tradition of philosophy know of the classical definition of truth as the correspondence of mind and external reality (*adaequatio intellectus et rei*). From that viewpoint, something is true if the mind reflects reality, and if the words chosen reflect the known facts. For a carpenter or architect, however, something is true if it is simply aligned properly with sharp corners. The Hebrew approach to the concept of truth begins from yet another perspective, seeing something as "true" if it is solid and strong enough to bear weight and to hold up under pressure. The basic root of the Hebrew word *'emet* therefore signals firmness, stability, and perpetuity. Such witness is true if one

can confidently lean up against it without fear of falling through it, as might be the case, for example, with some fake painted-stage scenery. Truth by biblical definition is something one can trust. Our liturgical word *amen* comes from the same Hebrew root, signifying agreement with something one can trust. The gift of the Spirit of truth is promised by Jesus to the entire community of his followers (v. 26). This ensures that their convictions will be community convictions and that their combined witness will be strong enough for others to lean against it. It will make their testimony secure and worthy of acceptance.

The truth of the Gospel is revealed in the lives of believers. The fact that we continue as believers testifies to the truth of God's word and the Spirit's wisdom. We freely trust because people who have gone before us, individuals and groups whom we know and respect, have entrusted their lives to the truth of the Gospel. We have come to realize that when we live by God's word, life unfolds more smoothly than when we do not. We are less conflicted and more at peace. It is the role of the church community of believers to consider carefully what comes from God and what does not, what is consistent with our core beliefs as Christians and what is strangely aberrant, what is consistent with the gospels and what seems contradictory. This is similar to the gift of prophecy, which always requires the discerning response of the community because not everyone who comes running over the hill with an alleged command from God necessarily speaks for the true God. Final discernment may require much time as well as serious prayer.

Resistance and Rejection: A Price to Be Paid

When the Gospel of John was finally written and edited, over a half century had passed since the death

> Monday
> of the
> Sixth Week
> of Easter

and resurrection of Jesus. Persecution had already begun as Christian theology of the mission and identity of Jesus developed and as Jewish leadership began to separate themselves from their Christian coreligionists. The polemics of the late first century and its tensions created problems for everyone. Interreligious debates within Judaism were remembered and probably hardened. The words spoken by Jesus, especially the sharpest in his disputations with some Pharisees, were recalled. The passionate exclamations that had been readily understood within Jewish circles seemed harsh and definitive to Greek ears. Earlier debates became expulsions, so that by the time of the story of the man born blind (John 9:22) and this portion of the Last Supper discourse, excommunications may well have already occurred. Even in his own day Jesus clearly saw that one's witness in faith might have a cost; his life and death were ample evidence of that reality. Jesus offered encouragement to strengthen his disciples for the hard times to come (16:1). Today's gospel passage from the Last Supper discourses speaks soberly of expulsions and possible execution as the price for one's faithful discipleship. Just as Jesus had laid down his life because authorities feared that his message might be too disruptive, subsequent disciples might be required to do the same. The proclamation of his words should offer similar support for more modern Christians who gather at weekday Mass to strengthen their faith and to find the courage of their convictions. At some point in life, belief comes at a price. The sacrament of confirmation is also given for this same purpose.

In the face of conflict the Spirit strengthens us to testify to Jesus and the truth. The past fifty years of Christian witness to fundamental justice and basic respect for human dignity in Latin America, as well as those more recently beheaded by ISIS for refusing to recant their faith, have produced countless martyrs for their faith. God's truth and God's charity eventually come with a price tag. Knowing that such moments will come does not necessarily make it easier, only that we know what is taking place.

Monday of the Sixth Week of Easter

1. S. P. Somtow, *Jasmine Nights* (New York: St. Martin's, 1994), 202–3.

Tuesday of the Sixth Week of Easter

God's Story Proclaimed

ACTS 16:22-34
Believe in the Lord Jesus and you and your household will be saved.

Apostolic Discernment

Anyone visiting the ruins of Philippi today is shown the cave under the ancient acropolis and told that it was the prison that held Paul and Silas (v. 23). As Luke told the tale, there was an earthquake so severe (in itself not surprising for that mountainous area of Greece) that the prison doors were jarred open and the prisoners' chains ripped loose from the walls (v. 26). Paul and Silas could have interpreted that quake as some sort of divine intervention on their behalf and walked out of their prison cell into freedom. They freely chose to remain in place, however, in order to give witness to their integrity and to protect their jailer who would have been executed for dereliction of duty had the prisoners escaped. Later that same morning, Paul and Silas were freed and encouraged to leave town quietly. In that second case, they refused in order to insist on their rights to due process as Roman citizens (vv. 35-39; this element of the story unfortunately was not included in the Lectionary readings). Two different decisions were made. Both decisions were to remain in prison, yet each for very different reasons. The former was to protect the jailer; the latter was to insist on their own legal rights. The questions of "what" and "why" walk with disciples in every age of history. In each case they present themselves with an eye toward selecting the strategy that best serves the Gospel of justice and charity. Had Paul and Silas walked away quietly, they might have jeopardized the future rights of other Roman citizen disciples!

God's Story Made Present

Faith spurs believers to do the right thing for the right reason. In the early part of the twentieth century, Mahatma Gandhi mused over the fate of human life when goodness wanes because of a lack of faith. Gandhi thought about it in terms of those ways that bring an imbalance to our daily living. He called them the seven deadly social sins:

- politics without principle;
- wealth without work;
- commerce without morality;
- leisure without conscience;
- education without character;
- science without humanity; and
- worship without sacrifice.

People of faith seek to do these activities out of a faith-based motivation; that is, to enter into political activity with principles of justice, to provide commerce that is morally just, and to educate in a way that builds character. Every such activity has of its own nature a distinct purpose and set of ethics.

The Fruitful Witness of Charity

Paul and Silas gave evidence of their deep love of neighbor by staying in place even after their chains had been broken (v. 28). It was a decision taken even though they had been treated unjustly. The jailer in turn expressed his own charity by tending the prisoners' wounds from the prior day's beating (v. 33). Charity begets charity. The jailer also gave evidence of his admiration for their witness, probably by exploring the reasons for their having remained in place, and then requested to share their faith by baptism. The subsequent meal was undoubtedly accompanied by the celebration of the Eucharist (v. 34), thus bringing the Christian initiation of the jailer full circle, all inspired by the witness of Paul and Silas. We never know the full effects of any witness we give, even in situations when we are treated unjustly. "All things work for good for those who love the Lord" (Rom 8:28).

151

By God's grace decisions and actions of faith give strong witness to the values of a new and different world of charity and justice. There are many who find themselves "chained" to a life situation and choose to remain for the greater good of others: an adult child who chooses to remain home and care for aging parents; teachers who commit to teaching in difficult schools for the sake of disadvantaged children; those who opt to live in the city rather than the suburbs in order to bring stability to a neighborhood; the employer who keeps a less productive worker knowing that to dismiss the worker would prove difficult for that worker to find another job. In so many instances it is the Spirit at work when people of faith endure much pain themselves in order to create a new and better world.

ANTIPHON—PSALM 138:7C
Your right hand saves me, O Lord. (or: Alleluia)

Psalm 138

Psalm 138 is a brief hymn of praise for having had one's prayer heard by God (vv. 1, 3). The psalm explicitly attributes that divine intervention to God's kindness (*hesed*, God's mutual covenantal fidelity in vv. 2, 8). The original Hebrew text speaks of giving thanks "in the presence of gods" (v. 1). The Greek Septuagint version, however, prefers to translate it as "in the presence of angels," presumably so as not to confuse their readers and in order to refer to heavenly beings completely subordinate to God. The liturgy has chosen these words of praise and thanksgiving as a communal response and placed them on the lips of Paul and Silas newly freed from prison by God's right hand (v. 7). The verb is in the present tense, thus suggesting that God's gift of salvation is repeatedly and constantly offered at all times and in every place. The same words could easily be appropriate, therefore, on the lips of anyone

Tuesday of the Sixth Week of Easter

in the parish congregation who had recently been freed from worries, troubles, or burdens of any sort.

GOSPEL ACCLAMATION—JOHN 16:7, 13
The acclamation combines phrases taken from two different verses in the teachings of Jesus, first regarding sending the "Advocate" (v. 7 in today's pericope), and the second regarding the Spirit of truth who will guide the disciples to all truth (v. 13 from tomorrow's passage). This serves to prepare the community for the fact that Jesus speaks the truth (v. 7) and promises the Spirit to help them understand that truth (v. 13). The congregation is thus immediately prepared for thinking about truth.

JOHN 16:5-11
For if I do not go, the Advocate will not come to you.

"Making Way" for the Advocate

Throughout his public ministry, Jesus is filled with the Holy Spirit, which had first descended upon him at his baptism in the Jordan and had remained with him throughout his public ministry (John 1:31). Jesus also spoke of the Spirit that could only come after his glorification (7:39). After his resurrection, Jesus breathed upon the disciples in the Upper Room and gave them the gift of that Spirit (20:22) in a new way. Just as Luke differentiated between the public ministry of Jesus, on the one hand, and the post-Pentecost gift of the Spirit upon the entire early church (Acts 2), on the other, John had a similar view of the stages of salvation history. Today's passage speaks clearly of the necessity for the "departure" of Jesus so that the presence of the Holy Spirit might become more manifest in the life of the disciples and their community (v. 7). To speak clearly of the utter mystery of the interrelationships of the three divine persons is not easy (nor even possible) for the limited human mind. The gospels speak of the age of Jesus coming to climax in his glorification on the cross, and the subsequent age of the Spirit of Jesus, which brings forgiveness, unity, and vitality to the communities who remain in his love (15:9). Each age of God's providence must cede to its successor.

The glorified Jesus sends his Spirit to create a new community of truth and love. It's been said that we never grow up until both parents have died. There is a certain amount of truth in that. At such a time there is no longer any "going home." The future is upon our shoulders then. In much the same way every genuine community of faith struggles to "grow up," to live with the Spirit of the teacher. Each community finds itself asking how to be church at this time in history. The homilist might name some of the questions faced by the local community.

Convicting the World

Precisely because it is the Spirit of truth whom Jesus promises to send, he can speak with assurance of the judgment that Spirit will render over the world (v. 8). We need to recall that the world (*kosmos*), though loved by God, was by definition in John's gospel fundamentally opposed to God's will for all people. Though evil in its actions, this world is not irredeemable or beyond God's grace. Why did John's Jesus consider the world evil? This passage lists three reasons for God's negative judgment:

(1) the world *refused to believe* even when the grace of belief was offered (v. 9) and for that reason it was initially condemned;

(2) the world existed without a basic attitude of *righteousness* (*tzedeqiah*, v. 10), was not itself in right relation-ship with all other creatures, and even opposed Christ's relationship with creation; and

(3) the world was intimately *associated with the evil "ruler of this world"* who had been condemned by God (v. 11).

Jesus insists that sin and evil should be labeled as such. God's love can overcome the world's sin, but the dismal reality of sin must first be acknowledged before forgiveness can be extended. John's Jesus is already and always Lord and Master of the world and its eventual redemption.

Throughout the rhythms of time the Spirit pulls us into truth. As each of us negotiates life, we are forced to confront life and its twisting turns and carve truth and wisdom from what comes our way. That is seldom an easy task, if it ever is. Yet it is also the milieu in which the Spirit pulls us into truth.

God's Spirit of truth will never pretend that sin is virtue nor allow us to mask evil intent with pious words. Any idolatrous treatment of money, pleasure, or political power as an ultimate value in life as if it were more important than anything else is always a deceptive instinct. Deliberately mistreating and harming others always wreaks havoc. Speaking untruth in order to deceive eventually brings life down upon our heads. Whenever any of these actions occur in human behavior, and whenever we find ourselves confronted by the struggles that ensue, it is then that the Spirit sent into our lives makes itself known.

Tuesday
of the
Sixth Week
of Easter

Wednesday of the Sixth Week of Easter

God's Story Proclaimed

ACTS 17:15, 22–18:1
What therefore you unknowingly worship, I proclaim to you.

Literary note: The Lectionary has chosen to omit any reference to Paul's insistence on his rights as Roman citizen in Philippi (16:35-39) and his farewell visit to the home of Lydia (v. 40) before traveling to Thessalonica, where at least three weeks of polite synagogue conversation occurred before a religious riot broke out within the Jewish community (17:1-13) and Paul was escorted out of town and taken to Athens. Even though Acts attempts to present Christians as stable neighbors and productive citizens, Paul seems to have a consistent charism for passionate conversation and eventual disruption. It was in Athens that Paul was invited to the public forum at the Areopagus for discussion with the famous philosophers of that city (vv. 17-21). The tale begins anew in today's reading with the words of Paul's speech.

Speaking the Language of the Audience

Athens was arguably the intellectual center of Paul's first-century world. As Acts describes this first apostolic visit to that city, Paul seems to have decided to use their mode of sophisticated rhetoric as he announced his Gospel, and indeed does so on the Areopagus, the religious center of that splendid ancient metropolis, perhaps even near the city's famed Parthenon. Using the marble shrines of its sacred area as a background, Paul cites poets as he speaks about the mystery of God (v. 28). Paul shows himself willing to use the cultural language of his listeners in order to appeal to their interest and keep their attention. In so doing he demonstrates some affinity with the Hellenistic approach also found in the biblical book of Wisdom. One might even suspect that these words of Paul laid the foundation for the later

Thomistic arguments for the existence of God from the order of the universe and from human yearning for happiness. God has entered our lives and taken to himself absolutely everything human except sin. No mode of thought or expression is alien to God except falsehood.

God's Story Made Present

God hides in the common flow of life. The search for meaning in life and the search for God seem to be a common quest. In time the believer comes to realize they are one and the same.

Jewish tradition tells a story about the rebbe whose young son once came running to him, crying inconsolably. Between huge sobs, he manages to say, "Father, I've been playing hide-and-seek with the other children. It came my turn to hide, but after I found a good place, I sat there in the woods for hours waiting for the others to find me. No one ever yelled into the woods to tell me to come out. They just left me there alone." His father put his arms around the child and held him close, rocking him back and forth. "Ah, my son," he said, "that's how it is with God, too. God is always hiding, hoping that people will come to look for him. But no one wants to play. He's always left alone, wanting to be found, hoping someone will come. But crying because no one seeks him out."[1]

Altar to the Unknown God

At first Paul's reference to an "Unknown God" (v. 23) may seem to be an acknowledgment of the Athenians' efforts to cover all bases and offer honor to any god who may have been overlooked amid the multiplicity of altars scattered around the Areopagus. For us as believers some twenty centuries later, however, the phrase may have a deeper significance. God always remains beyond human ability to comprehend. No matter what we may think we know about our God, the divine remains robed in mystery and beyond our limited human understanding. Christian mysticism even has a technical term for our fundamental ignorance before the utter mystery of God—the *apophatic* approach to God, which refers to our inability to speak of God except in a totally limited fashion. Apophatic theology narrows down what God is by naming what God *is not*. Only God's own Spirit can guide us to the truth (John 16:13). If we struggle to know our own motivations and often find ourselves puzzled by friends and colleagues, how much more of a mystery is our God?

God's Story Made Present

God's Spirit trips us into stumbling upon God. God speaks to us in the events of our lives and in the circumstances that surround us every day, and yet so often do we miss it.

There is a scene in Thornton Wilder's *Our Town* in which Emily implores the stage manager whether she might return to the land of the living from the land of the dead so that she might relive her twelfth birthday. He agrees, but it doesn't turn out the way Emily had envisioned, and so before she leaves she offers her farewell to the world. "Oh Earth, you're too wonderful for anyone to realize you!" she says in awe and then wonders aloud to the stage manager, "Do any human beings ever realize life while they live it—every, every minute?" His wistful reply, "No—saints and poets maybe—they do some."

ANTIPHON—ISAIAH 6:3
Heaven and earth are full of your glory. (or: Alleluia)

Psalm 148

Although the refrain stems from a different source as noted below, the Lectionary has chosen Psalm 148 as today's congregational response. Scholars suggest that Psalm 148 may well have been the original pattern for the famous hymn of praise found in the third chapter of the book of Daniel. There the three young men in the fiery furnace call upon every element

of creation to join in endless praise of God. The Lectionary, however, has chosen to omit the psalm's list of material creation (vv. 3-10) in order to focus on the angels of heaven (v. 2) and the human leaders of Israel (v. 11) who are invited to praise the sacred name of God (v. 13). In selecting these verses as the church's liturgical response to Paul's speech to the Athenians on the hill of the Areopagus, the parish community joins heaven and history in praise of God. By the mystery of God's power, therefore, all the ages of human history and all creatures join the heavenly praise of the Creator of this world and the next.

The Refrain

It is an unusual decision that results in the Lectionary's choice of a phrase from outside of the Psalter to serve as the refrain for today's responsorial psalm. The actual words that were chosen as the refrain for the psalm's hymn sung by the creatures of heaven and earth—and also for the worshiping weekday community at the parish—are taken from the earth-shaking theophany granted to Isaiah in the temple (Isa 6:3) but with "heaven" added to Isaiah's poetry. In this way all of creation, earthly as well as celestial, is invited to share the praise that Paul's speech in Athens gives to the eternal God. These are the same words that the congregation will proclaim at the end of the introductory preface at every daily Mass. The words serve to unite the Christian congregation to the entire history of Israel's praise for their God. The parish congregation is transported, as it were, back to the temple with Isaiah and actually joins in the hymn that he witnessed.

| Wednesday of the Sixth Week of Easter |

GOSPEL ACCLAMATION—JOHN 14:16
Using words chosen from an earlier section of the farewell discourse, Jesus promises to ask the Father for another advocate (*parakletos*) who will remain with the disciples forever.

JOHN 16:12-15
When the Spirit of truth comes, he will guide you to all truth.

Guided to All Truth

Today's gospel begins with Jesus wisely noting that he had many other things to say, but the disciples were not ready to hear them (v. 12). At the same time, Jesus promised that the Spirit of truth would prepare their spiritual soil for a fuller harvest of God's truth. On occasion in classroom discussions or family conversations a person can be guided to "all truth" (v. 13) by a leading question or an observation that seems to open doors. A similarity can suddenly seem striking and enable us to understand very different situations from a completely new perspective. Sometimes a very painful experience can help us see events with new clarity. The Spirit of God is subtly involved in each of such human experiences. Many things guide us to truth, and all of them are used by God to bring us to a better understanding of ourselves and the world in which we live. Once we know the truth, we can have greater confidence in what we lean against (see also the earlier commentary for Monday of this week). The fifty days of Eastertide are designed so that the recently baptized might continue to ponder the mysterious ways of God, especially through their mystagogical conferences (as their post-baptismal meetings were called), and come to a fuller appreciation for the truth into which they had been initiated. Each year the entire church grows in utter awe for the truth of God's saving love at work in our world.

Wednesday of the Sixth Week of Easter

God's Story Made Present

God's Spirit guides us to all truth. In one of the classic *Calvin and Hobbes* comic strips, the panel opens with Calvin filling a water balloon at a tap. Already the reader knows there's going to be trouble. The frames unfold with Calvin bargaining with the universe. "In order to determine if there is any universal moral law beyond human convention, I have devised the following test. I will throw this water balloon at Susie Derkins unless I receive some sign within the next 30 seconds that this is wrong. It is in the universe's power to stop me. I'll accept any remarkable physical happenstance as a sign that I shouldn't do this." And so Calvin begins timing the universe's response. When there is none, he cries with glee, "Time's up! That proves it! There's no moral law!" And off he goes in great delight to find his nemesis, Susie Derkins. With sinister abandon he hits her with the water balloon square in the back, only to find himself running from her irate clutches as he screams "Help! Help! Help!" Of course there is no help forthcoming, and the last frame finds Calvin dazed and pummeled by Susie and wondering, "Why does the universe always give you the sign *after* you do it??"

Not Speaking on One's Own

There are moments during this Easter season when believers are confronted by the profound truth of the mystery of God in a new and perhaps astonishing fashion. The three persons of the Trinity speak out of a common truth that they desire to communicate to all human beings in every time and place. They speak out of mutual love for each other and for the fullness of truth that they are. No member of the Holy Trinity—Father, Son, or Spirit—ever acts in isolation or unilaterally (v. 13). They speak what they hear. They reveal what they know. They embrace what they love. The Spirit of truth reveals what belongs to the Son (v. 14) and declares it to the human faith community that we call the church. There is a profound and enduring unity to the saving actions of our Triune God that give glory and praise to the very actions of that same God. Because of God's transforming love for us, that divine unity is shared with us. Therefore, we are likewise united in truth. No disciple should speak on his or her own either, but rather should speak in the name of the community of faith and charity within which he or she lives.

Like expressions of human affection, God's truth unites and transforms us. We who gather together so often live with very different spiritualties, and yet we do pray as one to God. We have different understandings of God's presence and yet we gather to share in one Eucharist. We have different ways of living the Gospel, and yet we find ourselves united in living holy lives.

1. Jerome R. Mintz, *Legends of the Hasidim: An Introduction to Hasidic Culture and Oral Tradition in the New World* (Chicago: University of Chicago Press, 1968), 344.

Thursday of the Sixth Week of Easter

God's Story Proclaimed

[In US provinces where the celebration of Ascension is transferred to the Seventh Sunday of Easter, the following readings are used on this Thursday.]

ACTS 18:1-8

Paul stayed with them and worked and entered into discussions in the synagogues.

Literary note: In this case, the editors of the Lectionary have chosen to repeat the last verse of yesterday's reading as an introduction to today's account of Paul's first experience in Corinth. One can't help but wish that the practice had been used more often for the sake of continuity and clarity in contemporary liturgical assemblies who hear successive portions of Acts during Eastertide.

A God Who Keeps Calling

Many miles and no small amount of time earlier, Paul had once before turned from his Jewish colleagues in order to speak to the Gentiles. It was in Pisidian Antioch (central Turkey), after a very successful initial presentation followed by a violent rejection on the part of some synagogue leaders, that Paul and Barnabas had turned to the Gentiles (13:46). Obviously that decision was neither permanent nor final because Paul and Silas are back in the synagogue, this time at Corinth, facing similar resistance from some traveling Jewish leaders. Paul again turned to the Gentiles (18:6). Wherever Paul went, he began in the synagogue of the town because Jewish communities always welcomed visitors and showed a willingness to talk about the religion they shared in common. Like their ancestor Abraham, they valued hospitality (Gen 18:1-5). Synagogue members understood the biblical language that Paul used when he spoke about Jesus the Christ. A god in human form, however, was troubling to many Jews who had suffered much for their dedication to strict monotheism amid the paganism of that world. Nevertheless, God would not allow Paul to give up because Israel was and remained the chosen people whose covenant was irrevocable (Rom 11:29). If Paul and Silas turned to the Gentiles, their decision was temporary because they were convinced that final reconciliation was God's plan from the beginning for Jews and Gentiles alike.

God's Spirit weaves a new vision to life as we bumble along. Life paths are often one step back before there are two steps forward. Seeming failures are scattered along many paths. Ty Cobb's batting average of .366 still stands as the highest of any player in baseball, yet the reality is that he made out two out of every three times at bat. It is said the Madame Curie made 437 experiments before she discovered radium. Faith is little different. The journey of faith is not a smooth, straight path to God. Nor does everyone share the faith vision by which we seek to live—not those in our families, not all of society, and so sometimes even we compromise. To expect that seems unrealistic. Paul's initial failure in Corinth was followed by the conversion of a synagogue official when he moved to a new residence next door. The Spirit's success seems to be uneven at best, yet enough to make the world new.

Faith-Seeking Companions

At Antioch the Great, Paul and Barnabas had formed their initial missionary team (13:2), which seemed to function very successfully. Later some sort of disagreement broke out between them over Mark, and Silas was selected to become Paul's prime companion for the second missionary journey (15:36-40). Although Paul may have been stubborn in his convictions at times (a consoling reminder for anyone with similar personality quirks), Paul always knew his need for companions to enhance the witness. When he arrived in Corinth he met Priscilla and her husband Aquila and quickly came to cherish their friendship (18:2). The arrival of Silas and Timothy filled out the team (v. 5). Each in his or her own way but united in purpose, they gave testimony to Jesus the Christ wherever they went. There are very few lone rangers in Acts. The mission of evangelizers "in pairs" (Luke 10:1) was no accident. The gifts of the Holy Spirit work best between companions and colleagues. Each mini-group is a church community in miniature.

God seems to search us out in the midst of groups. Peace Corps volunteers are sent to foreign lands as teams. The young missionaries of the Church of Latter Day Saints do so in pairs. Small faith-sharing groups in parishes abound. The New Evangelization presumes that faith is not a private affair but something to be expressed publicly and in a social context. It does seem that those who talk about what they believe have a stronger faith than those for whom it is only personal and private.

Apportioning Responsibility Where It Belongs

As one might recall from Matthew's account of Pilate's final judgment in the case of Jesus, the people in the courtyard of the procurator's palace in Jerusalem accepted responsibility when Pilate refused and washed his hands of the matter (27:24). They did so by accepting "his blood on their heads." The same phrase is now uttered by Paul as he turned from the Jews in Corinth to their Gentile neighbors (v. 6). It is a surprisingly stark way of accepting or allocating the consequences of whatever decision is taken. It would seem, however, to be very specific to the action in question that day. Although we may not share that custom in contemporary Western culture, the same reality occurs whenever we accept responsibility for a decision. Paul laid the consequences

of turning to the Gentiles on some of the heads of the Jewish community, whatever their motive at the time. The positive response in faith from Crispus, the synagogue official, and his entire household (v. 8) clearly shows division in the Jewish community in this matter and the impossibility of universalizing the guilt upon the entire people.

God's Story Made Present

God spins our lives into unimagined whirlwinds. A half mile down Mushroom Road and off into a field belonging to Mike stands an old and knurled oak. As Mike tells it, his grandfather would tell the story of how back in 1888, when Mike's grandfather and his twin brother were eight years old, they sat under that oak tree and watched their father plant crops in that field—which means that the tree is at least 150 years old. It has a long history of marking history, he says—the history of the farm, the history of his family, the history of the local community. History gives perspective on the movements of God in our lives.

For each of us there does seem to be a purpose beyond our understanding. For Paul it was the understanding that rejection of the message by some of the Jews meant a redirection of his ministry to the Gentiles. In our lives it may be the loss of a job or the disappointment in a relationship or the unexpected turns in the unfolding of our lives. All such events echo the wisdom of the Portuguese proverb, "God writes straight with crooked lines." History reveals the purpose of such events.

Thursday of the Sixth Week of Easter

Antiphon—Psalm 98:2b
The Lord has revealed to the nations his saving power. (or: Alleluia)

Psalm 98

Curiously, the Lectionary had also chosen Psalm 98 as the response to the story of Paul and Barnabas turning from the Jewish leaders to the Gentiles back in Pisidian Antioch (13:46; see Saturday of the Fourth Week of Easter). Moreover, the verses of the response are exactly the same in both instances. They celebrate the revelation of God's salvation to the nations (v. 2) but also note that God has remembered his kindness (*hesed*, perennial covenantal mercy) and faithfulness toward the house of Israel (v. 3). Apparently the liturgy does not want any modern eucharistic congregation to forget God's enduring love for his chosen people, no matter how individual members may act on various occasions.

The Refrain

 It is in the day's refrain where differences may be found between Saturday of the Fourth Week of Easter and Thursday of the Sixth Week. Whereas the former celebration suggested that the congregation proclaim, "All the ends of the earth have seen the saving power of God," today's refrain shifts the focus from the earth *seeing* (v. 3) to God *revealing* (v. 2) that same saving power to the nations. The refrain celebrates the fact that it is saving power that God reveals, not his ability to condemn and destroy. Two different subjects are indicated, one a contingent creature and the other a divine agent. The divine intention in today's refrain includes all the Gentile nations, even from the very beginning of the world's salvation. Paul's decision reflects and embodies God's plan. In our contemporary world, perhaps because of sheer numbers, Christians constantly (and unfortunately) forget or overlook the priority of Judaism in the history of our salvation.

JOHN 16:16-20
You will grieve, but your grief will become joy.

A Little While

The Greek word for "little while" (*micron*) is mentioned seven times within these few verses. Time is relative, we

Thursday of the Sixth Week of Easter

know, as any child can attest while eagerly awaiting Christmas morning: a few hours can seem like a million years. Conversely, those who look back on a rich life spanning almost a century see everything as if it were just yesterday! The Johannine Jesus, though certainly incarnate (1:14), often seems pictured as supremely transcendent over human realities, entering the world effortlessly and passing through time and space with ease. This sequence of "little whiles" serves to offer a bit of balance to that smooth journey, and it underscores the fact that Jesus has truly entered human history with its sequence of times and stages. Like the contrasts celebrated in the great poem in the book of Ecclesiastes (3:1-9), there is a time for presence and a time for absence—which is not really absence at all, but only signals a different type of the Lord's presence in our midst each day. The prayer for the annual blessing of a new paschal candle at the Holy Saturday Vigil sings the bigger picture:

> Christ yesterday and today
> the Beginning and the End
> the Alpha
> and the Omega.
> All time belongs to him
> and all the ages.
> To him be glory and power
> through every age and forever. Amen.

God's Story Made Present

God slips into the rhythm of history's times and stages. On a warm summer day John took his five-year-old, Ben, to the neighborhood park. Sitting on the swings, John tells of how a conversation began to unfold:

> Dad, it's true, isn't it, that God is in everything?
> You're right, Ben, God is in everything.
> So then God is in that tree over there.
> That's right, Ben, God is in that tree.
> And God is in all the grass that's around here, too.
> That, too. Ben, where are you going with all this?
> Well then, God is in that picnic table, too. Isn't that right, Dad?

I suppose you're right about that, too, Ben.
And that means that God is in you, too.
That's right, Ben. God is in me as well. Ben, where are you going with all this?
And that means that God is in me too. Isn't that right, Dad?
You're right, Ben. God is in you, too.
Well then, Dad, shouldn't you be respecting me?

John says it was a question he'd never expected, as if what it meant to be a parent had been disassembled and put back together again right before his eyes—and right before his son. Every "little while" of life seems to bring us to new understandings of who we are and of what it is to which God calls us.

Talking to One Another

The response of the disciples to the multiple references of Jesus to a "little while" clearly signaled their confusion. They posed their questions to each other (v. 17), almost in private and off the record, rather than directly to Jesus himself. It may be helpful to recall that the farewell discourse in John's gospel also features several clarifying questions posed by individual disciples directly to Jesus: Peter in 13:25, 36, 37, Thomas in 14:5, Philip in 14:8, and Judas in 14:22. In this instance, however, they may have been embarrassed to reveal their ignorance yet again, especially after all their time together with him. On the other hand, there is value in initially speaking among themselves to sort things out at a less formal level. Conversation within the community of believers, a.k.a. the church, can be helpful, and the Holy Spirit constantly operates on that level. Such discussion can occur because the ministry of teaching is found within the community as Paul reminded the Ephesians (4:11-13). Each individual believer helps to build up the ecclesial Body of Christ. Moreover, the Holy Spirit, using such discussions, gradually brings the church to an ever deeper understanding of Christ and his redemptive work. Ecumenical councils only achieve consensus after prolonged probing discussion of the issue at stake. Doctrine is developed over time through patient conversation within the church under the guidance of the Spirit.

God maps paths of faith out of confusion and uncertainty. The gospel paints confused disciples who did not understand what Jesus meant when he said to them, "A little while and you will not see me, and again a little while you will see me." Although Mark's gospel is best known for that repeated puzzlement (see 6:52; 9:32), John also gives testimony to the repeated lack of understanding on the part of the disciples. Our own paths of faith and trust are not always so certain and clear, nor are we always comfortable with not understanding. And yet God brings us to faith often through the questions we pose to each other.

Thursday of the Sixth Week of Easter

Friday of the Sixth Week of Easter

God's Story Proclaimed

ACTS 18:9-18
I have many people in this city.

The Shadow of Jeremiah

Paul's night vision in Corinth sounds rather like the word that came to Jeremiah some six hundred years earlier (Jer 1:4-10, 17-19). Jeremiah was summoned by God to announce Jerusalem's destruction by the Babylonians, a message bitterly opposed by the city's leadership. God encouraged Jeremiah, however, to remain strong and courageous because God was with him. Paul was similarly and regularly confronted by those individual Jews who opposed his outreach to the Gentiles. In Corinth the opponents even got into a fistfight in the presence of the proconsul's judgment seat (still standing today amid the ruins of Corinth's forum, v. 17). Gallio seems to have invoked a separation of church and state and refused to be involved. Paul understood, however, the power of personal conscience. His integrity was at stake and he refused to back down, remaining in Corinth about a year and a half before moving to the harbor at Cenchreae (about twenty miles away) whence he sailed for Ephesus.

The Spirit paves faith with courage. Like the month of March that can come in like a lamb and leave like a lion, last year's pride of eighth-grade lions was released to the wilds of approaching high school. For the most part they had spent this last year of grade school like every other class of parish eighth graders, each sheepishly trying to be like everyone else and looking for ways to suppress what made them different. Yet in spite of their instincts to fit the teenage mold, they had already begun to strike their own chords, listening to an inner voice calling them to stand their own ground in their own lives. Steven dreamed of being a financial analyst; Shelly, a pediatrician; Gabby, a psychologist; Emily, a third-grade teacher; Liz M., an art teacher; Liz P., a doctor; and both Jerome and Jeremiah, physical therapists. In time those inner voices will also challenge them to be true to their faith and to the lifestyles that faith shapes. It will not be the first time they will need the Spirit's gift of courage.

Enduring Misunderstanding and Division

One of the major issues in Paul's life was the relationship of Jews and Gentiles, and—more specifically—how the Gospel should best be proclaimed to each group properly and effectively. Thoroughly Jewish himself by education and faith conviction, Paul knew how to address the Jewish members of any synagogue. He had to learn by experience, however, how (and why) to engage Gentiles. He sought their ultimate unity in Christ and suffered because of their divisions. There were some Jews who hounded Paul from city to city for the sake of argument as was noted at Antioch (13:45-50), Iconium (14:5), Lystra (14:19), and Thessalonica (17:4-9). Some of the new converts like Sosthenes, however, were very Jewish as evidenced by his role as a synagogue official (18:17). At Beroea it was the Jewish leadership who received Paul with great courtesy and listened carefully, even becoming disciples of Jesus (17:11). Initially all Christians were Jews. A careful reading of the text shows that the Jewish people as a whole did not reject Paul's message, and our contemporary preaching should be very careful not to suggest otherwise.

God stands present in the midst of conflict. The rhythms of any faith community are filled with tensions as they struggle with how God's presence unfolds in the midst of life. The past holds wisdom and the future holds deepening life. Yet God stands faithful in the midst of it all, not taking sides. No one has a corner on wisdom. No one has a corner on life. No one has a corner on God.

Each age has its own differences and divisions. The bitter antagonisms of the Protestant Reformation have finally found some new understanding through the dialogues that have taken place since the Second Vatican Council. International antagonisms between the hostile nations of the First and Second World Wars have discovered mutual benefits through friendship and economic cooperation. Today's most virulent debaters might yet become friends through the gift of God's patient wisdom.

God is king of all the earth. (or: Alleluia)

Psalm 47

A somewhat surprising sense of enthusiasm runs through the portions of Psalm 47 used as the congregation's response to the morning's first reading. The reading itself, especially its account of the near riot within sight of the proconsul's tribunal (18:17), certainly seems sobering by contrast. The psalm itself was used for Israel's annual New Year Festival each autumn, celebrating God's enthronement as king of Israel and the entire world. Clapping of hands and shouting (v. 2) serves as an initial poetic bookend to the joyful shouting and trumpets at the end of the psalm (v. 6). Perhaps the editors of the Lectionary wanted to remind congregations that there is a larger context to all human disagreements and finite arguments—namely, the supreme authority of God who protects his servants from the negative effects of petty human opposition or jealousy.

The Refrain

Apparently this refrain served as a congregational chant at Israel's annual enthronement festival (v. 8). In its current Christian liturgical context the verse might also serve as a contrast to the limited Roman authority exercised by Pro-

consul Gallio who chose to ignore the fist-fight that broke out in his courtroom (v. 17). The same sense of God's royal authority over all the earth (echoing the chant of the seraphim before God's exalted heavenly throne as cited in Isa 6:3) is renewed each day in the modern congregation's response to the preface of the Eucharist. Sometimes only God's truth can reconcile human differences.

JOHN 16:20-23
No one will take your joy away from you.

Sorrow into Joy

The gospel uses the metaphor of birth pain transformed into the joy of receiving a child to emphasize the transitional nature of all human grief and sorrow (v. 21). In the Upper Room Jesus still faced his passion and death at the hands of the city's authorities, Roman and Jewish. From the very beginning, however, he wanted to insist that the pain would be transitional and would exist merely as a way of entering into the rejoicing that accompanies the experience of the fullness of God's glory, which can never be taken away (v. 22). The paschal mystery, which stands at the very heart of Christian faith, is not only characterized by the combination of the Lord's death and resurrection but also includes the fact that his disciples also share both realities. The sorrow of pain for doing the right thing is transformed by God into life and is common to all the disciples of Jesus. That life lasts forever. Transformation and participation are the keys to understanding the mystery.

God is constantly dismantling and rebuilding creation. Creation coming into fruition seems to be marred in the becoming. There is pain and grief and suffering. When we are immersed in it all, we tend to conclude that something has gone awry. Yet it seems that conflict and struggle are endemic to the process, even necessarily so. Chaos theory proposes that for growth to take place, something must first be dismantled. The challenge is to be able to step back and look for the hand of God in the process, though most of the time it is faith that we rely upon rather than clarity and understanding.

**Friday
of the
Sixth Week
of Easter**

Saturday of the Sixth Week of Easter

God's Story Proclaimed

Acts 18:23-28
Apollos established from the Scriptures that the Christ is Jesus.

A Community Effort

Paul's third missionary journey (18:21–21:16) was undertaken to strengthen the faith and resolve of his recent converts (v. 23). One traditional definition of theology is "faith seeking understanding." Over the years many early Christian leaders contributed to that development in each other's life. Yesterday's reading reported that Paul left Corinth for Ephesus in the company of his friends, Priscilla and Aquila (v. 18), a faith-filled couple from Rome whom he had met in Corinth (18:2). They were schooled enough, as we learn today, to take Apollos aside, eloquent and educated as he was, to share further and more accurate instruction about the mystery of Jesus. Although already knowledgeable about the Scriptures, Apollos only knew the story of Jesus up to his baptism by John (v. 25); so Priscilla and Aquila provided him with the rest of the Gospel story (v. 26). Throughout Acts we encounter countless situations in which the first disciples devoted to the Way deepened their own personal knowledge and understanding of the Christian faith, beginning with the gifts of the Holy Spirit at Pentecost (2:36). Paul himself had much to learn in his personal journey into Christianity before he was brought by Barnabas to Antioch in Syria as a catechist for that community (11:25). Perhaps that was the purpose for his time in Arabia prior to returning to Damascus and eventually going up to Jerusalem (Gal 1:17). Growth in faith is clearly a lifelong community project. If it takes a community to educate a child, it takes a congregation to educate a believer. Continuing faith formation is everyone's task, formator and formed alike, lifelong and constantly more fruitful.

God taps everyone as evangelists in passing on faith. The local YMCA has begun inviting members to join exercise teams. They recognize that the groups provide support and encouragement toward staying committed to one's well-being. Toward that end they have scattered posters around the facility encouraging members to "Join a Team to Become the Individual You Want to Be." Parishes and faith communities recognize that same wisdom toward growing in faith.

While it often seems that the one who pastors a community is the prime teacher and spirit-filled leader, in reality there are many who participate in that role—youth ministers and parish coaches who form relationships and lead to faith by their caring presence; catechists and RCIA staff who share their own faith on a very personal level; pastoral councils that pray together and inspire one another by their commitment; small faith-sharing groups. Individuals like Apollo regularly come into contact with members of faith communities, each of whom inevitably leaves an impact upon the lives of others.

Jesus the Christ

Apollos came to Ephesus from Alexandria (v. 24), a city long famous for pagan and Jewish intellectual life. In that city about two centuries earlier the Scriptures had been translated from Hebrew into the famous Greek version known as the Septuagint. Apollos brought great zeal and religious knowledge from the Egyptian metropolis and its thriving Jewish community. He still needed, however, to understand the fullness of the paschal mystery and how Jesus was the long promised Messiah (v. 28), the one anointed by God for his unique mission to Israel and the larger world. A bit later in the story of Acts Luke would tell his readers of the little community of believers in Ephesus who only knew of John the Baptist's mission to Israel and didn't even know there was a Holy Spirit (see 19:1-7, next

Monday's first reading). The early Christian knowledge of Jesus had two primary foci of deeper understanding—namely, that he was the long promised anointed son of David sent for the restoration of Israel and that he would do so by his death and resurrection. Jesus as the Messiah (the anointed royal son of David in Acts 2:34, citing Ps 110:1) and Jesus as the suffering but victorious Victim (Acts 2:25-28, citing Ps 16:8-11; Isa 52:13–53:12) were both themes found in the Scriptures of Israel. Only under the inspiration of the Holy Spirit, however, would the early Jewish Christians untangle those significant threads of thought in their Scriptures and see the unique fulfillment of these truths in the life and ministry of Jesus of Nazareth. Even that intellectual journey eventually took centuries until the teachings of the Council of Nicea in AD 325!

God's Story Made Present

The faith journey of Apollo is the faith journey of each of us. A recent five-year study by CARA (the Center for Applied Research in the Apostolate at Georgetown University) reported on the role of Catholicism in the lives of Catholics. The study indicates that four percent are core Catholics who attend Mass weekly and are involved in the parish beyond Sunday Mass. Forty-five percent attend Sunday Mass at least monthly and perhaps weekly but are not involved with the parish beyond that. Religion for the remaining fifty-one percent is on the periphery of their lives. Among this latter group

> 35 percent say religion is still "somewhat" or "very" important in their lives, and 71 percent believe in God. They continue to talk to God; 42 percent say they pray a few times a month or more often. Three-quarters pray with some frequency. In other words, there is still a weak gravity that keeps them within reach of the Catholic Church. . . . Some do come back as "reverts." About one in 10 Catholics today say there was a point in their life when they left for a time.[1]

Saturday of the Sixth Week of Easter

It seems that all individuals in every age must discover for themselves who Jesus is and what role he will play in their lives. For some he is the one who came and died for our sin. For some he is the one who reveals the fullness of God to us. For some he is divine love made flesh. For some he is the fullness of what it means to be human.

ANTIPHON—PSALM 47:8A
God is king of all the earth. (or: Alleluia)

Psalm 47

As the worship of the temple developed under the influence of Babylonian religion, and as their mode of celebrating the new year grew in importance in Jerusalem, Psalm 47 became the special psalm for the New Year's Festival each autumn. At the end of each major harvest season God was again acclaimed annually as the great king by whose supreme authority over nature the annual harvest was received. Psalm 47 was perfect for use as a hymn on that occasion because of its invitation to songs of joy (v. 2), celebration of divine royalty (v. 3), universality (v. 8), and its recognition of the diversity of roles within the nation—namely, princes in leadership and the entire family of Abraham (v. 10). The verses focus on God rather than the harvest. The psalm's ecstatic praise for God's awesome transcendence over all human nations, as highlighted in the refrain (v. 8), provides yet another thread from the Jewish Scriptures for the teaching of Apollos regarding Christ the royal Son of God and his redemptive mission to the world.

GOSPEL ACCLAMATION—JOHN 16:28
By choosing the final verse of today's gospel passage, the editors of the Lectionary provide an introduction and focus for the liturgical proclamation of its message to all who gather for Saturday's Eucharist. This verse can also serve to orient the community's prayer toward the liturgical celebration of the feast of the Ascension wherever it has

been transferred to the Seventh Sunday of Easter (tomorrow).

JOHN 16:23-28
My Father loves you because you have loved me and believed in me.

Asking the Father in the Name of Jesus

We may recall that in Matthew's Sermon on the Mount the disciples of Jesus are invited to "ask and you shall receive" (Matt 7:7). To understand the subtleties of that teaching more fully, however, it may be helpful to explore the nuances of the Greek language—namely, the difference between the present and aorist verbal forms. Matthew's verb for "ask" was in the present tense (which presumes something repeated regularly and perhaps often), not the aorist. The implication of the present tense in the Sermon on the Mount therefore was "keep asking." The purpose of repeated requests is for our sake, not God's. When we repeat a request, we are somehow forced to recognize more fully our profound dependence on someone else. We also are given the opportunity to take the time necessary for sorting out our surface wants from our deeper needs. Here, however, in John's Last Supper discourse Jesus uses the aorist; this suggests a single action that is done once and for all. By using the aorist tense, John's Jesus says that whatever we ask for *definitively*, once and for all, presumably after careful thought and with full knowledge, he will give us (v. 23). In John's gospel, Jesus seems to expect that one has thought the request through carefully and knows precisely what is truly needed. Moreover, in both the Sermon on the Mount and in today's text the "you" is *collective* and plural—that is, "whatever you [all] ask" (v. 23). This presumes therefore a community prayer, not merely an individual's selfish *gimme* petition. Definitive petitions of the entire community are always granted, but in God's way and in God's time.

Jesus promises that thoughtful requests of the community receive a response. When prayer flows from the entire community, there tends to be a broader wisdom than what might be present in individual prayer. Differing needs, the complexity of implications, various visions—they all become woven into communal prayer.

Figures of Speech

Jesus acknowledges that prior to this, the moment of his final solemn teaching to his disciples on the occasion of the Last Supper, he had spoken in "figures of speech" (v. 25, *paroimìas* or proverbs, the word used in John's gospel for parables). On an earlier occasion in the Jerusalem temple at the feast of Hanukkah (10:24), some of the Jewish leaders had begged him to speak more frankly, but he would not do so at that time since they would not understand the way his mission as Messiah differed from their merely political aspirations and expectations. Each of the Synoptic Gospels offers, for example, a small collection of his parables of the kingdom, illustrations of how God works in our world. Now Jesus tells his disciples that he intends to speak with *parresìa*—that is, frankly, candidly, and boldly (v. 25), a decision that the disciples receive with gratitude and some degree of relief (vv. 29 and 33 as will be repeated in next Monday's gospel passage). This directness and clarity is the very same characteristic that marked the speech of Peter after the gift of the Spirit on Pentecost (Acts 2:29). The urgency and intensity of the moment requires an unambiguous description of his identity and mission—namely, that he came from the Father into the world and was now leaving the world and returning to his Father (v. 28). Jesus suddenly speaks out of his divine transcendence without mincing words, reminiscent of his early statements to Nicodemus about coming to save the world rather than condemn it (3:16). The

> **Saturday of the Sixth Week of Easter**

gift of the Holy Spirit enabled Peter to speak clearly at Pentecost, and that same Spirit enables people to understand with equal clarity and "be taught by God" (6:45). It may also be helpful to recall that the real gift of Pentecost is not the speaking in tongues (no matter what pious tradition may assume or popular preaching proclaim), but of hearing and understanding. After all, each person truly heard the apostles in his own native tongue (2:9). Languages and figures of speech were no longer obstacles!

God's Story Made Present

When God speaks, it seems most often to be mysterious rather than with clarity. We wonder what God is saying in a particular event. We try to discern God's wisdom in the process of decisions. We do not always understand why life is the way it is. The clarity seems to come in retrospect, or perhaps not all at once.

Andrew was a college senior participating in a discussion group exploring the quality and nature of the college experience. At one point in the conversation he was asked what novels he had read during the past year.

Saturday of the Sixth Week of Easter

Andrew lamented the fact that he had read none, even though he has always enjoyed reading novels in the past. But college is so demanding, he explained, and so much filled with reading for coursework that he never quite got to doing what he enjoyed.

Somewhat later in the conversation and in response to another person's question about goals and dreams, Andrew began to relate his passion for the trilogy film *Lord of the Rings*. In the context of his excitement he told of how he had seen the first film twenty-three times, the second fourteen times, and the third and most recent six times. For Andrew *Lord of the Rings* had become a way for understanding his life, one that totaled 150 hours of viewing time in a lifestyle that seemed for him too encumbered for reading novels.

People of faith use the gospels to understand life. Andrew used *Lord of the Rings*. In the course of our lives we all explore ways of understanding what our lives are about and how it is that God moves and shapes us.

Leaving the World

In those ecclesiastical provinces where the liturgical celebration of the feast of the Ascension has been transferred to tomorrow (Seventh Sunday of Easter), the final verse of this passage offers the perfect liturgical transition. Jesus announces that he is "leaving the world and going back to the Father" (v. 28; next Monday's gospel text, however, will continue to develop these same themes). The departure as described, however, refers only to his physical presence in the world of human activity and in the life of his church. His Spirit will continue to be active in Peter's missionary activities as exemplified in the miraculous catch of fish (21:11) and in Peter's loving and shepherding the residential communities committed to his care (21:15-17). In spite of their naïve claim to full understanding, like Peter (Mark 9:32) the disciples still have much to suffer and to learn. They will be scattered by their fear and weak in their faith. Even though the disciples had finally realized that Jesus had come from God (v. 27), they will still need the strength and gifts of the Spirit to be consistent and cogent instruments of witness and forgiveness (20:21-23).

God's Story Made Present

Jesus is present to us not physically but really and mysteriously, often not recognized.

Like many fly fishermen in western Montana where the summer days are almost Arctic in length, I often do not start fishing until the cool of the evening. Then in the Arctic half-light of the canyon, all existence fades to a being with my soul and memories and the sounds of the Big Blackfoot River and a four-count rhythm and the hope that a fish will rise. Eventually, all things merge into one, and a river runs through it. The river was cut by the world's great flood and runs over rocks from the basement of time. On some of those rocks are timeless raindrops. Under the rocks are the words, and some of the words are theirs. I am haunted by waters.[2]

As you and I make our ways through life, we do have the sense that we are not alone, that there is a presence that speaks, and perhaps guides, but also knows us.

**Saturday
of the
Sixth Week
of Easter**

1. Mark M. Gray, "Your Average American Catholic," *America* 212, no. 17 (May 18, 2015): 16–19.
2. Norman Maclean, *A River Runs Through It* (Chicago: University of Chicago Press, 1976).

Seventh Week of Easter

———

Monday of the Seventh Week of Easter

God's Story Proclaimed

Acts 19:1-8

Did you receive the Holy Spirit when you became believers?

The Edge of Ignorance

An attentive listener can find a bit of wry humor in this morning's first reading. To Paul's inquiry regarding whether the Ephesians had received the Holy Spirit, they replied that they didn't even know there was one (v. 2)! John's baptism had been a prophetic summons to Israel's national renewal before God. John had made the Jordan his preferred location of ministry because it was at the same place where the fledgling people of God had first entered the promised land under Joshua (3:1-17) a thousand years earlier. John called them back to the site of their origins in the hope that they might rediscover there a faith clear and courageous enough to make that once-new land a place of true lasting spiritual fruitfulness. Unfortunately, however, their experiences over the centuries had been fraught with sin and disaster. John constantly spoke of the need for repentance (*metanoia*; literally, "change of mind," v. 4). The years had taught them how much they didn't know about God's plans and expectations for his chosen people. The small Ephesian community's question about the role of the Holy Spirit was one more example of that lack of knowledge. Paul spoke boldly and persuasively, however, about the fullness of the kingdom (v. 8). Because modern generations still need instruction and guidance, humbly admitting at times our own lack of knowledge, we are very properly and perpetually called disciples and apprentices. So often we find ourselves saying sheepishly like the Ephesians, "We didn't even know there was one!" The long litany of areas of our ignorance about God links us to those first Ephesians and constantly reminds us of how much we still have to learn.

God's Story Made Present

God's spark to faith is only a spark and not yet a conflagration. The poet Maya Angelou understood that we don't always understand or recognize all of the aspects of faith. We don't always recognize the work of the Spirit or even avert to the Spirit's workings. "Many things continue to amaze me, even well into the sixth decade of my life," she writes. "I'm startled or taken aback when people walk up to me and tell me they are Christians. My first response is the question 'Already?' It seems to me a lifelong endeavor to try to live the life of a Christian. I believe that is also true for the Buddhist, for the Muslim, for the Jainist, for the Jew, and for the Taoist who try to live their beliefs. The idyllic condition cannot be arrived at and held on to eternally."[1]

Imposition of Hands

Paul's initial response to the acknowledged ignorance of that little band of Ephesians was to offer instruction about the essential role played by Jesus of Nazareth in the world's redemption (v. 4). That was followed by baptism and the imposition of his apostolic hands (v. 5). It might be helpful to know that the imposition of hands was a familiar traditional gesture in early Judaism. When rabbinic students had successfully completed their studies in the Torah, they were welcomed by that action into the long line of scribes and Pharisees who over the years had placed their knowledge of God's will at the service of their respective communities. The imposition of hands, therefore, was a gesture of welcome and a sign of sharing the ancient mission of learning and teaching. It was a sign of Paul's official recognition that the new student teachers in Ephesus could be trusted with the spiritual traditions of Israel. Paul's action signaled that the group of twelve could claim the authority of knowledge regarding God's work in the world.

The power of God's Spirit is set free in the communal ritual of prayer.
When any aspect in a person is ritually recognized and endorsed by the community, it becomes real in a new and concrete way. Because of the ritual of a wedding, even the civic community begins dealing with a couple differently, and the couple sees themselves in a new light. The same is said of a graduation ceremony, where a person feels "promoted," as well as standing on the podium having won a gold medal at the Olympics. Rituals, whether cultural or faith-filled, set a new reality free within us. The imposition of hands is a symbol that creates a new reality—at confirmation, at the ordination of presbyters, and in blessing over those who have been wed.

Speaking in Tongues

Among the writings gathered into the book of the prophet Isaiah, we find an obscure passage regarding incomprehensible speech. Scholars have attempted to make sense out of the strange sounds that Isaiah describes as "a strange language spoken with stammering lips" (28:11). In Isaiah's time the issue was foreign invaders who spoke unknown languages. At Ephesus, however, it seems that the spiritual experience of baptism and the reception of the gift of God's Spirit was overwhelming. For these new converts, the mystery of God was so exalted and incomprehensible that any attempt to describe the works of God only resulted in garbled communication (v. 6). Intense experiences are often beyond normal patterns of human communication. Paul tried to explain to the Romans that those who have received the firstfruits of the Spirit can only groan within themselves (8:22) as they struggle to find adequate language for the new experience of God in their lives. So many experiences of hymns, affection, gratitude, praise, or anguish leave us stuttering and virtually speechless.

Monday of the Seventh Week of Easter

God's Story Made Present

God's Spirit dumbfounds our humanity. There once was a frog from the ocean that came to visit a frog that lived in a little ditch, three feet by four feet by two feet. After the little ditch frog jumped down into the ditch, swam across, and went up the other side, he said to the ocean frog, "How do you like that? Isn't that something? What is it like where you live?" And the ocean frog said, "I couldn't tell you. You have to go there. I'll take you there someday." Try putting into words the experience of falling into love, or the first warm day of spring, or a piece of art that leaves you in awe. The words always fall short. We find ourselves at a loss as well to explain, much less to convince someone else, what it is that faith brings to our vision of life. Our very wordlessness attests to the presence of the Spirit.

ANTIPHON—PSALM 68:33A
Sing to God, O kingdoms of the earth. (or: Alleluia)

Psalm 68

Scholars consider Psalm 68 one of the more confusing hymns in the entire Psalter. As a result diverse and sometimes contradictory interpretations abound over the years. Things don't always seem to fit together easily. Note that the Lectionary's editors have decided to use successive portions of this same psalm for the responses of the first three days of this final week of Eastertide, using the same refrain for each of the days. Three different thoughts dominate today's response from the first section of the psalm. First, the congregation is reminded that Israel's enemies are scattered like smoke or melting wax when God enters the scene (v. 2). This is contrasted by a reference to the just who rejoice and break into songs of praise (v. 4) because the God of Israel is the father of orphans, defender of widows, and liberator of prisoners (v. 6). The first Christians at Ephesus certainly praised God's majesty and care for the poor as does every contemporary parish congregation.

The Refrain

As noted above, the refrain comes from the final section of the psalm that will be used as the response on Wednesday. Each day the words of the refrain (v. 33) describe the sung praise of Gentile nations for God's goodness. Today in particular, however, they echo the song of the just (v. 4) whose ancient praise in the temple was renewed by the praise of the Ephesians who had recently received the gifts of God's Spirit (19:7).

GOSPEL ACCLAMATION—COLOSSIANS 3:1
This invitation (or perhaps even a command) addressed to all baptized Christians encourages them to seek the heavenly world where Christ is seated at God's right hand. The statement prepares for the relieved acclamation of the disciples in that Upper Room who rejoice that Jesus is finally speaking clearly.

JOHN 16:29-33
Take courage, I have conquered the world.

Plain Talk Has Consequences

The Synoptic Gospels noted that Jesus often used parables in his teaching (Mark 4; Matt 13). They were stories about how God works in our world. Those brief vignettes served to invite his listeners into discussion with him about the topic at hand. Together they then explored the implications of the story and unpacked his meaning. They formed a learning community. Mark's gospel, however, suspected that Jesus used parables at times to keep outsiders from fully understanding the purpose of his work; for that reason modern scholars speak of the "messianic secret" (Mark 7:10-12). The audiences of his day were all too eager for a political revolutionary against Roman domination, something quite contrary to the mission of Jesus. Here, however, the disciples rejoice at the clarity and directness of his speech. The Greek word used is *parresìa*—that is, boldness, directness, frankness, and candor (v. 29; also used by Paul in today's first

reading, see Acts 19:8). Plain speech, however, has consequences as Jesus notes, sometimes brutal and severe. Because Roman authorities tolerated no hint of rebellion or civic unrest and killed Jesus as a precaution, the disciples would be scattered by his crucifixion (v. 32). Jesus takes consolation from his Father's abiding presence and from eventual victory over the hostile forces around him (v. 33). He understands his destiny very clearly, and he faces it with courage.

God's Story Made Present

God grows with us into living the truth. When is it that we really grow up to the point of taking difficult stands? Do we ever really decide or is it all about God bringing us to that point in life, that somehow we are lived into it like springtime into summer without our even realizing?

When I was five years old I hoped for a six-shooter for my birthday, one that would shoot Nerf bullets. It would make me the hero in my neighborhood forays into the land where good and bad met in combat. My birthday came and went that year, but I never got the six-shooter that shot Nerf bullets.

When I was eight I watched Peter Pan on television. And when Tinkerbell tossed fairy dust on all of us who were watching and told us that if we believed we, too, could fly, I climbed on a footstool, spread my arms, and jumped off—thinking just maybe it was true. I landed on the floor.

One by one life dispels our fantasies and brings us to the truth of living the difficulties of life and facing the harsh realities of living the Gospel. In the process God grows us into being who we're meant to be.

Monday of the Seventh Week of Easter

Trouble in the World

Not everyone immediately responds positively to the teaching of Jesus. In the theology of John, the world (*cosmos*) usually represents human society, attractive but fundamentally hostile to God. As noted on Wednesday of the Second Week of Easter, however, God so loved even that enemy as to give his only Son to save the world, not condemn it (3:16). One should not be surprised therefore if a resistant world should marshal obstacles to Jesus, his teaching, and his representatives. In today's reading Jesus assures his eleven in the Upper Room that they would certainly encounter opposition. The word used is "trouble" (*thlipsis*, v. 33), the very same negative reality that Paul insisted was necessary to enter the kingdom (14:22; see Tuesday of the Fifth Week of Easter). Both Luke in Acts and John in this gospel see the inevitable necessity of opposition and affliction as part of the reality we call the paschal mystery. Such opposition helps to clarify our motives and make it clear that the success is due to God's grace, not our mere human effort. Christ's victory over the resistance of the world is a source of hope for all who have become members of his body through baptism.

God's Story Made Present

God confounds the birth of new life. We don't always understand why what happens, happens. Sometimes that understanding comes much later, but sometimes not even then. Anne Lamott writes of "this man [who] worked for the Dalai Lama. And he said—gently—that they believe when a lot of things start going wrong all at once, it is to protect something big and lovely that is trying to be born—and that this something needs for you to be distracted so that it can be born as perfectly as possible."[2]

Monday
of the
Seventh Week
of Easter

1. Maya Angelou, *Wouldn't Take Nothing for My Journey Now* (New York: Random House, 1993), 73.
2. Anne Lamott, *Traveling Mercies: Some Thoughts on Faith* (New York: Pantheon, 1999), 107.

Tuesday of the Seventh Week of Easter

God's Story Proclaimed

Acts 20:17-27

I am finishing my course and the ministry that I received from the Lord Jesus.

Inner Changes

Miletus (v. 17) was a thriving ancient port city some forty miles from Ephesus. Although today thoroughly silted by the mouth of the Meander River, the site once boasted of four harbors, and therefore it was a very practical site for Paul to meet the elders of Ephesus while he was traveling from Philippi (v. 6) toward Caesarea (21:8) and on toward Jerusalem. Paul's speech to the elders is liturgically divided by the Lectionary with its conclusion postponed until tomorrow's reading. In this first section Paul makes two references to being a witness (vv. 21, 24). We know from our own life experience that there are two differing types of witness. Some, for example, like young Paul are witnesses to a historical event, such as the stoning of Stephen, because he was there on the spot and saw everything. He even held the cloaks of the perpetrators of that deed (7:58, Tuesday of the Third Week of Easter); his memories and words constitute the witness. Others, however, like Paul in this passage at a later age, are personal witnesses to their own inner growth and experience in the sense of knowing firsthand the positive effects of receiving fraternal charity and living community in Christ. The person himself became the evidence. In this pericope Paul refers to his own witness (*marturia*) in both senses—that is, the inner change "to repentance before God and to faith in our Lord Jesus" (v. 21) and then "to the Gospel of God's grace" (v. 24). He saw the risen Lord (Acts 9; 22; 28) and knew the life-giving blessing of having changed his attitude (*metanoia*) about the person and ministry of Jesus. Moreover, he saw firsthand the way life was radically transformed for others in one young community after another who had accepted the Gospel lived in charity and peace.

God's Story Made Present

As with Paul so with us, the Spirit compels us to give witness. Annie Dillard offers an image of living by one's commitments and the witness it gives. When one is committed to one's faith and committed to living it out, it takes over one's vision and purpose and very existence.

Once, a man shot an eagle out of the sky. He examined the eagle and found the dry skull of a weasel fixed by the jaws to his throat. The supposition is that the eagle had pounced on the weasel and the weasel swiveled and bit as instinct taught him, tooth to neck, and nearly won. I would have liked to have seen that eagle from the air a few weeks or months before he was shot: was the whole weasel still attached to his feathered throat, a fur pendant? Or did the eagle eat what he could reach, gutting the living weasel with his talons before his breast, bending his beak, cleaning the beautiful airborne bones?

. . . I think it would be well, and proper, and obedient, and pure, to grasp your own necessity and not let it go, to dangle from it limp wherever it takes you. Then even death, where you're going no matter how you live, cannot you part. Seize it and let it seize you up aloft even, till our eyes burn out and drop; let your musky flesh fall off in shreds, and let your very bones unhinge and scatter, loosened over fields, over fields and woods, lightly, thoughtless, from any height at all, from as high as eagles.[1]

Compelled by the Spirit

In speaking with the elders from Ephesus, Paul gave a brief account of his missionary journeys and his years of witness to the grace (v. 21) and Gospel of God (v. 24). The speech also served as a farewell to the people whom he had come to love during his two years of residence in their city (19:10). Paul admitted that he felt "compelled by the Spirit" (v. 22) to conclude his third and final missionary journey and return to Jerusalem. It was there that he had received an initial blessing and the approval of the apostles for not imposing the full Judaic law upon Gentile converts (15:22). Along the way several individuals expressed a general and often repeated concern that he should not go to Jerusalem; they felt that he would be returning to a time of special hardship and difficulty (21:4, 12-14). With characteristic stubbornness Paul insisted on moving forward in his plans. On two occasions Paul admitted that he did not shrink from doing the task to which he had committed his life (vv. 20, 27), no matter what it might cost him or his converts. Perhaps he felt an urgent need to give final witness to the graces received during his life. The result is clear, even if Paul's inner motives remain hidden in his heart. Paul felt compelled to travel onward to the Holy City. The Spirit is at work in each of our lives, urging us to do the right thing and providing opportunities for faith expressed in action.

The Spirit compels us to do good works. When St. John Paul II was pope, he would often refer to the "culture of death"—that is, the fact that there are many forces in culture that dehumanize us as human beings. While there is much truth in that, there is also a culture of life among us, though perhaps that is paid less attention. Yet many bring forth a culture of life:

- grandparents who find themselves raising grandchildren when they had hoped that life would be easier when they grew older;

- husbands and wives who remain faithful in marriage even though it is not what they once dreamed it would be;

- adult children who care for their aging parents, surrendering their own lives;

- professional people with responsibilities forced to make decisions that few

if any will agree with or understand, simply because they are not in their position;

- individuals in jobs who make decisions because it is the right thing to do, though at great expense to themselves, only because if they do not, no one else will; or

- caring about relatives or neighbors who have no one else to look after them, even when those relatives or neighbors may not be appreciative.

All of us become an echo of St. Paul who said he felt "compelled by the Spirit, warning me that imprisonment and hardships await me. . . . Yet I consider life of no importance to me, if only I may finish my course" (vv. 22, 24). It is in all of this that we give glory to God and that God in turn glorifies us, even if no one else sees it.

ANTIPHON—PSALM 68:33A

Sing to God, O kingdoms of the earth. (or: Alleluia)

Psalm 68

Although (as noted yesterday) the antiphon remains the same for the first three days of this week (v. 33), the verses selected from Psalm 68 are new. The initial responsorial verses cited here give praise for the rains of the season that produce abundant crops (v. 10) and enable the flocks to flourish (v. 11). Perhaps it was primarily the verses that speak of God's authority over the "passageways of death" (v. 21) that caught the eyes of the editors of the Lectionary. If Paul felt that he did indeed face serious consequences, even punishment and death, for his ministry to the Gentiles, this verse would offer him (and us) a sense of apostolic confidence in the face of any negative reaction for doing the right thing. The God who controls nature is also Lord of history. God remains supreme over the life of each person and over the manner in which each individual's personal history unfolds across the seasons.

Tuesday of the Seventh Week of Easter

The Refrain

Today's refrain is the same as that proclaimed by the assembly yesterday, so it will be helpful to review the commentary for the Monday of the Seventh Week of Easter.

Gospel Acclamation—John 14:16

At the end of the morning's gospel passage Jesus will announce his forthcoming departure from this world. The acclamation, therefore, anticipates that statement and offers the consolation of another Advocate who will remain with the disciples always.

John 17:1-11a

Father, glorify your Son.

The Gift of Giving Glory

The seventeenth chapter of John's gospel has often been called the "priestly prayer" of Jesus because of its stress on his personal unity with the will of his Father (v. 4), his care for the mutual harmony and well-being of all his disciples and believers (v. 21), and his mission to reveal God's name to them (v. 6). These same characteristics could also describe every pastor and all who share concern for their people's well-being. Much has been written about the "glory" that Jesus asked for himself (v. 1) and that he had shared with the Father from all ages (v. 4). We know that each human language has its own subtleties. The Hebrew word for glory (*kabōd*), for example, stresses the weightiness and value of this transforming gift from God, almost like a precious metal. The Greek word for glory (*doxa*) highlights our human judgment of that value, and the Latin word for glory (*gloria*) stresses the praise that is elicited from its human recipient. Perhaps it is the latter meaning of "glory" that is predominant in this passage from John's gospel. The same notion is found in daily parish liturgy. The prime example is the hymn of praise so familiar to Catholics because of its frequent use in response to the preface prayer of each Eucharist, which acclaims that "heaven and earth are filled with your glory." In typical Johannine fashion the gospel weaves in and out with the theme of "glory," gradually deepening and extending its meaning in each verse. There is no doubt, however, that this transforming and uniting gift ultimately comes from God alone because the Lord's reflection in this passage begins with a request for that gift (v. 1).

God glorifies us in times of faithfulness. One of the signs of maturity is the ability to postpone immediate gratification for a greater and more distant good. In that context, everyone at some point in their lives faces the task of doing something they would rather not do, and doing it simply because it needs to be done. It may be boring or distasteful or demanding or whatever, but a person does it simply because it is necessary. Beyond such moments, there are also those times when what needs to be done will knowingly elicit anger and rejection from others. Still we commit to the task at hand.

It is today's story of Paul. "I am going to Jerusalem. What will happen to me there I do not know, except that in one city after another the Holy Spirit has been warning me that imprisonment and hardships await me" (v. 23). It is also the prayer of Jesus in today's gospel. "I glorified you [Father] on earth by accomplishing the work that you gave me to do" (v. 4).

For any of us, having done what needed doing in spite of the response of others does give glory to the Father, for it has been done with a sense of being called to the task. And in that we find ourselves glorified, which is to say we find ourselves in relationship to the Father by our being faithful.

Tuesday of the Seventh Week of Easter

Knowledge and Eternal Life

Jesus describes his mission as that of giving eternal life to his disciples (v. 2). They had received and accepted his word (v. 8) as well as his unique origin from God. Buried amid the verses of this Johannine prayer of Jesus on the eve of his passion is a remarkable description of the eternal life that he offers to his disciples. It is life filled with transforming radiance and glory (*doxa*, v. 5). The images are almost desperate human efforts to describe the unspeakable. In the midst of the gospel's faltering description of those realities, this passage makes a clear relationship between that knowledge and eternal life—that is, *hê aiônios zôe*, (literally) the life of the next age (v. 3). Jesus insists that eternal life is essentially comprised of finally and fully knowing the Father as "the only true God and the one he sent, Jesus Christ" (v. 3). Somehow, knowing that truth is already sharing in the life of the next age. That Jesus should thus refer to himself by name in the third person suggests that the words may already have been very familiar to early Christians, perhaps phrases from their communal prayer. It is also important to understand that the Semitic sense of "know" includes personal involvement and concern for the object known as well as the intellectual process of understanding it. A physician, for example, may bring his expert knowledge to any professional study of an X-ray (our contemporary sense of "knowing"), but he may also bring his personal concern when the picture in question belongs to a spouse, parent, or daughter (the Semitic understanding of "know"). Only then does he "know" the X-rays in this fuller sense. The personal relationship completely changes the nature of the knowledge. Only if one cares does one really *know*. Both aspects are present when we Christians "know" the Father and the Son (v. 3). Jesus states that the essential fullness of the type of eternal life that he promises is not endless existence without conclusion, but rather full and grateful personal appreciation of God's goodness to one's self and all creation. Jesus both knows his Father (v. 3) and shares that

<aside>
Tuesday of the Seventh Week of Easter
</aside>

knowledge with his disciples (v. 6); both experiences signal a participation in the life of the next age. As his mission in this world comes to a conclusion, his disciples know everything about him (v. 7), and they belong to God in a new and lasting way (v. 8).

God's gift of knowledge, especially of knowing him, changes us. Possessing a scientific knowledge of cosmic space, for example, changes us because we suddenly see ourselves as citizens of the universe in a new way. Having an educated understanding of human physiology gives us a great reverence for the delicate balance of functions that compose our physical bodies. Knowing the disastrous effects of smoking or drug use upon our heart, respiration, and circulation truly changes how we view the activities of those around us and may make us very different in attitude from colleagues or acquaintances. In each case, we are changed by what we know. All the more are we changed by an understanding of the person of our God who has chosen us as partners in service to the larger world in which we live, love, and work. Knowing God, we are elevated to a new level of existence with God, and in mysterious ways we become like God. As a result we begin to love difficult persons in a new way, perhaps the way God does. We become more generous with personal treasures, perhaps like God's selfless generosity. We spend the night in vigil at the bedside of a dangerously ill neighbor, perhaps the way God tends to us.

In and Out of the World

The notion of world (*cosmos*) runs through the five chapters of the extended reflections of Jesus on the occasion of the Last Supper. Back in Genesis the world was called "very good indeed" (1:31). Since then much had happened and the history of human sin was appalling. Early in John's gospel the flawed nature of our world was acknowledged. That new insight was incorporated into the liturgy on Wednesday of the Second Week of Easter, when we were introduced to the shocking truth that God loved the world, even though it remained intrinsically hostile to him, and even gave his Son for its salvation (3:16)! Curiously, almost by way of contrast, in today's passage Jesus says that he does not pray for that world (v. 9). Today Jesus insists that his true disciples had been summoned out of that unfriendly and antagonistic society (v. 6). He had revealed God's identity to them (v. 6) in a unique fashion, and as a result they belonged to God in a special way. With his glorification Jesus is no longer "in the world," but his disciples remain in its midst (v. 11). For that reason Jesus here insists that he continues to pray for them (not the world) in the hope that they will not be infected by disbelief and the negative rejection of that larger world in which they live (vv. 9, 11). Jesus explains that he continues to receive glory and praise (v. 10) by their fidelity to him and his teaching.

God has planted our feet both in and out of the world. Thomas Merton observed, "If you want to identify me ask not where I live, or what I like to eat, or how I comb my hair, but ask me what I am living for, in detail, and ask me what I think is keeping me from living fully for the thing I want to live for. Between these two answers you can determine the identity of any person. The better the answer he has, the more of a person he is."[2] We do live both with the convictions of faith and the reality of being compromised by the world.

Tuesday
of the
Seventh Week
of Easter

---

1. Annie Dillard, *Teaching a Stone to Talk: Expeditions and Encounters* (New York: Harper & Row, 1982), 58, 62.

2. Thomas Merton, *My Argument with the Gestapo: A Macaronic Journal* (New York: Doubleday, 1969), 160–61.

Wednesday of the Seventh Week of Easter

God's Story Proclaimed

ACTS 20:28-38

I commend you to God who has the power to build you up and to give you an inheritance.

Presbyters and Overseers

Forms of leadership within the early Christian community and the titles that designated their roles developed gradually over the first century. Initially they varied from one local church to another. Paul's letter to the Philippians, for example, was in fact addressed "to the holy ones at Philippi with the overseers (*episkopoi*) and ministers (*diakonoi*) (1:1). Those who were already elders (Greek: *presbuteroi*; Hebrew: *zakenim*, literally, "bearded ones") within their respective family structures were quickly recognized as also having some shared responsibility for the larger community of faith. For that reason they were sometimes called "overseers." Today the Lectionary presents the concluding portion (vv. 28-38) of Paul's final exhortation to the elders of Ephesus, also called "overseers" (v. 28), as they met in the port city of Miletus. He encouraged them to care for the truth of their teaching and to be mindful of the needy. Every Christian community is organically structured with responsibilities designated and delegated according to the abilities of the individuals and the needs of the group. Leadership in the church is always a servicing of its needs. It is incorrect to think of these groups as higher or lower. Such officeholders are equal to other members of their community, and they are only differentiated by function. Hierarchy signifies a sacred interrelated order of *servants*.

God's Story Made Present

Service initiated by the Spirit empowers others to further service. The time came for Paul to surrender control over the communities he had founded and move on, knowing that they would struggle. The sculptor Henry Moore once made the observation that "the secret of life is to have a task, something you devote your entire life to, something you bring everything to, every minute of the day for your whole life. And the most important thing is—it must be something you cannot possibly do."[1]

Vigilance for Truth

Differing structures in early Christian communities quickly appeared on the scene. Some like the first believers at Ephesus only focused on John the Baptist's ministry (19:3-5); others like the Jewish Ebionites concluded that Christ's baptism, not his passion, was the sacred event that redeemed the world. Many groups struggled with giving undue stress to either Christ's humanity or his divinity, and thus they presented a skewed picture of the fundament truth of Jesus and his paschal mystery. Unfortunately, sometimes the preaching was really for the personal gain of those speaking. Paul called the latter "savage wolves" in the flock (v. 29). Pastoral vigilance had to be maintained in order to protect the health of the community's faith. The mystery of Christ's identity and mission remains profound, and only gradually was it understood by human believers. In fact it took centuries for the church to find the best words for such a profound truth, as evidenced in the history of the Council of Nicea (AD 325). Paul admonished the elders from Ephesus to be vigilant about the faith of their community members (v. 28). It is a never-ending task for the church, one that includes the duties of parish catechists and pastors in every age.

Faith is the thread by which God keeps our lives in balance. The path through the woods was marked by cairns, each fifty yards or so beyond the one before. Someone had taken the time and made the effort, balancing one stone upon another, each held in place by that one thread of instinct called gravity that ran through the very center of the column and kept it from toppling. There was a harmony to each one, five or six stones one atop another, something that made you stand with a bit of wonder before their simplicity and the mystery of their balance that defied the logic of why they did not fall. At times it seems that all of life, too, is held together by one thin invisible thread, somehow keeping our lives in balance when they seem ready to topple. I think perhaps for believers it is faith that is that thread. And so the cairn of one's life stands.

Hard Work for the Weak and Needy

Paul was legitimately proud of the fact that as much as possible he supported himself during his many journeys to establish young Christian communities throughout his part of the world. At Corinth he had teamed up with Aquila and Pricilla as tent makers (18:2). They supported themselves by sewing leather shelters for nomadic merchants and travelers. In supporting his apostolic mission by the work of his hands (v. 34), Paul found freedom from dependence on others, and thus he defended himself from the charge of catering to the whims of wealthy patrons. Though not demanding that lifestyle of others, he saw its value for his own ministry. In that fashion he also found the means to share with the needy. In this way Paul encouraged the elders of Ephesus to be generous givers to those without sufficient means of their own (v. 35). Responsibility both for the content of faith and generosity to the needy were the two special "commandments" that he gave to his colleagues at Ephesus.

Falling in love with the Lord colors our entire lives. It was so with Paul's ministry, it was why he continued as a tent maker, and it was how he cared for the weak and the needy. It all seems to reflect the insight of Teilhard de Chardin: "The day will come when after harnessing the ether, the winds, the tides, gravitation, we shall harness for God the energies of love. And on that day for the second time in the history of the world, man will have discovered fire."[2]

ANTIPHON—PSALM 68:33A
Sing to God, O kingdoms of the earth. (or: Alleluia)

Psalm 68

The third segment of this psalm differs from the sections used as responses on the past two days. Today's verses from Psalm 68 celebrate the great and truly awesome power (*uz*) of God, a word used six times in this brief portion of the psalm. In response to everything that God has and continues to do, the Gentile nations are invited to use the refrain (v. 33) to sing their praise of respect and honor to the almighty God of Israel. Most nations only respect physical and military might greater than their own. On the docks of ancient Miletus, however, surrounded by merchant ships of every size and shape, as well as amid the commerce inherent in the worlds of our contemporary Mass attendees, God's infinite power demands humble recognition and praise from everyone. The refrain is the very same as that used earlier on Monday and Tuesday of this week. Perhaps today the refrain should actually be sung in obedience to its command.

GOSPEL ACCLAMATION—JOHN 17:17B, 17A
Today's acclamation prepares the congregation for understanding that God's word is truth, and it reminds them that they have been made holy and somehow set apart by that truth. Curiously, perhaps to establish a premise and then a petition, the phrases are inverted from the order found in the gospel itself.

JOHN 17:11B-19
May they be one just as we are one.

Wednesday of the Seventh Week of Easter

Protected in God's Name

The ancient world of Israel had a great respect for any name that truly represented the person in a quasi-physical sense, and particularly there was a reverence for the name of their God. To know God's name was to have power, and to pronounce it was somehow to invoke that power and unleash it into the world of the believer. The second commandment of the Decalogue prohibited misuse of that name and in particular forbade applying the name to any vain, empty object (Exod 20:7; Deut 5:11). In this portion of the great priestly prayer, Jesus insisted that his disciples are both united (v. 11) in their praise for God's name and protected by it ("kept in your name," v. 12). A scroll (*mezuzah*) with the name of God and his commandments was written and attached to the door of every house, and it was even worn as a phylactery on the brow and hand of the devout worshiper at times of personal prayer (Deut 6:8). It served as clothing that marked off sacred time, and it probably functioned as a protective amulet for the users. Jesus had revealed God's true name to his disciples (v. 6), and their knowledge of God's name protected them from full and final harm. Earlier in this Easter season—when considering the lame man healed by Peter's invocation of God's name (3:1-10, Wednesday of the Octave of Easter)—we heard of the healing property of God's name. Today we are reminded that God's name also protects. Against that background, all the more does the causal and disrespectful use of God's name in our contemporary society become deeply troublesome.

Wednesday of the Seventh Week of Easter

God protects those who invoke his name. The quiet mention of the name of a loved one, be it spouse or child, inspires renewed courage to tackle a tough job as means of supporting them, even when we might much rather be elsewhere. The mere utterance of their names reminds us of our motivation. Similarly, the mention of God's name keeps us focused on the task at hand and may protect us from distraction or discouragement. Moreover, the mention of God's name prevents (and protects) us from thinking that it is by mere human effort that we accomplish any of life's important tasks. Our work, however menial, is always part of the larger picture of the world working smoothly under God's providence. Devout Jewish adults often wear a medallion with the two Hebrew letters that form the word *chay*, short for *El Chay* ("living God"). Like the miraculous medals of Catholic Christians, the object marks the wearer as a believer and provides a concrete reminder of the person's faith in God's protective presence, especially in times of hardship or physical danger. Without superstition, the object serves as a reminder of a larger and often invisible dimension of our existence.

Consecrated "in" Truth

Jesus made a point of praying that all his disciples near and far be "consecrated in truth" (v. 17). The basic notion of any "consecration" is that the object is somehow set aside from daily profane use for some special purpose. It is therefore no longer available for whatever secular purposes may be needed at any given moment. The object so blessed is especially preserved and reserved. It is to be treated therefore with the respect it deserves. Jesus sees his disciples as consecrated and set apart by and for their mission. Peering through the phrase "in truth," scholars can see the Semitic background behind it. In Hebrew and related languages, the same preposition can mean both location and instrument. For that reason, Jesus is not saying that "truth" is a place where consecration occurs, but rather that truth is precisely what consecrates and set his disciples apart. It is knowing the full truth about God that makes the disciples of Jesus different and therefore "holy." This difference, however, is not something that creates an isolation of arrogance or superiority. True holiness includes by definition an impetus toward the mission of sharing that truth with the larger world. Because the disciples have been blessed to know the truth, they are sent forth just as Jesus was sent forth from the Father into our world. One can't help but think of all the situations when knowing the truth makes us eager to share it with others, either in trivial gossip or in more substantial forms of help and healing.

God's Story Made Present

God sends each into the world to be Truth. Near the end of *The Fellowship of the Ring,* the first in the Lord of the Rings trilogy, Frodo stands at the water's shore, having just escaped the pursuing Orcs. He has come to realize that he has been given the ring in order to return it to its fiery place of birth and so destroy the power of cosmic evil held in the ring. Yet Frodo is also very much aware that evil roams the earth and seeks the very ring he carries. He knows well that they will stop at nothing to possess it. The journey ahead will sap all his strength, and he is afraid. He would gladly turn from the task.

"I wish it need not have happened in my time," he says. "So do I," replies Gandalf the wise wizard, "and so do all who live to see such times. But that is not for them to decide. All we have to decide is what to do with the time that is given us." And with that Frodo climbs into the boat and rows to the other side where the journey into the battle with darkness will continue.

1. "Henry Moore: An Interview by Donald Hall," *Horizon* 3, no. 2 (November 1960): 102–15.

2. Teilhard de Chardin, "The Evolution of Chastity," in *Toward the Future,* trans. René Hague (New York: Harcourt, 1975), 86–87.

Thursday of the Seventh Week of Easter

God's Story Proclaimed

ACTS 22:30; 23:6-11
You must bear witness in Rome.

Lectionary note: In order to conclude the readings from Acts by the feast of Pentecost, and to include its more significant final passages for the pastoral reflection of the faithful during the Easter season, the editors of the Lectionary have omitted some fascinating sections of Luke's narrative: the journey by sea from Miletus to Caesarea on the coast of Palestine (21:1-7); warnings regarding Paul's determination to go to Jerusalem (21:8-14); Paul's meeting with James and his firm resolve to prove his faithful obedience to the Jewish law by prayer in the temple (21:15-26); the malicious gossip against Paul, the near riot in the temple, and Paul's arrest, followed by Paul's second account of his vision on the way to Damascus (21:27–22:24); and Paul's arrest and his speedy release with apologies upon the discovery of Paul's Roman citizenship (22:25-29). These passages should be read prior to this morning's Mass for a fuller understanding of the background to the situation described today. The narrative resumes with Paul standing before the Sanhedrin in Jerusalem. They formed an official body of leaders in Jerusalem, and Paul knew only too well the importance of the moment.

Hearing the Other Side of the Debate

Pharisees and Sadducees of the first century shared fidelity to the faith of Israel, its covenant, and its commandments. They differed, however, because the more traditional Sadducees (most of whom were associated with the high priestly families) gave priority to the first five books of the Pentateuch and downplayed anything not found therein. That meant that any thoughts of resurrection or spirits were discounted if not rejected. Pharisees by contrast gave considerable attention to oral tradition, which included belief in the resurrection of the dead (23:8) and spirits that had already experienced that new mode of existence. In a genuine effort to understand the issue, the cohort commander convened the Sanhedrin and ordered Paul to stand before them (v. 30) to state his case. Instead of speaking about his passionate views regarding the law and Gentiles, however, Paul shrewdly highlighted the differences among the Sanhedrin members in his audience. Emphasizing the disagreement in fact aided Paul's case at the moment. Elsewhere, however, his constant effort in all the synagogues that he visited during his missionary journeys usually provided occasions for emphasizing Jewish unity in faith before God's plan for the salvation of the larger world. This desire of Paul to remain as a stable synagogue teacher whenever possible was evidenced, for example, by his year and a half in Corinth (18:11) and his two years in Ephesus (19:10). His deep respect for Judaism even led Paul to apologize for his quick harsh language to the high priest (23:5). Even Paul lost his temper sometimes! In this passage we hear Paul's side of the story.

God's gifts include both unity in faith and possible diversity in practice. A useful contemporary example of the differences between Jewish Pharisees and Sadducees might be found in the various Christian communities. Catholics offer a global vision of being a community of faith, the Eastern Orthodox stress the mystery of God in liturgy, Lutherans emphasize our need for Christ's redemption because of human sinfulness, United Methodist hymns and preaching highlight the work of the Holy Spirit, Episcopalians have a strong sense of their national identity as Christians, Baptist spirituality centers on the effects of that fundamental sacrament, and so on. United by the grace of Christ's death and resurrection, each Christian group brings its own gifts to the table. Unfortunately, ancient and often bitter arguments between such religious groups eclipse the fact that far more unites than divides us. The Second Vatican Council invites us to rediscover our unity and explore those differences in peace and mutual admiration. Dialogue between these groups has revealed that many variations need not really be church-dividing at all.

On Trial for Hope in the Resurrection

As noted above, the Pharisees and Sadducees differed in the delineation of the sources they accepted for God's revelation and the basic truths they each held dear. Jesus himself had taught from within the Pharisaic tradition, and Paul's apostolic witness continued the trajectory. Paul went beyond the Pharisee–Sadducee doctrinal differences of that day, however, because he insisted on the full implications of the resurrection of Jesus. Not only did Paul, like his fellow Pharisees, believe in the possibility of the resurrection, he proclaimed that Christ's resurrection was in fact the inauguration of the end time and the opportunity through the grace of baptism to share in the beginning of that last age. This risen Jesus is the one who had appeared to Saul on his way to Damascus and claimed to be the "one whom you persecute" (9:5), and he is not only risen from the dead but now newly and profoundly identifies with his disciples! To proclaim the resurrection, as Paul did, was therefore to invite his audience to see the history of the world as radically changed and to respect Christians as the new enduring sign of the presence of Jesus. Proclaiming Paul's hope in the resurrection (v. 6) meant heralding that final phase of human history and asserting his own ministry as an instrument in the grand sweep of God's work in this world. Paul became a herald of the eschaton and was persecuted for that "crime," which risked unsettling the established social order in Roman-controlled Palestine. God had called Paul to the service of the Gospel and equipped him with gifts of faith, energy, and zeal for that lifelong task.

His experience on the way to Damascus years earlier finally came full force as Paul stood before the Sanhedrin after his years of missionary travel and preaching.

God continues to prod this last age of human history into life. Communities of faith continue to be signs of this new and final age. They exist as countercultural to the existing culture. Communities are just that—communities—and not simply gatherings of individuals. They profess the word of God to be normative and not the prevailing cultural mores. All of life is held as sacred in its own right, whatever the consequences of preserving life. The common good is treasured and fostered. The worker does not exist for the sake of production, but production is to benefit the laborer. In so many ways the communities of faith continue to promote the new and final age initiated by Jesus.

Another Nighttime Vision

Paul's commitment to the principle of things and his wholehearted and energetic dedication to his ministry to the Gentiles often seemed to create controversy. He regularly received encouragement from his Lord, however, as he struggled in prayer and worry during the long nights on the road. At the port of Troas Paul had been encouraged to turn to Europe (16:9) and continue his efforts at Corinth in spite of opposition (18:9). God can speak to individuals in their dreams, often revealing their deep and as yet unrecognized sentiments and convictions. Paul's visions served to confirm and approve his approaches and offered comfort amid the controversies that he encountered. Somewhat like the experiences of the prophet Jeremiah (Jer 1:18), God's fidelity gave Paul added strength toward perseverance amid the struggles of the moment. The risen Lord always remained at Paul's side, not only offering assurance but promising even greater

Thursday of the Seventh Week of Easter

future opportunities for his ministry in Rome (v. 11).

God sustains amid the conflicts of our lives. Abba Anthony was one of the Desert Fathers who lived in the fourth century. One of his sage observations was that the time is coming when people will be insane, and when they see someone who is not insane they will attack that person saying: "You are insane because you are not like us." Life is always filled with people who disagree with our vision for life. Expecting them to change can be unrealistic. God's presence, then, becomes the stabilizing keel for the vessel of our lives.

ANTIPHON—PSALM 16:1
Keep me safe, O God, you are my hope. (or: Alleluia)

Psalm 16

The Lectionary has chosen to use today precisely the same verses from Psalm 16, including its same liturgical antiphon, as it did for the very first day after Easter. In the former situation the verses of this psalm had been applied to the experience of Jesus as he trusted his Father's support and promise of freedom from the corruption of death (v. 10). In today's liturgy the same verses are applied to Paul as he faces continuing opposition. Finally, these same sentiments might be adopted by any contemporary believer in the midst of society's occasional hostility toward strong ethical values and contrary convictions. For further comments, see Monday of Easter Week.

> **Thursday of the Seventh Week of Easter**

GOSPEL ACCLAMATION—JOHN 17:21
This morning's acclamation highlights three things: Christ's prayer for unity among his disciples, and then his reminder that his own unity with the Father is both the model for the disciples and their unity a motive of credibility for the larger (terribly divided) world to which they are sent.

JOHN 17:20-26
May they all be one.

The Gift of Unity

In this biblical passage as used in today's eucharistic liturgy, the entire church continues to eavesdrop, as it were, on the prayer of Jesus, overhearing him pray for the unity of all his disciples throughout history (v. 20). That includes all those who will believe as a result of the witness of countless other future disciples in all times and places. If such unity is the object of prayer, that same unity is ultimately a gift from God, not a mere human accomplishment. By the time that John's gospel was written toward the end of the first century, the early church had already experienced various differences of faith and been afflicted by heretical aberrations, most of which were christological. Belief in the full humanity and full divinity of Jesus were often compromised in each direction by such errors. Greek philosophies struggled with the Christ of faith, and Jewish monotheism was often unable to find categories capable of affirming such complete unity between Father and Son as to allow him to apply the "I AM" of God to himself (John 18:5, 8). Jesus prayed for the same type of unity among his disciples as existed between himself and his Father. As the church approaches the conclusion of the Easter season each year and is again blessed by seven weeks of profound reflection on the Lord's death and final exaltation, unity in faith is the object of special petition in our prayer. Because this unity remains God's gift, we hope that such a deep degree of communion will be our constant possession as we return to Ordinary Time and daily life throughout the rest of the liturgical year.

The hunger to be one is a hunger for God. A basic human yearning is to be at peace with one another, to be one. Parents deeply want their children to get along, even as adults. Tensions at work unsettle us. Holidays can be ruined by disagreeable relatives and family. At its heart human sexuality is not only a uniting of bodies but also a hunger at a deeper level to unite our spirits. The prayer of Jesus that all be one is our prayer as well. It is a divine instinct that echoes our hunger to be one with God.

Transcending the Divisions of History

The profound bond of unity that Jesus proclaims and asserts in these verses of his farewell "priestly" discourse also includes all "who will believe" (v. 20) throughout all the centuries long after the historical edges of his earthly ministry. John's gospel presents a figure of Jesus that transcends the limitations of human knowledge and ultimately even the boundaries of time and space. Future generations of men and women are suddenly invoked as if already present in the mind of Jesus and embraced by his loving sacrifice for their salvation. The various cultures and ethnic groups that had already embraced the message of Jesus by the time that John's gospel was written at the end of the first century were implicitly recognized and celebrated as present to the mind of Jesus at the Last Supper.

The life-giving love of Jesus embraces the entire human history and all its vast populations. Every culture expresses that life-giving love in a way that makes it real for them, even if it seems not to speak to other cultures. Italians process through the streets of their cities carrying life-size statues of saints in procession as they pin money to ribbons flowing from the statues. Mexican Catholics celebrate the Day of the Dead on November 2 by gathering in cemeteries with family at the gravesites of relatives, bringing baskets of food to share in a kind of picnic that unites them with their deceased loved ones. In southern India on every Friday during Lent Catholics take part in a sixteen-kilometer Way of the Cross as each person carries a large cross on the long walk. In the United States Native Americans begin a Eucharist with smudging by burning sweet grass and wafting the smoke over the congregation akin to the use of incense.

Motive for Belief

In two instances this prayer of Jesus returns to the fact that the unity of Father and Son, together with that of all disciples, is a motive of credibility for the evangelization of the larger world. Jesus insists on the importance of such unity "that the world may believe" (v. 21) and that "the world may know" (v. 23). John's gospel struggles with such unity because human division in faith always renders the witness of believers less credible. The famous Edinburgh Missionary Congress (1910) was summoned precisely because the internecine bickering of Christian missionaries in Africa and Asia during the nineteenth century left their pagan audiences puzzled and ultimately disinterested. The annual Octave of Prayer for Christian Unity each January since 1908 has been a concerted attempt on the part of all Christian churches to take these words of Jesus seriously. Without ecumenical unity, the witness of missionaries is compromised, even on a local level. As the once popular song would have it, "They'll know we are Christians by our love." Absolute uniformity, however, is neither necessary nor even desirable because the mystery of God is always beyond the ability of human language or practice to express adequately. Ecumenical diversity, for example, can be another blessing before the world if also clearly embraced by the fullness of charity for each other. The rich gift of unity among believers is a prerequisite for successfully heralding the Lord's resurrection.

> **Thursday of the Seventh Week of Easter**

God's Story Made Present

God instinctively tears down the walls we build. In his poem "Mending Wall," the poet Robert Frost tells of how each springtime he and his neighbor meet by the stone wall that divides their adjoining fields. With each of them on either side, together they walk along replacing the stones toppled by the heaving ice and snows of winter. To his neighbor he muses, "Something there is that doesn't love a wall." The wall makes little sense to Frost for his neighbor has all pine trees and Frost himself has all apple trees. He wonders what purpose the wall serves. He can't imagine his apples going over to eat the pinecones and says again, "Something there is that doesn't love a wall, that wants it down." Yet his neighbor only says, "Good fences make good neighbors." In the end Frost's musing is to no avail. The neighbor likes having walls. In spite of our human tendencies to divide, there is something at the heart of creation that seeks to unite. Believers are inclined to say it is God.[1]

Divine Presence

The passage concludes profoundly with Jesus affirming that he has revealed God's name as Father to his disciples (v. 26). Authentic Jewish tradition had already spoken very beautifully of God as Father (Isa 63:16; 64:7), but John's gospel uses the term in a new and more substantial fashion. As a result of Jesus sharing his knowledge of God with them, his disciples possess the same love in their communal lives that Jesus shared with his Father. This is a great mystery and an extraordinary gift. The categories of love, life, faith, and glory become so mutually interrelated in John's gospel as to become the very elements that unite us and transform us. When God's love dwells in human lives in any of these ways, God is present.

God's Story Made Present

To experience being loved is to experience the presence of God.
There is an old Hasidic tale that says when we are conceived in the womb of our mother and over the coming months God whispers to us all the secrets of the universe. During that time God tells us where birds go when they fly so high that we are no longer able to see them, and why it is that waves always come into the shore and never out. God explains why snowflakes always have six sides, never any more and never any less, and whether zebras are black with white stripes or white with black stripes. God tells us, too, who it is who bends the bow in the heavens and where its ends are tied. In such ways and for nine long months God whispers to us all that there is to know. Then having revealed to us all the wisdom of creation, God tells us one final secret, that God loves us, always has and always will. And with that we are born into life, except that in the process of being born we forget all that we first heard in the womb of our mother. Thus we spend the rest of our lives trying to remember. Perhaps it also explains why we sense that we have met God whenever we find ourselves loved.

**Thursday
of the
Seventh Week
of Easter**

---

1. Robert Frost, *The Poetry of Robert Frost* (New York: Holt, Rinehart & Winston, 1969), 33–34.

Friday of the Seventh Week of Easter

God's Story Proclaimed

ACTS 25:13B-21
Jesus was dead, whom Paul claimed to be alive.

Historical note: Most Christians are familiar with the name of Pontius Pilatus, the Roman procurator in Palestine (AD 26–36) at the time of the death of Jesus. This was the title given to the Roman governor who was entrusted with full authority by the emperor, especially in financial and military matters. Procurators collected tribute for Caesar and maintained public order in his name, residing either in Herod's former palace in Caesarea or in Jerusalem. The two individuals mentioned in today's reading are Antonius Felix (AD 52–60) and Porcius Festus (AD 60–62). Felix was notorious for his cruelty and lust, and under his administration (according to Josephus) Jewish hostility deepened immensely. Felix is also remembered for having punished many robbers by public crucifixion in an effort to impose order upon the area. By contrast, Festus, sent by Nero, tried to be an honest administrator, but the political situation was apparently beyond repair and spiraled toward the Jewish revolt of AD 66–70. Agrippa II ruled portions of Galilee from AD 52 until his death in AD 93 or shortly thereafter. His relationship with his sister Bernice II caused considerable scandal in Rome.

Following the Rules to Seek Justice

Curiously, this first reading seems to be a transcription of a memo written by Festus, the Roman procurator (v. 14), by way of courtesy, giving King Agrippa the background to Paul's legal status. Festus (and Paul) was determined to stay on good terms with local authorities. As evidenced by this case, Roman law was known for its fairness in judicial procedures, and it is not surprising that the Code of Canon Law subsequently adopted and developed by the Catholic curial offices in Rome and Constantinople over the centuries followed much of its procedures. The point of Festus was his insistence that a person had a right in Roman law to face his accusers and defend himself against any charges (v. 16). The Romans understood that no binding decision should be made in a controversy *nisi audiatur alia pars* ("unless the other party be also heard"). For that reason, Festus was unwilling to simply condemn Paul on the basis of the accusations alone. In writing for the educated classes of his day, Luke wanted to make sure that his readers appreciated the legitimacy of Paul's actions as well as the fairness with which Paul had been treated by Roman authorities. Wherever possible Luke praised the pagan practices of his day. By the eighth decade of the first century, it had become important to demonstrate that Christians were law-abiding people and good citizens, even if (like the Jewish populace) they were unwilling to participate in the daily religious rituals of local pagan temples.

Through our instinctive God-given sense of fairness God nudges the world into greater goodness. Paul, like all the disciples of Jesus, ancient and modern, tried to follow the standards of the day for good citizenship, as did Festus, the Roman procurator. This was—and always is—really God at work. Little children instinctively know when something isn't fair and say so with conviction, sometimes even petulantly. Rather than separating and secluding themselves from the injustices of society, adult Christians work hard to promote a more just world by serving on juries, running for membership on school boards, and opposing discrimination and prejudice of all kinds. Inspired by God's grace they try to become models for their neighbors in opposing racism and all forms of social sin. The example of "blessed" Festus, like so many truly good people around us, should not be forgotten.

Appeal to Caesar

The actual historical details are very unclear, and no precise reason is offered for Paul's appeal to Caesar. He may have feared an unfavorable verdict if he went to Jerusalem to have his case heard by the Sanhedrin (v. 20). In any case, Paul had long been planning eventually to go to Rome on his way to Spain and had even written the letter to the Romans—probably from Corinth (15:24, 28) sometime between AD 56–58 for that purpose. As a Roman citizen, Paul had the right to appeal his legal situation to the emperor for personal judgment. He shrewdly took advantage of the safety and travel resources that such legal custody would provide. He didn't have to pay for his travel expenses. Being able to proclaim the Gospel of the risen Jesus at the center of his world was an opportunity too good to miss! Paul therefore used his rights according to Roman law to support and sustain the mission that he and Barnabas had first embraced back in Antioch many years earlier (13:2). Although Paul's actual legal action is only mentioned in the last verse of this passage (v. 21), the entire narrative gradually sets the stage for this climax and provides the background for Paul's request. The favorable good will of Procurator Festus provided the backdrop for Paul's appeal.

God's Story Made Present

Friday of the Seventh Week of Easter

In God's own ways all aspects of human history unfold to bring about the goodness of the kingdom. The preamble to the US Constitution states what Americans as a nation intend to be: "We the people of the United States, in order to form a more perfect union, establish justice, insure domestic tranquility, provide for the common defence, promote the general welfare, and secure the blessings of liberty to ourselves and our posterity, do ordain and establish this Constitution for the United States of America."

In stating what we as a nation propose as our tasks, we are proclaiming that to which we intend to commit ourselves—to being a union of peoples, striving to bring forth justice, ensuring peace in our homes and our cities, securing our borders against transgressors, caring for the good of the populace, and assuring freedom now and for the future. It is the work of God's kingdom. "All things work for the good of those who love God" (Rom 8:28).

ANTIPHON—PSALM 103:19A

The Lord has established his throne in heaven. (or: Alleluia)

Psalm 103

Psalm 103 is a remarkable statement of praise for the supreme authority of Israel's God, who always deals with human history wisely and graciously. Virtually every action of rescue (v. 4), providential care (v. 6), and paternal compassion (v. 13) is generalized in this psalm and described as if that's the way God always works. Although the full body of the hymn is not used in this liturgical responsorial psalm, its litany of praise explains the initial invitation to bless God's holy name and not forget his benefits (v. 2). The highest heavens are also invited to join in praise for God's kindness (covenantal *hesed* or mercy, v. 11) and forgiveness. Today's congregational response concludes with the recognition that even the heavenly messengers do God's bidding (v. 20). The psalm's invitation to praise is a response to the way God uses human decisions, like Paul's appeal to Caesar, for the salvation of the entire known world.

The Refrain

With this refrain (v. 19) the congregation, both ancient and contemporary, is lifted beyond the limits of earthly experience to the very heavenly throne of the transcendent God, whose kingdom is universal and whose vision is comprehensive. Everything remains within the parameters of the Lord's view. In the ancient world a throne is the place for teaching wisdom and exercising authority. As commentators have noted, this verse seems to share a bit of the experience reflected in Isaiah's famous temple vision where seraphim surround the divine throne and sing God's praises (Isa 6:1-4; 40:6-8). The grass dries and withers, but the Lord and his creative Word remain forever. For situations like Paul's decision to preserve and extend his apostolic voice by appealing to the Caesar, the reminder of God's enduring presence, personal interest, and supreme power is consoling. Sometimes the power of a supportive community at prayer can lift up and transform its human participants, even in the most difficult situations.

GOSPEL ACCLAMATION—JOHN 14:26
Almost by way of encouragement for Peter who will receive Christ's commission to tend and feed the Lord's sheep, the congregation is reminded of the task of the Holy Spirit—namely, to teach and remind them of everything Jesus had said. Peter will not be alone or unguided in his mission.

JOHN 21:15-19
Feed my lambs, feed my sheep.

Lectionary note: The original Gospel of John concluded with an editorial summary that clearly signaled the end of that gospel's initial composition, explaining that the purpose of the work was the increase of faith in its readers (20:30). Early church authorities, however, added this final inspired chapter to report Peter's humble reconciliation with Christ after his prior cowardly denials (18:25-27) and to describe his double divine appointments as itinerant fisher–missionary (21:1-14) and resident shepherd–pastor (vv. 16-19). The initial account of the appearance of the risen Lord at the seashore and the apostles' miraculous catch of fish was the gospel text already used on Friday of the Octave of Easter. Now at the end of Eastertide, on the edge of the liturgy's resumption of Ordinary Time, the Lectionary returns to proclaim Peter's pastoral role in Christian community life.

More than These

As noted above, John's account of the Lord's passion had included Peter's triple denial. Because Semitic pat-

terns of communication used the triple repetition of anything to signify a superlative (as in "holy, holy, holy," Isa 6:3, and the liturgical refrain at the end of each preface to the eucharistic prayer), that thrice-repeated denial was very important. It had to be resolved, therefore, for the integrity of the gospel's story. The Lord's initial appearance to the disciples in the Upper Room had included the gift of the Spirit for the forgiveness of sins (20:22), but the specific sins of Peter still required his Lord's acknowledgment and formal forgiveness—and indeed in corresponding triplicate. He was asked about the sheep three times. It would seem important to note that the reference to Peter's love as more than "these" (v. 15) was not a comparative reference to the other disciples who had gone fishing with Peter and now stood nearby. Peter, especially after his humiliating denial, would never have dared to say anything so falsely presumptuous or arrogant as to suggest that his love was greater than that of his companions—especially after the humiliation of his denials! Scholars suggest that the reference was rather to the boats and fishing and everything of his former "professional" life to which he had so readily returned after the resurrection. Before Peter could be commissioned as shepherd, he had put aside his former life and all the human satisfactions they may have afforded. These verses were an account of a deep, enduring vocational decision on the part of Peter. Any true fisherman experienced in savoring the quiet stillness of a stream and the patient wait for an early morning nibble at the bait or tug on the nets understands the point and the price.

God nudges us into going where we would rather not go.
Life is filled with commitments, and many of them are commitments to love in one way or another. The first time we commit to a person or cause or need, such as in marriage vows, always seems to be the easiest. It is the recommittals that follow a second, third, and fourth time and all the times thereafter that call us to ever renewed love

and faithfulness. It is at such times that we can be distressed, like Peter, as we wonder why it needs to be so difficult and demanding. Yet perhaps it is such times that are the markers of being followers of the Lord Jesus—being led where we do not want to go.

Feeding the Lambs and the Sheep

Young David had actually and perhaps providentially been employed as a shepherd of his father's flocks when he was chosen by Samuel and anointed as king of Judah (1 Sam 16:4-13). The kings of the ancient Near East were sometimes given the formal title of shepherd of a nation. Likewise, the pharaohs in Egypt were often pictured as carrying a shepherd's staff and a harvester's flail. The collected visions and messages of the book of Ezekiel contain some harsh words of divine rejection against the ancient royal shepherds of Israel who used their flocks selfishly and didn't care for the needs of their sheep (34:1-16). Shepherding was therefore an ancient and preferred image for leadership and community service. The God of Israel was celebrated as the "Good Shepherd" (Ps 23:1). In rejecting the priests and kings of his day, Ezekiel insisted that God would take up the task himself! When Peter was asked about the depth of his love for his risen Lord, therefore, and then thrice commanded to feed the flock, he received a commission to teach them and to care for their material and spiritual needs. Young lambs and mature adults alike were to be the object of his new apostolic responsibility. The same duties are confided to every local parish priest and pastor today. The task, however, is also shared by pastoral councils and lay pastoral leaders.

Friday of the Seventh Week of Easter

God empowers shepherding in each person. The tasks of shepherding and guiding are always about giving focus without becoming overly rigid or controlling. The challenge is always to keep a balance between the two, realizing that different situations call for differing emphases—as children grow, as couples shepherd one another in a marriage, as friends mutually mentor one another, and as the teaching aspect of the church offers wisdom. The challenge is always how to keep a middle ground of encouragement without indifference or domination. Perhaps the answer to that challenge is to keep asking the question.

Stretching Out His Hands

By the time that the Gospel of John had achieved the form we currently possess, Peter had been dead for almost a quarter of a century. Tradition would claim that Peter had died as a martyr under Nero in about AD 68. In fact, the bones traditionally venerated as those of Peter, buried under the Roman basilica that bears his name, were scientifically analyzed in the middle of the last century at the request of Pius XII and judged credible to that tradition. Yet the event was described in this passage as if it still was in the future. The point of the gospel remains that Peter's pastoral vocation, like all vocations in service to others, included suffering from the beginning. The text presents itself as a prediction. Scholars suggest that a common proverb about old age (v. 18) is cited here because it bore surprising similarity to the actual circumstances of Peter's death, allegedly by crucifixion upside down. The text concludes by noting that Jesus explicitly used the comment to illustrate Peter's eventual death (v. 19). Each parishioner at morning Mass is likewise invited to stretch out her hands daily in submission to God's unfolding will. As symbolized and anticipated in baptism, God's will includes the paschal mystery of suffering and resurrection for each of us.

God creates classrooms for learning how to live. The theologian Karl Rahner made the observation that one of the tasks of life is to learn how to die well. Such learning opportunities abound throughout our lives. If we learn well, then our final journey will be eased.

Saturday of the Seventh Week of Easter

God's Story Proclaimed

ACTS 28:16-20, 30-31
Paul remained at Rome, proclaiming the Kingdom of God.

Jewish to the Core and to the End

From the very beginning of Paul's missionary life—when he arrived with Barnabas at the port of Salamis on the island of Cyprus and proclaimed the word of God in their synagogue (13:5)—until his invitation to Jewish leaders in Rome (28:17), he never forgot his mission to Jews first and then to the Gentiles. His initial words to the Jews in Rome insist on his innocence of any disrespect toward "our people or our ancestral customs" (v. 17), no matter what false accusations or rumors may have preceded his arrival. After his arrest in Jerusalem and in his appearance before the Sanhedrin, Paul had declared that he was a Jew from Tarsus, "strictly educated in ancestral law under Gamaliel and zealous for God" (22:3). Although he is usually celebrated in Catholic tradition as the apostle to the Gentiles, he never forgot his Judaism or its crucial gift of faith to the history of the world's salvation. In his meeting with the leaders of the synagogue in Rome, he reminded them that he had no accusation to make "against my own nation" (v. 19). Christians who hear the accounts of these first missionary journeys each year should never forget the privileged place of Judaism in the history of God's love, the Jewish profile of Christ's human mission, or the work of the Holy Spirit in human history. Paul was very clear in asserting that "it is on account of the hope of Israel that I wear these chains" (v. 20). As Paul said regarding the Jewish people when writing to the Romans prior to his actual arrival in their midst, "the gifts and the call of God are irrevocable" (11:29). The truth of Paul's enduring fidelity toward his native Judaism should be remembered and once again made a part of our own Christian tradition as well. Paul, like his countrymen (and all Catholics who recite the Divine Office), regularly used Psalm 136 in synagogue worship; in this psalm each action of God in the history of Israel is repeatedly met with the congregation's response: "for his great love (*hesed*, or covenantal fidelity) is without end." The book of Acts comes to its climax with Paul's witness to the Jewish community in Rome. Unfortunately, this portion of our Christian faith was forgotten prior to the Holocaust with disastrous and evil results.

God yokes Jews and Christians as partners in the work of his kingdom.
For the past fifty years Christians have struggled with the horror of the Holocaust and have been confronted with our own historical contributions to that tragedy. A new respect and appreciation for Judaism has arisen throughout the Christian world. Popes like Sts. John XXIII and John Paul II have insisted on the importance of the witness of Judaism to our modern world. Good Friday rituals of Roman Catholicism have been changed to preclude blaming all Jews then—and all Jewish leaders throughout the centuries—for the crucifixion of Jesus. It has become imperative to begin anew and see our Jewish neighbors as partners in the work of God's kingdom on earth and in human history rather than rivals or culprits.

Proclaiming and Teaching with Complete Assurance

For the sake of brevity, or perhaps to avoid any distraction, the editors of the Lectionary chose to omit from this final passage several verses that describe Paul's daily passionate teachings from early morning until evening regarding Jesus and the law of Moses (vv. 21-29). Thus without repetition this first reading on the last day of Eastertide concludes with the two final verses from Acts and succinctly summarizes the content and purpose of Paul's witness in Rome (v. 30). Not only did

Paul speak without hindrance from Roman authorities (whose good will Luke consistently wished to highlight) but once again he did so "with complete assurance" (*parresìa*, or candor, frankness, and boldness, v. 31). This same word has been deliberately used by Luke from the very first speech of Peter on Pentecost in describing his own confidence (2:29) in speaking about David's death and Christ's resurrection. Confident boldness and directness has characterized the witness of the early church from the very beginning. The apostolic missionaries knew what they believed and were convinced of its importance for the whole world. Paul has boldly brought the message to the political center of his world. He stands proclaiming, "Mission Accomplished!" Apparently Luke felt no need to distract from that witness by any reference to Paul's death at the hands of Nero's soldiers. Even as it was in the first century, Paul's faithful witness continues as a mark of authenticity in every word of faithful testimony by contemporary Christians.

God's grace makes bold witnesses. The age-old joke that asks, "Why did the chicken cross the road?" and its well-worn response, "To get to the other side," in one way or another echoes our own human instincts. The fact is that life is filled with inner calls: to make a difference, to find love, to live peacefully and without conflict, and to find and experience beauty. We all wish to get to that other side.

The book of Acts brings to conclusion the story of Paul's journeys and faithful witness to his call as a disciple. Every believer in his or her own way answers a similar call to be faithful: to live in the image of Jesus, to build up life where we live it, to care about the weak among us, and to carry the crosses of life.

Saturday of the Seventh Week of Easter

ANTIPHON—PSALM 11:7B
The just will gaze upon your face, O Lord. (or: Alleluia)

Psalm 11

Psalm 11 seems to have come out of an intense experience of physical persecution and harm by those described as "wicked" (vv. 2, 5, 6). Against that background this brief prayer speaks of the psalmist's utter confidence in God as refuge (v. 1) and compassionate judge who punishes the wicked with fire, brimstone, and scorching winds (v. 6). That section is omitted, however, in the responsorial verses selected by the editors of the Lectionary in order to focus on God's universal vision, which misses nothing (v. 4), rejects violence (*hamas*, v. 5), and loves just deeds (v. 7). This psalm serves to highlight in a final fashion God's blessings for Paul's faithful witness over the decades.

The Refrain

In this refrain, the original Hebrew word translated as "just" (v. 7) is *yashar*—that is, "straight or upright." Similarly in English we contrast those who are morally good with the "crooked," those who are bent toward evil. People who are ethically grounded can stand straight before God and neighbors, looking them in the eye without fear or shame. Such people are promised the eventual reward of being able to see God's face. It is unfortunate that the fundamental nuance of the Hebrew original has been generalized and lost in this translation as "just." Scholars often feel that the version of the Psalter currently used in the Lectionary still needs further work.

GOSPEL ACCLAMATION—JOHN 16:7, 13
Once again the liturgy returns to Christ's promise of the Holy Spirit. Yesterday's words focused on teaching and reminding, but today's promise underscores the profound and complete truth of what the Spirit will teach. Perhaps the reference to being "guided into all truth" is a subtle liturgical allusion to the Catholic belief in doctrinal development—that is, the grace by which the church gradually and ever more profoundly understands the truth we attempt

to live and share. These words certainly prepare the church for tomorrow's celebration of the gift of the Spirit at Pentecost.

JOHN 21:20-25
This is the disciple who has written these things and his testimony is true.

Mutual Care and Concern

The nameless disciple "whom Jesus loved" (v. 20) has been a regular participant in many of the events described throughout the Gospel of John. While a few commentators have opined that the reference is deliberately vague so as to represent every believer throughout all of history, most have identified the figure with the apostle John himself. They have assumed that John's personal humility discouraged using his own name, thereby downplaying his identity and importance in these events. Most of the figures in John's gospel, however, do in fact represent larger groups of people. Thus John could be using himself as an unnamed, though typical, example of all those whom Jesus loved dearly—that is, everyone! To a casual gospel reader, this final scene and Peter's question, "What about him?" (v. 21) might sound like idle curiosity. Peter and John had been constant companions throughout the gospel, perhaps even good friends with complementary personalities. Peter's eventual fate had just been described as being led where he did not wish to go (v. 18). It would make sense therefore for Peter to ask his question out of genuine care and concern for a brother in the new creation. The response of Jesus, by introducing the reference to remaining "until I come" (v. 23), may have alluded to John's legendary advanced age at the time of the final editing of this gospel. Whether Peter's question reflected the fact that he truly cared about John, he is chided to take care of his own relationship to God's will and not to be preoccupied with the destiny of others. Finding the right balance between genuine care for others and nosiness is one of life's enduring challenges.

God personalizes each journey of faith. It seems almost by instinct that we compare ourselves and our lives to that of others. Our homes and our children, our titles and our salaries, how we are perceived as male or female—they all seem subject to comparison. It is little wonder, then, that we can be inclined to do so in our faith lives as well. Whether we are more prayerful or less, more justice oriented or less, more biblically versed or less, more committed or less, each person's journey is unique and designed by God.

Many Other Things

Although the gospels have a deliberate historical basis, the events are arranged in various literary structures in order to make some clear catechetical points about the person and mission of Jesus. Some events are omitted in order to clarify and emphasize the teachings communicated by those accounts that have been chosen for inclusion in each of the gospels. The authors did not wish to distract the readers. For that reason, this second and final summary (v. 24) acknowledges the many other signs and teachings that filled the public ministry of Jesus. As noted above, chapter 20 had its own distinctive conclusion, which also referred to "many other signs" (v. 30) but added the purpose for the gospel: the movement to faith on the part of its readers and listeners. In a sense, the lives of all postapostolic generations could constitute an as-yet-unwritten third chapter concerning the lives of believers and witnesses to the work and mission of the risen Jesus in our world.

> **Saturday of the Seventh Week of Easter**

The signs and wonders of justice and charity produced by contemporary disciples and apprentices of Jesus give testimony to his living presence in our midst. Name those works of your own faith community that give such testimony.

We conclude this book with the solemn words used
to bless the Easter candle each year:

Christ yesterday and today
the Beginning and the End
the Alpha
and the Omega
All time belongs to him
and all the ages.
To him be glory and power
through every age and for ever. Amen.

—*The Roman Missal*

Index of Readings

Index of Antiphons

Index of Acclamations